T0225741

Database Principles and Technologies – Based on Huawei GaussDB

Huawei Technologies Co., Ltd.

Database Principles and Technologies – Based on Huawei GaussDB

Huawei Technologies Co., Ltd.
Hangzhou, China

ISBN 978-981-19-3031-7   ISBN 978-981-19-3032-4   (eBook)
https://doi.org/10.1007/978-981-19-3032-4

Jointly published with Posts & Telecom Press, Beijing, China
The print edition is not for sale in China (Mainland). Customers from China (Mainland) please order the print book from: Posts & Telecom Press.

This Springer imprint is published by the registered company Springer Nature Singapore Pte Ltd.
The registered company address is: 152 Beach Road, #21-01/04 Gateway East, Singapore 189721, Singapore

Preface

Nowadays, database technology has developed from the early stage of simply saving and processing data files to a rich, comprehensive discipline with data modeling and database management system as the core, as the foundation and core of modern computer application system. Entering the Internet era, the traditional database system began to show decadence in response to the storage needs of big data, and enterprise customers urgently need a new generation of database products, that is, products with dynamic expansion and contraction capacity, high throughput, low cost, and other characteristics. As a result, cloud computing-based databases have emerged and risen, showing the future-oriented trend of cloud-based, distributed, and multi-mode processing.

Based on Huawei's GaussDB (for MySQL) cloud computing-based database, this book focuses on various cloud computing-based features and application scenarios of cloud computing-based databases. The division of the book's eight chapters is as follows:

Chapter 1 mainly introduces databases, including database technology overview, database technology history, relational database architecture, and mainstream application scenarios of relational databases.

Chapter 2 mainly teaches database basics, including the main responsibilities and contents of database management, and introduces some common and important basic concepts of databases.

Chapter 3 introduces SQL syntax, including GaussDB (for MySQL) data types, system functions and operators, which aims to help beginners master get started with SQL syntax.

Chapter 4 focuses on SQL syntax classification and further explains SQL statements accordingly, covering data query, data update, data definition, and data control.

Chapter 5 focuses on database security fundamentals, including basic security management techniques for databases, such as access control, user management, permission management, object permissions, and cloud auditing services, which will be elaborated from basic concepts, usages, and application scenarios.

Chapter 6 focuses on the database development environment, including the use of all the tools of GaussDB (for MySQL), for the convenience of users to learn and view.

Chapter 7 mainly teaches database design fundamentals, detailing the specific work of requirements analysis, conceptual design, logical design and physical design in accordance with the New Orleans design methodology, and finally introducing the specific means of database design implementation with relevant cases.

Chapter 8 mainly introduces the features of GaussDB database, involving Huawei relational database and Huawei NoSQL database.

This book is edited by Huawei Technologies Co., Ltd., thanks to Ma Ruixin for the specific writing and final compilation of the whole book. We welcome readers' criticism and correction if there are any shortcomings in the book, due to the limited time for compilation.

Hangzhou, China   Huawei Technologies Co., Ltd.
December 2021

Contents

About the Author

Huawei Technologies Co., Ltd. Founded in 1987, Huawei is a leading global provider of information and communications technology (ICT) infrastructure and smart devices. We have approximately 197,000 employees and we operate in over 170 countries and regions, serving more than three billion people around the world.

Huawei's mission is to bring digital to every person, home and organization for a fully connected, intelligent world. To this end, we will: drive ubiquitous connectivity and promote equal access to networks to lay the foundation for the intelligent world; provide the ultimate computing power to deliver ubiquitous cloud and intelligence; build powerful digital platforms to help all industries and organizations become more agile, efficient, and dynamic; redefine user experience with AI, offering consumers more personalized and intelligent experiences across all scenarios, including home, travel, office, entertainment, and fitness & health.

Chapter 1
Introduction to Databases

Database technology is a technology developed earlier in computer science, having experienced nearly 60 years of history since its birth in the early 1960s. Now, database technology has developed from the early stage of simply saving and processing data files to a rich comprehensive discipline with data modeling and DBMS as the core, as the foundation and core of modern computer application system. With the continuous refinement of "Internet+", big data, AI and data mining technologies in recent years, database technology and products are changing day by day. This chapter will give a brief introduction to the basic knowledge and concepts of database.

1.1 Overview of Database Technology

Database technology is an effective technology used for data management. It studies how to manage data scientifically so as to provide people with shareable, secure and reliable data. It involves four important concepts, as shown in Fig. 1.1, which are introduced below.

1.1.1 Data

Data refers to the raw records that have not been processed. Generally speaking, data is not clearly organized and classified, and thus cannot clearly express the meaning of what things represent. Data can be a pile of magazines, a stack of newspapers, minutes of a meeting, or a copy of medical records. Early computer systems were primarily used for scientific calculations and dealt with numerical data, that is, numbers in the generalized concept of data, such as integers like 1, 2, 3, 4, 5, but also floating point numbers like 3.14, 100.34, and -25.336.

© The Author(s) 2023
Huawei Technologies Co., Ltd., *Database Principles and Technologies – Based on Huawei GaussDB*, https://doi.org/10.1007/978-981-19-3032-4_1

Fig. 1.1 Overview of
database technology

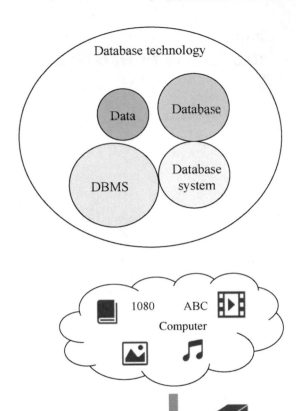

Fig. 1.2 Information is
stored in a computer after
being digitized as data

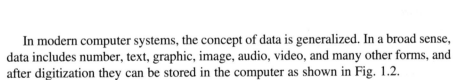

In modern computer systems, the concept of data is generalized. In a broad sense, data includes number, text, graphic, image, audio, video, and many other forms, and after digitization they can be stored in the computer as shown in Fig. 1.2.

In addition to its presentation, data also involves semantics, i.e., the meaning and implications of the data. Data and the semantics of data are closely related. For example, 88 as a data can indicate that the total number of employees in a department is 88, or that a student's score in a certain subject is 88, or that the price of a product is 88 yuan or a person's weight is 88 kg.

1.1.2 Database

Database is a large collection of organized and shareable data stored in the computer for a long time, with the following three characteristics.

Fig. 1.3 Database

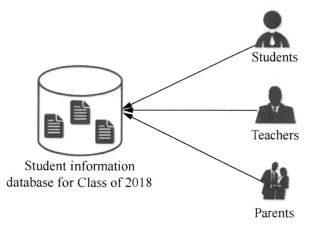

Student information
database for Class of 2018

(1) Long-term storage: The database should provide a reliable mechanism to support long-term data storage, so that data recovery is feasible upon the system failure to prevent data loss in the database.
(2) Organization: Data should be organized, described and stored in a certain data model. Model-based storage endows data with less redundancy, higher independence and easy scalability.
(3) Sharebility: The data in the database is shared and used by all types of users, not exclusive to a single user.

The student information database shown in Fig. 1.3 should be accessible non-exclusively to different users such as students, teachers and parents simultaneously.

1.1.3 Database Management System

Database management system (DBMS) is a system software located between the user and the operating system that can organize and store data scientifically, access and maintain data efficiently.

Like the operating system, the DBMS is also the basic software of the computer system, as shown in Fig. 1.4.

The DBMS mainly functions as follows.

(1) Data definition. The DBMS provides data definition language (DDL), through which the user can easily define the composition and structure of data objects in the database.
(2) Data organization, storage and management. The DBMS is responsible for organizing, storing and managing data in a classified manner, involving data dictionaries, user data, data access paths, etc. The DBMS also has to determine in which file structure and which access method to organize this data in the

Fig. 1.4 Hierarchy diagram
of computer system

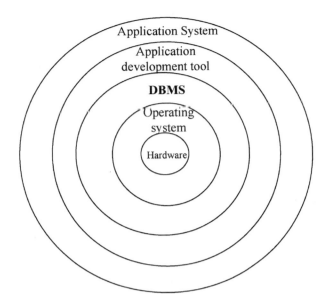

storage space, and how to realize the linkage between the data. The basic goal of
data organization and storage is to improve storage space utilization, facilitate
data access, and provide a variety of data access to improve access efficiency.
(3) Data manipulation. DBMS also provides data manipulation language (DML),
    with which users can manipulate data to achieve such basic operations as query,
    insert, deletion and modification on data.
(4) Transaction management and operation management of the database. The data-
    base is unified managed and controlled by the DBMS during establishment,
    operation and maintenance to ensure the correct operation of transactions, the
    security and integrity of data, the concurrent use of data by multiple users and the
    system recovery after a failure.
(5) Database establishment and maintenance. This function covers the database
    initial data input and conversion, database dump and recovery, database reorga-
    nization and performance monitoring, analysis function, etc. These functions are
    usually implemented by certain programs or management tools.

1.1.4   Database System

The database system (DBS) is a system for storing, managing, processing and
maintaining data composed of database, DBMS and its application development
tools, applications and database administrators.

In Fig. 1.5, the parts other than the user and the operating system are the
components of the database system.

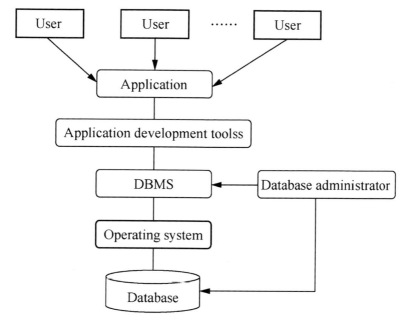

Fig. 1.5 Database System

 Though the operating system is not a component of the database system, the DBMS needs to call the interface provided by the operating system in order to access the database.

1.2 History of Database Technology

1.2.1 Emergence and Development of Database Technology

Database technology emerged in response to the need of data management tasks. Data management refers to the classification, organization, coding, storage, retrieval and maintenance of data, which is the core of data processing.

The development of data management has gone through three stages, as shown in Fig. 1.6.

(1) Manual management stage (from the emergence of computers to the mid-1950s). Before the mid-1950s, there was no software system responsible for data management. To perform data computation on a computer, programmers needed to design their own programs. Not only the logical structure of the data had to be

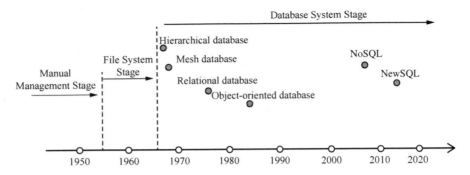

Fig. 1.6 Timeline of data management development

specified in the application, but also the physical structure, including storage structures, access methods, etc. had to be designed. Thus, on one hand, programmers had a very heavy workload, while on the other hand, non-programmers were incapable to use the computer system.

(2) File system stage (from the late 1950s to the mid-1960s). In this phase, data was organized into separate data files, which is accessed based on file name and saved and obtained based on record, with file opening, closing, and access support provided by the file system.

(3) Database system stage (from the late 1960s to present). In the late 1960s, database systems (proprietary software systems) emerged to allow large-scale data management. In this stage, with the development of the times, hierarchical databases, mesh databases, and classic relational databases have emerged successively. In the last 20 years or so, emerging databases such as NoSQL and NewSQL have also emerged.

1.2.2   Comparison of the Three Stages of Data Management

A comparison of the three stages of data management is shown in Table 1.1.

Among the three stages, the manual management is the most primitive stage, in which the data is not shareable. A set of application-oriented data corresponds to a program. Multiple applications processing the same data must be defined individually. They cannot use each other, so there is a large amount of redundant data between programs. In addition, the data lacks independence, which means that when the logical and physical structure of the data changes, the application must be modified accordingly. So, the data is completely dependent on the application.

The file system stage supports sharing to some extent compared to the manual management stage, but such sharing is still poor and redundant, so that the files are still application-oriented. In this phase, different applications must create their own files even if they use the same data. Given the lack of file independence, the same

Table 1.1 Comparison of the three stages of data management

		Manual management stage	File system stage	Database system stage
Background	Application background	Scientific computing	Scientific computing and data management	Large-scale data management
	Hardware background	No direct storage device	Disks and drums	Large capacity disks and disk arrays
	Software background	No operating system	File system	DBMS
Characteristics	Processing mode	Batch processing	Online real-time processing and batch processing	Online real-time processing, distributed processing, and batch processing
	Data administrators	Users (programmers)	File system	DBMS
	Data objects	A particular application	Applications	Real world (individual, department, enterprise, etc.)
	Degree of data sharing	No shareability, very high redundancy	Poor shareability, high redundancy	High shareability, low redundancy
	Data independence	No independence, complete dependence on programs	Poor independence	High physical independence and certain logical independence
	Data structure	Unstructured	Structured within records, but unstructured as a whole	Structured as a whole, and described by a data model
	Data control capabilities	Application control	Application control	Data security and integrity guaranteed by the DBMS, providing concurrency control and data recovery capabilities

data is stored repeatedly and data redundancy is high. Such separate management approach is prone to data inconsistency.

The lack of file independence means that the file serves a specific application and the logical structure of the file is designed for this application. If the logical structure of the data changes, the definition of the file structure in the application must be modified, because the data depends on the application. In addition, files do not reflect the intrinsic linkage between things in the real world because they are independent of each other. From file system to database system, data management technology has made a leap.

In the database system stage, database technology is applied to data management on a large scale and starts to use large-capacity disks and disk arrays for data storage. Dedicated DBMS has emerged that allows online real-time processing, distributed processing, and batch processing. At this stage, data is well shared and less redundant, and data files reach a high level of physical independence and certain logical independence. The overall structure of the data can be described by a data model, and the database system has the ability to ensure data security and integrity and provide concurrency control and data recovery.

1.2.3 Benefits of Database

The database delivers following benefits.

(1) Data structure as a whole. The data structure is for the whole organization, not for a particular application. The structure of records and the links between records are maintained by the DBMS, thus reducing the workload of programmers.

(2) High level of data sharing and easy expansion. Data can be shared by multiple applications, reducing data redundancy and saving storage space. Data sharing avoids incompatibility and inconsistency between data. The reason for achieving easy expansion is to take into account the overall needs of the system to form structured data, and a highly resilient and easily expandable database system can meet a variety of requirements.

(3) Strong data independence. In terms of physical independence, the physical storage characteristics of data are managed by the DBMS, which can be ignored by the application; the application only needs to deal with the logical structure, and does not need to make changes with the changes of the physical storage characteristics of data. In terms of logical independence, the application can remain unchanged when the logical structure of data in the database is changed. Data independence simplifies application development and greatly reduces the complexity of the applications. Data independence from the application is actually decoupling the data from the application, while the original strongly coupled approach presented the disadvantages of poor flexibility, high development volume, and heavy maintenance tasks.

(4) Unified management and control. The database system facilitates users to manage and control data in a unified manner, including data security protection, data integrity checking, concurrency control, data recovery, etc. Data security protection refers to the protection of data to prevent data leakage or damage caused by unlawful use. Data integrity checking refers to checking the correctness, validity and uniformity of data. It controls the data within valid limits and ensures that certain relations are satisfied between the data. Concurrency control refers to the control and coordination of concurrent access operations by multiple users when they access the database at the same time, so as to avoid

interfering with each other and affecting the results obtained from the access. Data recovery refers to the function that the DBMS restores the database from an error state to a known correct state when the database system has hardware failure, software failure, operation error, etc.

1.2.4   Development Characteristics of the Database

Database has become one of the important foundation and core technology of computer information system and intelligent application system, as shown in Fig. 1.7.

The development of database systems presents the following three characteristics.

(1) The database development is concentrated on the data model development. The data model is the core and foundation of the database system, so the development of the database system and the development of the data model are inseparable. How to divide the data model is an important criterion for database system division.

(2) Intersection and combination with other computer technologies. With the endless emergence of new computer technology, intersecting and combining with other computer technologies becomes a significant feature of the development of database system, such as the distributed database upon the combination with

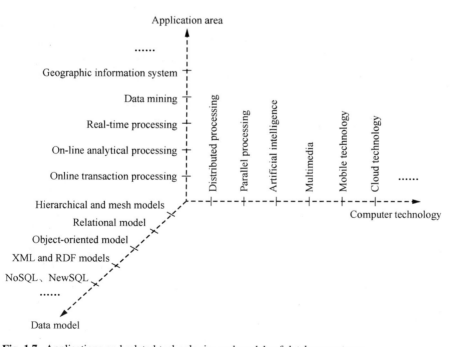

Fig. 1.7 Applications and related technologies and models of database systems

distributed processing technology, and cloud database upon the combination with cloud technology.

(3) Development of new database technology for application fields. The universal database cannot meet the application requirements in specific fields, and it is necessary to develop specific database systems according to the specific requirements of relevant fields.

1.2.5 Hierarchical Model, Mesh Model and Relational Model

The hierarchical model, mesh model and relational model are the three classical data models that have emerged throughout history.

1. Hierarchical model
   The hierarchical model presents a tree-like data structure, as shown in Fig. 1.8. There are two very typical features as follows.

   (1) There is one and only one node without "two parents" nodes, which is called the root node.
   (2) Each of the nodes other than the root node has one and only one "two parents" node, and this hierarchical model is often used in common organizational structures.

2. Mesh model
   The mesh model has a data structure similar to a network diagram, as shown in Fig. 1.9. In the mesh model diagram, E represents an entity and R represents the relation between entities. In the mesh model, more than one node is allowed to have no "two parents" node, and a node can have more than one "two parents" node. As shown in Fig. 1.9, E1 and E2 have no "two parents" node, while E3 and E5 have two "two parents" nodes respectively. The mesh model is able to map a lot of many-to-many relations in reality, such as students choosing courses and teachers teaching them.

Fig. 1.8 Hierarchical model

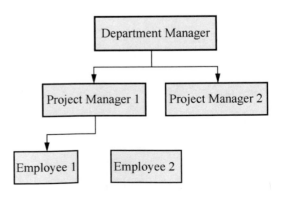

Fig. 1.9 Mesh model

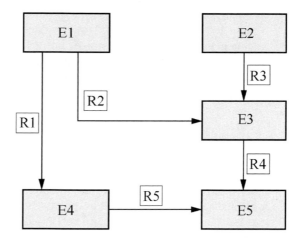

Fig. 1.10 Relational model

Key (Code)   Attribute

Student Number	Name	Age	Gender
2019004	Wang Si	19	Male
2019005	Li Wu	20	Female
2019006	Chen Liu	18	Male
2019007	Zhao Qi	19	Female
2019010	Song Shi	17	Male
......	......	......	......

——— Tuple

3. Relational model

A strict concept of relation is the basis of the relational model, and this relation must be normalized and the component of the relation must be an indivisible data item, as shown in Fig. 1.10.

Explanation	In 1970, Dr. Edgar Frank Codd, a researcher at IBM, published a paper entitled "A Relational Model of Data for Large Shared Data Banks" in the publication *Communication of the ACM*. He introduced the concept of relational model and laid the theoretical foundation for the relational model. Dr. Codd has published several articles on paradigm theory and 12 criteria that define how to measure relational systems. This laid the foundation of the relational model with mathematical theory.

Built on the set algebra, the relational model consists of a set of relations, each with a normalized two-dimensional table as its data structure. As the student information table shown in Fig. 1.10, a relation usually corresponds to a table. A tuple denotes a row in the table (a row denotes a tuple), an attribute denotes a column in the table (a column denotes an attribute); a key is also called a code, a domain is a set of values of the same data type, and a relational model is a relation name (Attribute 1, Attribute 2, Attribute 3,..., Attribute n), such as the relation in the example is student (student number, name, age, gender).

4. Comparison of the Three Models

Table 1.2 shows a comparison of the three models.

Both the mesh model and the hierarchical model are formatted models whose data structure is based on the basic hierarchical linkage as the basic unit. The basic hierarchical linkage refers to two records and the one-to-many (including one-to-one) linkage between them in a single-record operation. Entities in the formatted model are represented as records, the attributes of which correspond to the data items (or fields) of the records, and the linkages between entities are converted into linkages between records in the formatted model. The data linkage is reflected by the access path, in the sense that any given record value can only be viewed by its access path, and no "child" record value can exist independently of the "two parents" record value. The relational model, on the other hand, reflects data linkages not by access paths but by associative linkages, so it is more capable of reflecting the linkages between things in the real world.

The hierarchical and mesh models are efficient in querying because the application usually uses pointers to link the data, thus the record values can be found quickly by following the paths pointed by the pointers. Despite the efficient access, the hierarchical and mesh models are not easy to use for the average user because queries generally require a high-level or procedural language. Hence the poor experience for the average user. In the early days, the query efficiency of the relational model was relatively low; however, with the development of hardware, this deficiency in efficiency has been gradually overcome and compensated by the high flexibility and independence of the relational model. The structured query language provided by the relational model can greatly reduce the development workload for programmers and lower the threshold of use for general users. Therefore, the relational model can quickly replace the hierarchical and mesh models and become the dominant data model in recent years.

Each tuple in a relational database should be distinguishable and unique, which relies on entity integrity to achieve.

(1) Entity integrity: Simply put, the primary key cannot be null.
(2) Referential integrity: Simply put, it is the linkage between primary and foreign keys.
(3) User-defined integrity: for a specific constraint, such as a unique value.

Table 1.2 Comparison of hierarchical model, mesh model, and relational model

Features	Hierarchical model	Mesh model	Relational model
Data Structure	Formatted model with simple and clear tree-like structure	Formatted model	Normalization-compliant model
Data Manipulation	There is no "two parents" node, and no "child" node can be inserted; the "child" node will be deleted when the "two parents" nodes are deleted	Corresponding information (e.g. pointer) is also be added or deleted in the "two parents" nodes when adding and deleting nodes	Data operations are set operations, where the object and result of the operation are relations. Data operations must satisfy the integrity constraints on relations.
Data Linkage	The linkage between data is reflected by the access path	The linkage between data is reflected by the access path	The linkage between data is reflected by the relation
Advantages	1. Simple and clear data structure 2. High query efficiency 3. Good integrity support	1. Directer description of the real world, reflecting many-to-many relations 2. Good performance and high saving and access efficiency	1. Based on a rigorous mathematical theory 2. Single concept, with relations to represent entities and linkages between entities 3. Access path transparent to the user, with a high degree of independence and confidentiality 4. Simplification of development work for programmers
Disadvantages	1. Many non-hierarchical linkages that exist in the real world are not suitable for representation by hierarchical models 2. Representation of many-to-many linkages generates a lot of redundant data 3. Hierarchical commands tend to be procedural due to the tight structure	1. Complex structures become extremely complex as applications expand 2. The complexity of the object definition and manipulation language requires the embedding of high-level languages (COBOL, C), thus making it difficult for users to master and use 3. due to the existence of multiple paths, the user must understand the details of the system structure, thus increasing the burden of writing code	1. The hidden access path leads to less efficient queries than the formatted model 2. Optimization of the user's query is required

1.2.6 Structured Query Language

Structured query language (SQL) is a high-level, non-procedural programming language that allows users to work on high-level data structures without requiring them to specify data storage methods or to understand specific data access methods. This language allows various relational databases with completely different underlying structures to use the same SQL as an interface for data manipulation and management. That's why SQL has become the de facto universal language for relational databases, even until now. Considering the large user base of SQL, many NoSQL products also develop SQL-compatible interface forms to facilitate the use of a wide range of users.

SQL not only can be nested, but also can realize procedural programming through advanced objects, which has great flexibility and rich functions, and is known as the de facto universal language standard for relational databases. The development timeline of SQL standard is shown in Fig. 1.11.

1.2.7 Characteristics of Relational Databases

The ACID characteristics of relational databases are as follows.

(1) Atomicity. The transaction is the logical unit of work of the database; the operations in the transaction are either all done or nothing done.
(2) Consistency. The result of the execution of the transaction must be to move the database from one consistent state to another consistent state. For example, if User *A* transferring $100 to User *B* is a transaction, then it must ensure that Account *A* is reduced by $100, and Account *B* is increased by $100 at the same

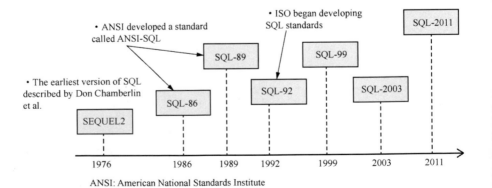

Fig. 1.11 Development timeline of SQL standard

time; there must be no consistency violation where Account *A* has reduced the amount of money but Account *B* has not increased..

(3) Isolation. The execution of a transaction in the database cannot be interfered with by other transactions, that is, the internal operation of a transaction and the use of data are isolated from other transactions; multiple transactions subject to concurrent execution cannot interfere with each other.

(4) Durability. Once a transaction is committed, the changes to the data in the database are permanent. Post-commit operation or failure will not have any effect on the result of the transaction.

1.2.8   Historical Review of Relational Database Products

The introduction of the relational model was an epochal and significant event in the history of database development. The great success in the research of relational theory and the development of relational DBMS has further promoted the development of relational database. The last 40 years have been the most "glorious" years for relational databases, during which many successful database products have been born, having a great impact on the development of society and our life. Some of the relational database products are shown in Fig. 1.12.

(1) Oracle is the database product of Oracle Corporation, which is one of the most popular relational databases in the world. In 1977, Larry Ellison and his colleague Bob Miner founded Software Development Labs (SDL), and they also developed the first version of Oracle in assembly language based on a paper published by Dr. Codd (released to the public in 1979).

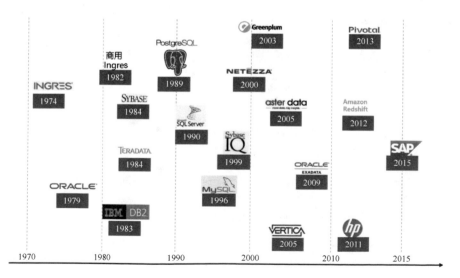

Fig. 1.12 Some of the relational database products

The Oracle's success can be attributed to the following reasons.

(a) High openness. It supported running on all mainstream platforms at that time, fully complied with various industry standards and was highly compatible.

(b) High security. It provided multiple security protections, including features for assessing risk, preventing unauthorized data leakage, detecting and reporting database activity, and enforcing data access control in the database through data-driven security.

(c) Strong performance. Under the open platform, the database has been a perennial leader in professional test results. In the 1980s to 1990s, it consistently followed and led the technical trend of relational databases. In addition, Oracle released Oracle EXADATA All-in-One product in 2009 to compete for the high-end online analytical processing (OLAP) market.

(2) Teradata is a database product launched by Tenet of the US. The first database computer DBC/1012, which was released in 1984, was the first database-dedicated platform with massively parallel processing (MPP) architecture. The Teradata database was primarily available in the early days as an all-in-one machine, positioned as a large data warehouse system. Proprietary software and hardware gave it excellent OLAP performance, but it was very expensive.

(3) DB2 is the database product of IBM. DB2 is the main relational database product promoted by IBM, which only served IBM mainframe and small machine at the beginning, and then started to support Windows, UNIX and other platforms in 1995. The reason why it is named DB2 is because DB1 is a hierarchical database.

(4) Ingres was originally a relational database research project initiated by the University of California, Berkeley in 1974, and the code of Ingres was available for free, so much commercial database software was produced based on it, including Sybase, Microsoft SQL Server, Informix, and the successor project PostgreSQL. It can be said that Ingres is one of the most influential computer research projects in history.

(5) Informix was the first commercial Ingres product to appear in 1982, but was later acquired by IBM in 2000 due to management failures by its owner. The source code of Informix was then licensed to GBASE from China, which developed the Chinese-made Gbase 8t product on the basis of its source code.

(6) Sybase is a database product of Sybase Inc. The company was founded in 1984, named after the combination of the words "System" and "Database", and one of its founders, Bob Epstein, was one of the main designers of Ingres. Sybase first proposed and implemented the idea of the Client/Server database architecture. The company began working with Microsoft in 1987 to develop the Sybase SQL Server product. After the termination of the partnership, Microsoft continued to develop the MS SQL Server and Sybase continued to develop the Sybase ASE. Its subsequent relational database, Sybase IQ, designed especially

for data warehousing, was a highly successful columnar database. In May 2010, Sybase was acquired by the German company SAP.

(7) MySQL 1.0, the internal version of the MySQL database product, was released in 1996, and MySQL 3.11.1 was released in October of the same year. MySQL is allowed to be distributed commercially for free, but may not be bundled with other commercial products. MySQL was acquired by Sun in January 2008, and the latter was acquired by Oracle in 2009, so MySQL is now an Oracle product, but is still available as a free open source product.

(8) PostgreSQL database was born in 1989, inheriting many ideas from Ingres, and its SQL engine was modified and formally communitized in 1995. Greenplum, Netezza, Amazon Redshift, and GaussDB (DWS) are all databases developed based on PostgreSQL versions.

(9) Greenplum and Netezza are both distributed databases adopting the MPP architecture based on PostgreSQL version 8.x. Greenplum was acquired by EMC Corporation as a pure software version and formed the Pivotal family together with other products, of which Greenplum is the relational database product.

(10) Netezza is a software and hardware all-in-one product with proprietary hardware optimization technology, which was later acquired by IBM.

(11) Aster Data is a relational database product based on Greenplum, similar to Greenplum, with the main feature of providing SQL-based data discovery algorithms and powerful statistical analysis functions. The product was later acquired by Teradata Corporation.

(12) Amazon Redshift is a cloud-based relational database from Amazon, developed based on PostgreSQL.

(13) SAP HANA is SAP's self-developed in-memory database product, using columnar storage, data compression and parallel processing technologies.

(14) Vertica is a columnar database, suitable for the OLAP.

1.2.9   Other Data Models

With the expansion of the database industry and the diversification of data objects, the traditional relational database model begins to reveal many weaknesses, such as poor identification capability for complex objects, weak semantic expression capability, and poor processing capability for data types such as text, time, space, sound, image and video. For example, multimedia data are basically stored as binary data streams in relational databases, but for binary data streams, the generic database has poor identification capability and poor semantic expression capability, which is not conducive to retrieval and query.

In view of this, many new data models have been proposed to adapt to the new application requirements, specifically the following.

(1) Object oriented data model (OODM). This model, combining the semantic data model and object-oriented programming methods, uses a series of object-oriented methods and new concepts to form the basis of the model. However, the OODM operation language is too complex, which increases the burden of system upgrade for enterprises, and it is difficult for users to accept such a complex way of use. So OODM is not as universally accepted as relational database except for some specific application markets.

(2) XML data model. With the rapid development of the Internet, there are a large number of semi-structured and unstructured data sources. Extensible markup language (XML) has become a common data model for exchanging data on the Internet and a hot spot for database research, and accordingly derived an XML data model for semi-structured data. Pure XML database, based on XML node tree model, supports XML data management, but the same requires to solve the various problems faced by traditional relational database.

(3) RDF data model. The information in the Internet lacks a unified expression, so the World Wide Web Consortium (W3C) proposes to describe and annotate Internet resources with the resource description framework (RDF). The RDF is a markup language for describing Internet resources, with triple containing resources (subject), attributes (predicate), and attribute values (object) as the infrastructure. Such a triple is also called a statement, where an attribute value can be a resource (either a resource or a literal; if it is a literal, it can only be an atomic value, such as a number, a date, etc.), and an attribute describes the relationship between the resource and the attribute value. Statement can also be represented as a graph: a directed edge points from the statement resource to the attribute value, with the attribute on the edge; the attribute value of a statement can be the resource of another statement.

1.2.10   New Challenges for Data Management Technologies

Although new data models are emerging from time to time, all of them have failed to replace the relational database model as the common basic model for database products due to problems such as lack of convenience and generality.

New challenges for data management technologies are as follows.

(1) With the automation, diversification and intelligence of data acquisition means, the volume of data is soaring, so the databases need to provide a high degree of scalability and scalability.

(2) The ability to deal with diverse data types is needed. Data can be classified into structured data, semi-structured and unstructured data, including texts, graphics, images, audio, videos and other multimedia data, stream data, queue data, etc. Diverse data types require database products to develop the ability of dealing with multiple data types and the ability to heterogeneous processing.

(3) The development of sensing, network and communication technologies has put forward higher requirements for data acquisition and processing in real-time.

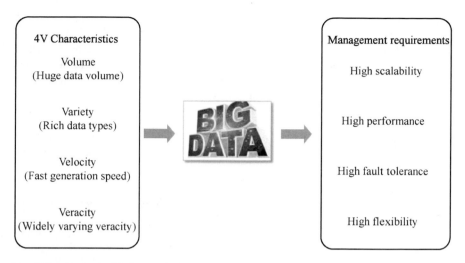

Fig. 1.13   Big data's 4V characteristics

(4) At the advent of the era of big data, data problems such as massive heterogeneity, complicated forms, high growth rate, and low value density have posed comprehensive challenges to traditional relational databases. NoSQL technology has flourished in response to the needs of big data development. Big data has 4V characteristics, as shown in Fig. 1.13.

The 4Vs are Volume (huge data volume), Variety (rich data types), Velocity (fast generation speed), and Veracity (widely varying veracity). Volume: The volume of data covered by Big Data processing is huge, having risen from the traditional terabyte level to the petabyte level. Variety: Big data processing involves a wide range of data types, where in addition to traditional structured data, Internet web logs, videos, pictures, geolocation information, etc. can also be found; moreover, semi-structured data and unstructured data also need to be processed. Velocity: The high processing speed in the Internet of Things (IoT) applications is particularly significant, with the requirement for real-time processing. Veracity: Big data processing pursues high quality data, i.e., mining valuable data from massive data with a lot of noise, and due to low data value density, high-value information needs to be mined among a large amount of low-value data.

1.2.11   NoSQL Database

To meet the challenges of the big data era, new models and technologies have sprung up, typically the NoSQL database technology, which first emerged in 1998 as a lightweight, open-source, non-relational database technology that does not provide SQL functionality. By 2009, the concept began to return, but it was a completely different concept compared to the original one. The NoSQL technology, or Not Only SQL, that is widely accepted today is no longer just SQL technology.

Many different types of NoSQL database products have been created over the years, and although they have different characteristics, non-relational, distributed, and not guaranteed to meet ACID characteristics are their unifying features.

NoSQL databases have the following three technical features.

(1) Partitioning of data (Partition). It can distribute data across multiple nodes in a cluster, and then conduct parallel processing on a large number of nodes to achieve high performance; it also facilitates the scaling of the cluster by scaling horizontally.

(2) Reduction of ACID consistency constraint. Based on the BASE principle, it accepts the eventual consistency constraint although it allows temporary inconsistency.

 Explanation	The BASE principle contains the following 3 levels of meaning. Basically available: Short-term data unavailability is tolerated, and no emphasis is placed on 24/7 service. Soft state: There is a period of state asynchrony, i.e. asynchronous state. Eventual consistency: It requires eventual data consistency and does not require strict full consistency.

(3) Backup for each data partition. The general principle of triple backup (three copies of data are kept on the current node, another node in the same rack, and another node in another rack against node failure and rack failure. The more backups, the greater the data redundancy. Based on the comprehensive consideration of security and redundancy, such triple backup of data is the most reasonable setting) is followed to cope with node failures and improve system availability.

The four common types of NoSQL database technologies are divided by storage model, including key-value database, graph database, column family database, and document database, as shown in Fig. 1.14.

Table 1.3 briefly introduces the main NoSQL databases. Key-value databases are generally implemented based on hash tables by pointing key to value; storing keys in memory enables extremely efficient key-based, or code-based, query and write operations, and is suitable for caching user information, session information, configuration files, shopping carts, and other application scenarios. Such products as column grouping database, document database and graph database also feature their own characteristics, but since this book is mainly concerned with relational databases, they will not be covered here.

NoSQL was not created to replace a relational DBMS (RDBMS), and while it has both significant advantages and disadvantages. It is designed to work with RDBMS to build a complete data ecosystem.

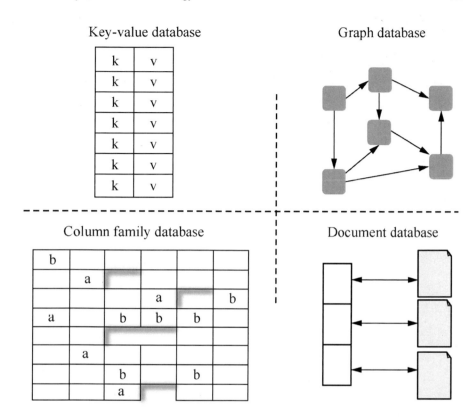

Fig. 1.14 Four common types of NoSQL database technologies

1.2.12 NewSQL Database

Since the introduction of NoSQL, a highly scalable product, its ease of use has been recognized. If applied to traditional databases, it can greatly enhance the scalability of traditional databases. Therefore, a relational database that combines the scalability of NoSQL with support for the relational model has been developed. This new-type database is mainly oriented to the online transaction processing (OLTP) scenario that shows high requirements for speed and concurrency. The database uses SQL as the main language, so it is called NewSQL database.

"NewSQL" is only a description of this class, not an officially defined name. NewSQL database is a relational database system that supports the relational model (including ACID features) while achieving the scalability of NoSQL, mainly oriented to the OLTP scenario, allowing SQL as the primary language.

The classification of NewSQL databases is as follows.

(1) Databases re-constructed with new architecture.

Table 1.3 Brief introduction of the main NoSQL databases

Type	Representative products	Typical application scenarios	Data model	Advantages	Disadvantages
Key-value database	Redis MemCahed	Caching user information, session information, profiles, shopping carts, etc.	Generally implemented based on hash tables by pointing key to value	Fast search	Unstructured data, such as strings or binary data
Column family database	HBase Cassandra	Logging and blogging platforms	Columnar storage	Fast search and distributed scalability	Not suitable for random updates or real-time operations with deletions and updates
Document database	DouchDB MongoDB	Logging platforms, which can store log information of different modes; data analysis based on weak patterns	Similar to pointing key to value, but the data structure of value is not strict, no requiring pre-definition of table structure	Variable table structure, high scalability, and suitability for unstructured objects	Some products do not support transaction operations
Graph database	Neo4j Infinite Graph	Recommendation engines and relationship graphs	Graph structure	Handling domain-specific problems with the help of graph theory algorithms	Restricted applications in non-graph domains

They may adopt technical architectures such as multi-node concurrency control, distributed processing, replication-based fault tolerance, and flow control. Such products include Google Spanner, H-Store, VoltDB, etc.

(2) Databases adopting the middleware technology of transparent shard.

The generation of data shards is transparent to users, and users do not need to make changes to their applications.

These products are Oracle, MySQL, Proxy, MariaDB MaxScale, etc.

(3) Database as a Service (DaaS).

The database products provided by cloud service providers are generally such databases with NewSQL features.

Such products include Amazon Aurora, Alibaba Cloud's Oceanbase, Tencent Cloud's CynosDB, Huawei's GaussDB (DWS) and GaussDB (for MySQL).

1.2.13   Database Ranking

Like programming languages, databases have popularity rankings, which are updated monthly and include overall database rankings and rankings under database types, such as special rankings for relational databases, key-value databases, temporal databases, graph databases, and so on, as shown in Fig. 1.15. The figure shows that in August 2019, the top 3 are firmly held by traditional relational databases; four NoSQL databases appear in the top 10; and the top 20 are generally evenly split between relational and NoSQL databases. Relational databases are extending their functionality and features.

351 systems in ranking, August 2019

Rank			DBMS	Database Model	Score		
Aug 2019	Jul 2019	Aug 2018			Aug 2019	Jul 2019	Aug 2018
1.	1.	1.	Oracle ➕	Relational, Multi-model ⓘ	1339.48	+18.22	+27.45
2.	2.	2.	MySQL ➕	Relational, Multi-model ⓘ	1253.68	+24.16	+46.87
3.	3.	3.	Microsoft SQL Server ➕	Relational, Multi-model ⓘ	1093.18	+2.35	+20.53
4.	4.	4.	PostgreSQL ➕	Relational, Multi-model ⓘ	481.33	-1.94	+63.83
5.	5.	5.	MongoDB ➕	Document	404.57	-5.36	+53.59
6.	6.	6.	IBM Db2 ➕	Relational, Multi-model ⓘ	172.95	-1.19	-8.89
7.	7.	↑ 8.	Elasticsearch ➕	Search engine, Multi-model ⓘ	149.08	+0.27	+10.97
8.	8.	↓ 7.	Redis ➕	Key-value, Multi-model ⓘ	144.08	-0.18	+5.51
9.	9.	9.	Microsoft Access	Relational	135.33	-1.98	+6.24
10.	10.	10.	Cassandra ➕	Wide column	125.21	-1.80	+5.63
11.	11.	11.	SQLite ➕	Relational	122.72	-1.91	+8.99
12.	12.	↑ 13.	Splunk	Search engine	85.88	+0.39	+15.39
13.	13.	↑ 14.	MariaDB ➕	Relational, Multi-model ⓘ	84.95	+0.52	+16.66
14.	14.	↑ 18.	Hive ➕	Relational	81.80	+0.93	+23.86
15.	15.	↓ 12.	Teradata ➕	Relational, Multi-model ⓘ	76.64	-1.18	-0.77
16.	16.	↓ 15.	Solr	Search engine	59.12	-0.52	-2.78
17.	17.	↑ 19.	FileMaker	Relational	58.02	+0.12	+1.96
18.	↑ 20.	↑ 21.	Amazon DynamoDB ➕	Multi-model ⓘ	56.57	+0.15	+4.91
19.	↓ 18.	↓ 17.	HBase	Wide column	56.54	-1.00	-2.27
20.	↓ 19.	↓ 16.	SAP Adaptive Server	Relational	55.86	-0.79	-4.57

Fig. 1.15 Database ranking

1.3 Architecture of Relational Databases

1.3.1 Development of Database Architecture

In the early days when the data size was not too large, the database system used a very simple stand-alone service, i.e., database software was installed on a dedicated server to provide external data access services. However, as business expands, the data size in the database and the pressure on the business are upgraded. This requires the database architecture to change accordingly. The architecture classification shown in Fig. 1.16 is a way to distinguish the database architecture according to the number of hosts.

An architecture with only one database host is a single-host architecture, while an architecture with more than one database host is a multi-host architecture. The single host in the single-host architecture deploys both database application and database on the same host; while the stand-alone host deploys them separately, with the database exclusively on a separate database server. The multi-host architecture enhances the availability and service capability of the overall database services by increasing the number of servers. This architecture can be classified into two models based on whether data shards are generated. One type is the group architecture, in which, depending on the role of each server, the servers are further divided into master-standby, master-slave and multi-master architectures. Regardless of the grouping method, the databases share the same structure and store exactly the same data, essentially replicating data between multiple databases with synchronization techniques. Another model is the sharding architecture, which spreads the data shards within different hosts through a certain mechanism.

1.3.2 Single-Host Architecture

In order to avoid the application services and database services from competing for resources, the single-host architecture evolved from the earlier single-host model to

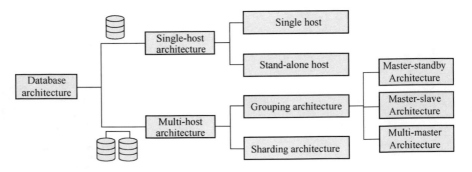

Fig. 1.16 Database architecture classification by number of hosts

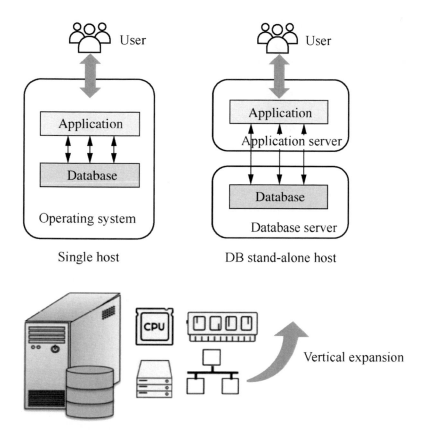

Fig. 1.17 Single-host architecture

stand-alone host for database, which separates the application services and data services. For the application services, the number of servers can be increased to balance the load, thus enhancing the concurrency capability of the system. The single-host deployment features such as flexibility and ease of deployment in R&D, learning, and simulation environments, as shown in Fig. 1.17.

The LAMP (Linux, Apache, MySQL, and PHP) architecture of the early Internet is a typical single-host architecture, with following obvious shortcomings.

(1) Poor scalability. The single-host architecture only supports vertical expansion, improving performance by increasing the hardware configuration, but there is an upper limit to the hardware resources that can be configured on a single host.
(2) Single point of failure. Expansion of the single-host architecture often requires suspension, and the service will also suspense. In addition, hardware failure can easily lead to the unavailability of the entire service, and can even cause data loss.
(3) As business expands, the single-host architecture is bound to encounter performance bottlenecks.

1.3.3   Group Architecture: Master-Standby Architecture

The master-standby architecture in the group architecture is actually born from the single-host architecture to solve the single point of failure, as shown in Fig. 1.18.

The database is deployed on two servers, where the server that undertakes the data read/write service is called the host, and the other server, standby, is used as a backup to copy the data from the host using the data synchronization mechanism. Only one server provides data services at the same time.

This architecture has the advantage that the application does not require additional development to cope with database failures, plus it improves data fault tolerance compared to a stand-alone architecture.

The disadvantage is the waste of resources, the backup and the host enjoy the same configuration, but the backup resources are basically in idle state; in addition, the performance pressure is still concentrated on a single server, which cannot address the performance bottleneck. When a failure occurs, the switch between the host and the standby requires some manual intervention or monitoring. So to say, this model only addresses the data availability and cannot break through the performance bottleneck; while the performance is still limited by the hardware configuration of a single server, cannot be improved overall by increasing the number of servers.

Fig. 1.18 Group architecture—master-standby architecture

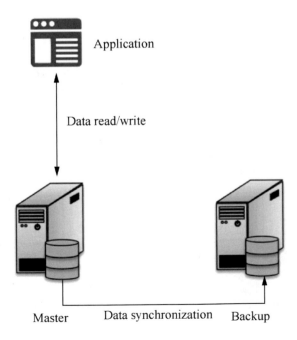

1.3.4 Group Architecture: Master-Slave Architecture

The deployment model of master-slave architecture is similar to that of master-standby architecture, but in which the standby is promoted to the slave role and provides certain data services. The application can adopt the read/write separation, and the development model needs to be adjusted accordingly at this time, i.e., the three write operations of write, modify, and delete are required to be done on the write library (host), and the query requests (read operations) are assigned to the read library (slave), as shown in Fig. 1.19.

This architecture brings the benefit of improved resource utilization and is suitable for application scenarios with more read operations and few write operations. In addition, it can be balanced among multiple slaves in scenarios with highly concurrent read operations. The slaves can be flexibly expanded, and the expansion operation generally does not affect the service.

However, the master-slave architecture also has the following disadvantages: first, data latency, i.e., there is a delay when synchronizing data to the slave database, so the application must be able to tolerate short inconsistencies, which is not suitable for scenarios with very high requirements for consistency; second, the performance pressure of write operations is still concentrated on the host; third, availability problems, i.e., when switching from the host to a slave due to host failure, such manual intervention costs time to respond, and the complexity to achieve automatic switching is high.

Fig. 1.19 Group architecture—master-slave architecture

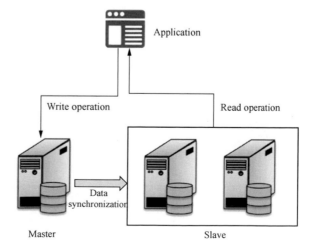

1.3.5 Group Architecture: Multi-Master Architecture

Multi-master architecture is also called active-active or multi-active architecture, in which the database and servers are master and slave to each other, and provide complete data services at the same time, as shown in Fig. 1.20.

The advantage of the multi-master architecture is to ensure higher resource utilization while reducing the risk of single point of failure; however, there is also the disadvantage that since both hosts receive write data, bi-directional synchronization of data must be achieved, but bi-directional replication also brings latency issues, and in extreme cases even the risk of data loss must be considered. When changing from dual hosts to multiple hosts, the increased number of databases further complicates the data synchronization issues, so the dual-host model is more common in practical applications.

1.3.6 Shared Disk Architecture

Next, we will introduce a special kind of multi-master architecture—shared disk. In this architecture, the database and servers share the stored data, and load balancing is achieved by multiple servers, as shown in Fig. 1.21.

The advantage of shared disk is that multiple servers can provide highly available services at the same time, thus achieving a high level of availability and scalability as a whole and avoiding a single point of failure of server clusters. This architecture supports easy horizontal scaling, which in turn enhances the parallel processing capability of the overall system.

The disadvantage is that it is quite difficult to implement the technology. In addition, when the memory interface bandwidth reaches saturation, adding nodes

Fig. 1.20 Group architecture—multi-master architecture

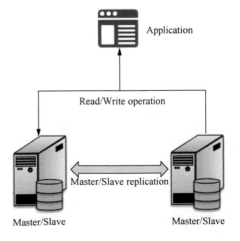

Fig. 1.21 Shared disk
architecture

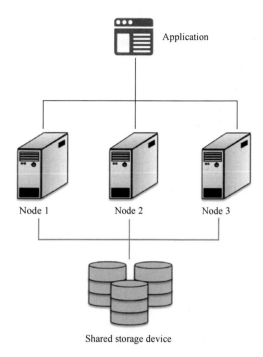

does not result in higher performance, and storage I/O can easily become a bottleneck affecting the overall system performance.

1.3.7   Sharding Architecture

The sharding architecture is primarily a horizontal data sharding architecture, which
is a sharding scheme that spreads data across multiple nodes. Each shard consists of a
part of the database. Multiple nodes in this architecture share the same database
structure, without intersection between the data in different shards, and the concat-
enation of all data shards forms the data aggregate. Common sharding algorithms are
those based on list values, range intervals, and hash values, as shown in Fig. 1.22.

The advantage of this architecture is that the data is scatted on the nodes within
the cluster, and each node can work independently, giving full play to the parallelism
of the cluster.

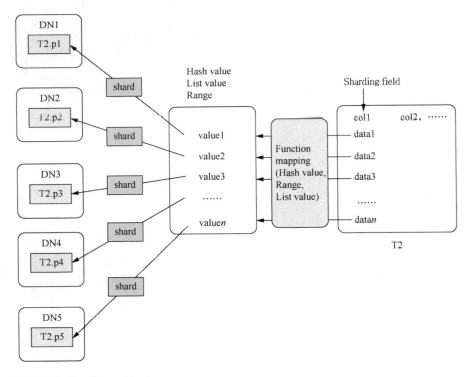

Fig. 1.22 Sharding architecture

1.3.8   Shared-Nothing Architecture

The shared-nothing architecture is a completely non-shared architecture in which each node (processing unit) in the cluster has its own independent CPU, memory and external memory, never sharing resources. Each node (processing unit) processes its own local data, and the results can be aggregated upward or circulated among the nodes through communication protocols. The nodes are independent of each other and have high scalability, so the whole cluster obtains a strong parallel processing capability, as shown in Fig. 1.23.

Hardware has evolved to the point where a node or a physical host can accommodate multiple processing units, so the smallest unit of the architecture may not be a physical host, but a logical virtual processing unit. For example, for a physical host with a quad-core CPU, four database instances can be deployed, which is equivalent to having four processing units.

Fig. 1.23 Shared-nothing architecture

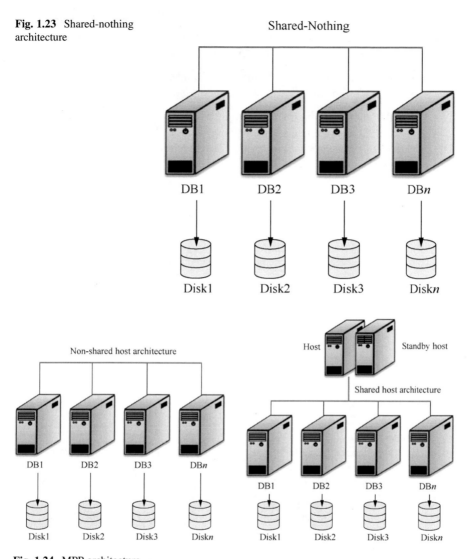

Fig. 1.24 MPP architecture

1.3.9   Massively Parallel Processing Architecture

The massively parallel processing (MPP) architecture spreads tasks in parallel across multiple servers and nodes. After the computation on each node is completed, the results of each part are aggregated into the final result, as shown in Fig. 1.24.

The MPP architecture is characterized by the fact that the tasks are executed in parallel, while the computation is distributed. Two minor variations exist here, one is the non-shared host architecture and the other is the shared host architecture. In the non-shared host architecture, all nodes are peer-to-peer, and data can be queried and loaded by any node, which generally does not have performance bottlenecks and single-point risks, but the technical implementation is more complex.

The common MPP architecture products are as follows.

(1) Non-shared host architecture: Vertica and Teradata.
(2) Shared host architecture: Greenplum and Netezza.

Teradata and Netezza are hardware-software all-in-one machines, while GaussDB (DWS), Greeplum, and Vertica are software versions of MPP architecture databases. The shared architecture is the basis of the shared-nothing architecture, and shared-nothing for clusters is only possible if data is sharded.

Explanation	The concept of shared-nothing describes the architecture from the perspective of resource independence, while the concept of shard describes the architecture from the perspective of data independence. The MPP describes the architecture from the perspective of parallel computing, which is the application and embodiment of parallel computing technology on distributed databases. The terms shard, shared-nothing and MPP can be regarded as the proper nouns of distributed database architecture.

1.3.10   Comparison of the Characteristics of Database Architectures

Finally, let's compare the characteristics of the above database architectures, as shown in Table 1.4.

In terms of high availability, the more hosts there are, the better the high availability will perform. As for read/write performance, both stand-alone architecture and master-standby architecture depend on single-host hardware, so both are affected by single-host hardware's performance bottleneck. While the master-slave architecture can use read/write separation to enhance read/write performance; the multi-master architecture and sharding architecture both have better read/write service capability and can provide strong parallel processing capability. In terms of data consistency, the stand-alone architecture excludes the data consistency issues, while the master-standby and master-slave architectures require data synchronization among multiple hosts because they increase the number of hosts, thus making it difficult to avoid data latency and data consistency issues. Multi-host architecture also faces the data inconsistency, unlike the shared disk architecture that benefit from shared storage. Inside the sharding architecture, data is scattered on each node and data synchronization is not required between nodes, so there is no data inconsistency. Finally, scalability. The stand-alone architecture and master-standby architecture only support vertical scaling, and both will encounter the stand-alone issues and hardware performance bottleneck. The master-slave architecture can improve concurrent read capability by scaling horizontally, and the multi-master architecture scales well, but increasing the hosts will lead to a sharp increase in the

Table 1.4 Comparison of the characteristics of database architectures

Characteristic	First-phone	Stand-alone architecture	Master-slave architecture	Multi-master architecture	Sharding architecture
Availability	Poor	Average	Fair	Good	Good
Read/write performance	Hardware performance dependent on a single host	Hardware performance dependent on a single host	With read/write separation, the write performance is limited by the host, while the read performance is enhanced by increasing the number of slaves to enhance concurrency	High read/write capability is achieved because multiple hosts can provide read/write services simultaneously	The non-shared architecture provides excellent distributed computing capabilities with strong parallel processing capabilities
Data consistency	No data consistency issues	The data synchronization mechanism is adopted to synchronize between master and standby, but there are data latency issues and data loss risks	Same as the master-standby mode, and with the increase of the number of slaves, the data latency issues and data loss risk will be more prominent	The data needs to be synchronized in both directions between multiple hosts, so it is prone to data inconsistency. But the shared disk architecture with shared storage does not have data consistency issues	Based on the sharding technology, data is scattered on each node, and data synchronization is not required between nodes, so there is no data consistency issues
Scalability	Only vertical scaling is supported, and will encounter hardware performance bottlenecks due to the single host	Only vertical scaling is supported, and will encounter hardware performance bottlenecks due to the single host	The slave can be scaled horizontally for better concurrent read capacity	Good scalability, but increasing the number of hosts will lead to a dramatic increase in data synchronization complexity	Linear scaling is theoretically possible, so scalability is best

complexity of data synchronization; while the sharding architecture can theoretically achieve linear scaling, and has the best scalability among these architectures.

1.4 Mainstream Applications of Relational Databases

1.4.1 Online Transaction Processing

Online transaction processing (OLTP) is the main application of traditional relational database, which is oriented to basic and daily transaction processing, such as access transaction and transfer transaction of deposit service.

Database transaction is a basic logical unit in the database execution process. The database system needs to ensure that all operations in a transaction are completed successfully and the results are permanently stored in the database.

For example, someone wants to buy something worth $100 in a store using electronic money. This involves at least two operations: the person's account is reduced by $100; the store account is increased by $100. A transactional DBMS makes sure that both of these operations (i.e., the entire transaction) either complete or are canceled together; otherwise, the $100 will disappear or appear for nothing. But in reality, the risk of failure is high. The execution of database transactions may encounter operation failures, database system or operating system errors, or even storage media errors. This requires the DBMS to perform recovery operations on a failed transaction execution to restore its database state to a consistent state (the state in which data consistency is guaranteed), for which the DBMS usually needs to maintain transaction logs to track all operations in the transaction that affect the database data.

OLTP is characterized precisely by high throughput, as evidenced by the ability to support a large number of short online transactions (inserts, updates, deletes), and very fast query processing, supporting high concurrency and (quasi-real time) real-time response.

The OLTP scenario places very high demands on the timeliness of response, requiring the database system to have the ability to quickly handle a large number of concurrent transaction operations, where the response of each transaction reaches millisecond level or even faster. Moreover, the transaction concurrency is very large, so high concurrency is also one of the most significant features in OLTP scenarios. For example, online ticketing systems, retail systems and flash sale campaigns are typical OLTP application scenarios.

1.4.2 Online Analytical Processing

The concept of online analytical processing (OLAP) was first proposed by Edgar Frank Codd in 1993 relative to OLTP system, and refers to the query and analysis operations on data. Usually, when querying and analyzing a large amount of historical data, the historical period involved is long, the volume of data is large, and the aggregation operations at different levels make the transaction processing more complex.

OLAP is characterized by its focus on complex queries and some "strategic" problem solving. In terms of data processing, it focuses on "analytical" data processing and operations such as data aggregation, grouping calculation, and window calculation, involving multi-dimensional data usage and analysis.

Common OLAP scenarios include reporting systems, customer relationship management (CRM) systems, financial risk prediction and early warning systems, anti-money laundering systems, data marts, data warehouses, etc. A reporting system is a platform or system that generates reports for a fixed period or in a fixed format, such as daily, weekly, and monthly reports, to provide electronic reporting data for business decision making. A CRM system is a comprehensive business system platform that provides customer maintenance services, stores customer-related information, analyzes customer behavior, responds to customers, and manages marketing activities. A data mart is generally an application geared toward the departmental needs of an organization, such as the analytical needs of a credit card department. Data warehouse is an enterprise-oriented analytic platform system created to build an analytic processing environment for the entire enterprise.

1.4.3 Database Performance Measurement Indicators

The particular architectural design and implementation of different databases will vary depending on the scenario. So to evaluate the merits of different databases in different scenarios, there is a need for a more authoritative standard. The Transaction Processing Performance Council (TPC) is responsible for developing benchmark specifications, performance and price metrics for business applications, and managing the publication of test results. It is a standard specification rather than a code, and any manufacturer can optimally construct their own system and evaluate it according to the specification. The TPC has introduced a number of benchmarking standards, including the following two specifications for OLTP and OLAP, respectively.

(1) TPC-C specification is for OLTP systems, including the traffic indicator tpmC (tpm: transactions per minute [test system transactions per minute]) and cost performance indicators (price [test system price]/tpmC), the latter is the cost to achieve a basic unit.

(2) OLAP-oriented system is the TPC-H specification, whose test metric is the traffic indicator qphH (qph: query per hour [complex queries processed per hour]) The TPC-H specification requires consideration of the size of the test data set, and the specification specifies 22 query statements for different test data sets, which can be fine-tuned according to specific products. The test scenarios include data loading, power testing and traffic testing; the specific test criteria are

Table 1.5 Comparative analysis of OLTP and OLAP

Item	OLTP	OLAP
Analysis granularity	Detailed	Detailed, aggregated and extractive
Timeliness	Accurate at the moment of access	Represents past data
Data update	Can be updated	Usually no update is required
Operation predictability	Operation requirements are known in advance	Operation requirements may be unknown in advance
Real-time	High performance requirements, millisecond or second response time	Relatively lenient performance requirements, minute or hourly response time
Data volume	Dealing with one or a few records at a time, small data volume	Dealing with a set at a time, large data volume
Drive method	Transaction-driven	Analysis-driven
Application type	Application-oriented	Analytics-oriented
Application scenarios	Supporting daily operations	Supporting management needs
Typical applications	Bank core systems and credit card systems	Analytical customer relationship management and risk management

explained by the test specification documents, which are publicly available online and can be accessed at the TPC website.

The comparative analysis of OLTP and OLAP is shown in Table 1.5, and similar analyses can be found on the web; they mostly refer to the relevant contents described in the book *Build in the Body to Y* by Iven, the proposer of the data warehouse concept. From the perspective of analysis granularity, OLTP is a detailed analysis, dealing with every most basic transaction event, while OLAP is a comprehensive analysis, in which there is more integrated and aggregated analysis. In terms of timeliness, OLTP emphasizes transient technicality, with transactions ending when they are completed. In terms of data update requirements, OLAP does not require updates in general.

To sum up, both OLTP and OLAP systems follow the ACID principle and use relational databases. Both are functionally similar in that they support SQL statements, can handle large volume of data, and implement highly consistent transactional processing. However, for application scenarios, OLTP places more emphasis on substantive requirements, while OLAP more on analysis of large-volume data. In general, due to the different goals pursued by the two in their respective application scenarios, it is currently not suitable to use them interchangeably, for example, using OLTP databases for OLAP analytics applications or using OLAP as a core transaction system with high requirements for real-time. But now an emerging hybrid transaction and analytical process (HTAP) database system aims to achieve a system that can host both OLTP and OLAP application scenarios. Related products applying this technology appear on the scene from time to time and are one of the trends in the development of NewSQL database technology. Readers can find related materials to expand their knowledge on their own.

1.5 Summary

This chapter introduces the basic concepts of database and data management system, reviews the development history of database for decades, details the development of database from early mesh model and hierarchical model to relational model, and introduces the emerging NoSQL and NewSQL concepts in recent years; provides a comparative analysis and introduction to the main architectures of relational database, and briefly explains the advantages and disadvantages of various architectures in different scenarios; finally, introduces and contrasts the mainstream application scenarios of OLTP and OLAP for relational data.

Through the study of this chapter, readers are able to describe the concepts related to database technology, enumerate the main relational databases, distinguish different relational data architectures, and describe and identify the main application scenarios of relational databases.

1.6 Exercises

1. [Multiple Choice] The characteristics of the data stored in the database are ( ).

   A. Permanently stored
   B. Organized
   C. Independent
   D. Shareable

2. [Multiple Choice] The components of the concept of a database system are ( ).

   A. Database management system
   B. Database
   C. Application development tool
   D. Application

3. [True or False] Database applications can read database files directly, without using the database management system. ( )

   A. True
   B. False

4. [Multiple Choice] What are the stages in the development of data management?
   ( )

A. Manual stage
B. Intelligent system
C. File system
D. Database system

5. [Single Choice] In which data model, more than one node is allowed to have no "two parents" node, and a node can have more than one "two parents" node. ( )

    A. Hierarchical model
    B. Relational model
    C. Object-oriented model
    D. Mesh model

6. [Multiple Choice] Which of the following are NoSQL databases? ( )

    A. Graph database
    B. Document database
    C. Key-value database
    D. Column family database

7. [True or False] The emergence of NoSQL and NewSQL databases can completely subvert and replace the original relational database systems. ( )

    A. True
    B. False

8. [True or False] The master-standby architecture can improve the overall read/write concurrency by separating read and write. ( )

    A. True
    B. False

9. [Single Choice] Which database architecture has good linear scalability? ( )

    A. Master-slave architecture
    B. Shared-nothing architecture
    C. Shared disk architecture
    D. Master-standby architecture

10. [True or False] The characteristic of the sharding architecture is that the data is scattered on each database node of the cluster through a certain algorithm, and the advantage of server number in the cluster is taken for parallel computing. ( )

    A. True
    B. False

11. [Multiple Choice] Test metrics used to measure OLTP systems include ( ).

    A. tpmC
    B. Price/tmpC
    C. qphH
    D. qps

12. [Multiple Choice] OLAP system is suitable for which of the following scenarios? ( )

    A. Reporting system
    B. Online transaction system
    C. Multi-dimensional analysis and data mining systems
    D. Data warehouse

13. [True or False] OLAP system can analyze and process a large volume of data, so it can also meet the processing performance requirements of OLTP for small data volume. ( )

    A. True
    B. False

Chapter 2
Basic Knowledge of Database

Various database products have different characteristics, but they share some common ground in the main database concepts, that is, they can achieve various database objects and different levels of security protection measures, and they also emphasize the performance management and daily operation and maintenance management of the database.

This chapter is about the main responsibilities and contents of database management, and introduces some common but important basic concepts of databases to lay a good foundation for the next stage of learning. After completing this chapter, readers will be able to describe the main work of database management, including distinguishing different backup methods, listing measures for security management and describing the work of performance management, as well as describing the important basic concepts of database and the usage of each database object.

2.1 Overview of Database Management

2.1.1 Database Management and Its Scope of Work

Database management refers to the management and maintenance of the DBMS, whose core goal is to ensure the stability of the database, security and data consistency, as well as the high performance of the system.

Stability refers to the high availability of the database. Master-slave, multimaster, distributed and other highly available architectures are used to ensure the availability and stability of the database system.

Security refers to the security of the content stored in the database to avoid illegal access and use of data content.

Data consistency refers to the database itself will provide many functions to ensure data consistency, such as foreign key constraints and non-null constraints on table, etc. Data consistency here is about the use of synchronization technology,

Huawei Technologies Co., Ltd., *Database Principles and Technologies – Based on Huawei GaussDB*, https://doi.org/10.1007/978-981-19-3032-4_2

replication tools, etc. provided by the database when building master-standby systems, master-slave systems and other multi-master systems to ensure data consistency among multiple databases. This assurance work is part of the database management work.

The high performance of the system mainly involves the optimization, monitoring, troubleshooting and other work inside the database management.

Database Administrator (DBA) is a collective term for the personnel involved in managing and maintaining the DBMS, not a particular person, but a role. Some companies also call the DBA database engineer. The work of the two roles is basically the same, ensuring 7/24 stable and efficient operation of the database.

Database management work includes management of database objects, database security, backup and recovery, performance and environment.

Database object management is actually the management of the data in the database, including physical design and implementation work. Physical design work refers to understanding the features and functions provided by different database objects, and transforming the data model in conceptual design and logical design into physical database objects on the basis of following reasonable relational design principles. Physical implementation work refers to the creation, deletion, modification and optimization of database objects.

Database security management refers to the prevention of unauthorized access to avoid leakage of protected information, as well as the prevention of security breaches and improper data modifications to ensure that data is available only to authorized users. Database security management work includes, but is not limited to, the management of system security, data security and network security. Enterprise database security strategy includes laying a solid foundation with authentication, authorization, access, control, recovery, classification, and batch management; encryption and desensitization through defensive data protection measures to protect critical information and data privacy without affecting program application functions; creating database intrusion detection with audit monitoring and vulnerability assessment, etc., while developing security policies and standards to ensure role separation and availability.

Backup and recovery management is said to develop a reasonable backup strategy to achieve regular backup function, so as to ensure the fastest recovery and minimum loss for the database system in case of disaster.

Database performance management means monitoring and optimizing the factors that affect database performance and optimizing the resources that the database can use to increase system throughput and reduce contention to handle the maximum possible workload. The factors involved in database performance optimization include workload, throughput, resources, and contention. Among them, the workload for the database is the user-submitted usage requirements, expressed in different forms such as online transactions, batch jobs, analytical queries, instant queries. The workload of the database varies from time to time, and the overall workload has a great impact on the database performance. Throughput refers to the overall processing capacity of the database software, i.e., the number of queries and transactions that can be processed per unit of time. Resources include CPU, I/O, network, storage, processes, threads, and all other hardware and software objects that are available and at the disposal of the database. Competition refers to the demand for the use of the same resource by multiple workloads at the same time, and this conflict arises because the number of resources is less than the demand of the workload.

Database environment management covers such database operation and maintenance management as installation, configuration, upgrade, migration and other management work to ensure the normal operation of the IT infrastructure, including database systems.

2.1.2   Object Management

Database object is a general term for the various concepts and structures used to store and point to data in the database. Object management is about a management process that uses objects to define languages, create tools, or modify or delete various database objects. Basic database objects generally include tables, views, index sequences, stored procedures and functions, as shown in Table 2.1.

The database product itself does not propose strict naming restrictions, but arbitrary naming of objects will lead to an uncontrollable and unmaintainable system, or even cause the maintenance difficulties to the entire system. The development of naming convention is a basic requirement for database design, because a good naming convention means a good start.

There are several suggestions for naming convention as follows.

(1) Unify the case of the names. The case of the names can be standardized on a project basis, such as all capitalization, all lowercase, or initial capitalization.
(2) Use prefixes to identify the type of object, such as the table name prefix "t_", view prefix "v_", function prefix "f_" and so on.
(3) Try to choose meaningful, easy to remember, descriptive, short and unique English words for naming, not recommended to use Chinese Pinyin.

Table 2.1 Basic database objects

Object	Name	Role
Table	Table	It is used to store the basic structure of data
View	View	It is a logical "virtual table" that reflects the data in the table in a different way and does not store data itself
Index	Index	It provides a pointer to the data value of a specified column stored in a table, like a table of contents of a book, and can speed up the query of a table
Sequence	Sequence	It is used to generate a unique integer database object
Store procedure, function	Procedure, function	It is a set of SQL statements used to accomplish a specific function. Procedures and functions can be called repeatedly after compilation, which can reduce the workload of database developers

Table 2.2 Database naming convention

Not recommended	Recommended	Description
Table_customer	t_customer	Table is a database-reserved keyword, not recommended
t_001	t_customer_orders	The original name has only numbers and meaningless letters, which cannot reflect the meaning of the object as a whole
v@orders	v_orders	The original name contains an illegal character
shitu_dizhi	v_address	The use of Hanyu Pinyin should be avoided

Not recommended	Suggested	Description
Special_customer_account_total_amount	acct_amt	Appropriate use of abbreviations is recommended to shorten the name length
T_Customer_Orders, v_customer_orders	t_cust_orders, v_cust_orders	Case rules should be unified

(4) Use the name dictionary to develop some common abbreviations on a project basis, such as "amt" for "amount".

Some commercial databases set length limits for table names and view names in early versions, for example, they cannot exceed 30 characters. Too long names are not easy to remember and communicate, nor easy for SQL code writing. Some public database naming specifications can be used as a blueprint to develop some industry- and project-oriented database naming conventions according to project characteristics, as shown in Table 2.2.

2.1.3 Backup and Recovery Management

There are many possible reasons for data loss, mainly storage media failure, user's operation error, server failure, virus invasion, natural disasters, etc. Backup database is to additionally store the data in the database and the relevant information to ensure the normal operation of the database system, so that it can be used to restore the database upon the system failure.

The objects of database backup include but not limited to data itself and data-related database objects, users, permissions, database environment (profiles, timing tasks), etc. Data recovery is the activity of restoring a database system from a failed or paralyzed state to one that is operational and capable of restoring data to an acceptable state.

For enterprises and other organizations, database systems and other application systems constitute a larger information system platform, so database backup and recovery is not independent, but should be combined with other application systems to consider the overall disaster recovery performance of the whole information system platform. This is the so-called enterprise-level disaster recovery.

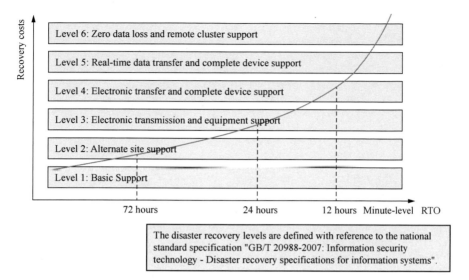

Fig. 2.1 Disaster recovery levels

Disaster backup refers to the process of backing up data, data processing systems, network systems, infrastructure, specialized technical information and operational management information for the purpose of recovery after a disaster occurs. Disaster backup has two objectives, one is recovery time objective (RTO) and the other is recovery point objective (RPO). RTO is the time limit within which recovery must be completed after a disaster has stopped an information system or business function. RPO is the requirement for the time point to which the system and data are recovered to after a disaster. For example, if the RPO requirement is one day, then the system and data must be recovered to the state 24 h before the failure caused by the disaster, and the possibility of data loss within 24 h is allowed in this case. However, if the data can be restored to the state only two days ago, that is, 48 h ago, the requirement of RPO = 1 day is not satisfied. The RTO emphasizes the availability of the service, and the smaller the RTO, the less the loss of service. The RPO targets data loss, and the smaller the RPO, the less the data loss. A typical disaster recovery goal of an enterprise is RTO <30 min, with zero data loss (RPO = 0).

China's *GB/T 20988-2007: Information security technology—Disaster recovery specifications for information systems* divides disaster recovery into six levels, as shown in Fig. 2.1.

Level 1: Basic support. The data backup system is required to guarantee data backup at least once a week, and the backup media can be stored off-site, with no specific requirements for the backup data processing system and backup network system. For example, it is required to store the data backup on a tape placed in another location in the same city.

Level 2: Alternate site support. On the basis of meeting Level 1, it is required to equip part of the data processing equipment required for disaster recovery, or to

Table 2.3 Disaster recovery levels

Disaster recovery level	RTO	RPO
1	More than 2 days	1–7 days
2	More than 24 h	1–7 days
3	More than 12 h	Several hours to 1 day
4	Several hours to 2 day	Several hours to 1 day
5	Several minutes to 2 day	0–30 min
6	Several minutes	0

deploy the required data processing equipment to the backup site within a predetermined time after a disaster; it is also required to equip part of the communication lines and corresponding network equipment, or to deploy the required communication lines and network equipment to the backup site within a predetermined time after a disaster.

Level 3: Electronic transmission and equipment support. It is required to conduct at least one full data backup every day, and the backup media is stored off-site, while using communication equipment to transfer critical data to the backup site in batches at regular intervals several times a day; part of the data processing equipment, communication lines and corresponding network equipment required for disaster recovery should be equipped.

Level 4: Electronic transfer and complete device support. On the basis of Level 3, it is required to configure all data processing equipment, communication lines and corresponding network equipment required for disaster recovery, which must be in ready or operational status.

Level 5: Real-time data transfer and complete device support. In addition to requiring at least one full data backup per day and backup media stored off-site, it also requires the use of remote data replication technology to replicate critical data to the backup site in real time through the communication network.

Level 6: Zero data loss and remote cluster support. It is required to realize remote real-time backup with zero data loss; the backup data processing system should have the same processing capability as the production data processing system, and the application software should be "clustered" and can be switched seamlessly in real time.

Table 2.3 exemplifies the disaster recovery levels defined by the Information security technology—Disaster recovery specifications for information systems.

The higher the disaster recovery level, the better the protection of the information system, but this also means a sharp increase in cost. Therefore, a reasonable disaster recovery level needs to be determined for service systems based on the cost-risk balance principle (i.e., balancing the cost of disaster recovery resources against the potential loss due to risk). For example, the disaster recovery capability specified for core financial service systems is Level 6, while non-core services are generally specified as Level 4 or Level 5 depending on the scope of service and industry standards; the disaster recovery level for SMS networks in the telecom industry is

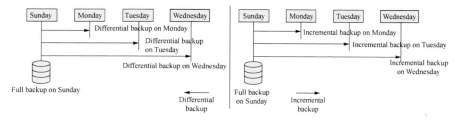

Fig. 2.2 Differential and incremental backups

Level 3 or Level 4. Each industry should follow the specifications to assess the importance of its own service systems to determine the disaster recovery level of each system.

Different databases provide different backup tools and means, but all involve various "backup strategies". Backup strategies are divided into full backup, differential backup and incremental backup according to the scope of data collection; or into hot backup, warm backup and cold backup according to whether the database is deactivated; or into physical backup and logical backup according to the backup content.

Full backup, also called complete backup, refers to the complete backup of all data and corresponding structures at a specified point in time. Full backup is characterized by the most complete data and is the basis for differential and incremental backups, as well as the most secure backup type, whose backup and recovery time increases significantly with the increase in data volume. While important, full backup also comes at a cost in time and expenses, and is prone to a performance impact on the entire system.

The amount of data to be backed up each time for full backup is quite large and takes a long time, so it should not be operated frequently, even with the highest data security. Differential backup is a backup of data that has changed since the last full backup. Incremental backup is a backup of the data that has changed after the previous backup, as shown in Fig. 2.2.

Given that incremental backups have the advantage of not backing up data repeatedly, each incremental backup involves a small volume of data and requires very little time, but the reliability of each backup must be guaranteed. For example, when a system failure occurs in the early hours of Thursday morning and the system needs to be restored, the full backup on Sunday, the incremental backup on Monday, the incremental backup on Tuesday, and the incremental backup on Wednesday must all be prepared and restored in chronological order. If Tuesday's incremental backup file is corrupted, then Wednesday's incremental backup will also fail, so that only the data state at 12:00 PM on Monday can be restored.

The differential backup shows the same advantage as incremental backup, the volume of data per backup is small and the backup time is short, but the availability of system data should be guaranteed. It only needs the data from the last full backup and the most recent differential backup. For example, if a failure occurs early

Table 2.4 Physical and logical backups

Category	Physical backup	Logical backup
Backup object	Physical files of the database (such as data files, control files, archived log files, etc.)	Database objects (e.g. users, tables, stored procedures, etc.)
Portability	Weak, even non-portable	Database object-level backup, with stronger portability
Space occupation	Large space occupied	Relatively smaller space occupied
Recovery efficiency	High	Relatively low
Applicable scenarios	Disaster recovery of large service systems or the whole system, and system-level full backup	Incremental data backup between primary and backup databases, data synchronization between different service systems, and online data migration during upgrade without business interruption

Thursday morning and the system needs to be restored, simply prepare the full backup on Sunday and the differential backup on Wednesday.

In terms of the volume of data to be backed up, the largest volume of data to be backed up is the full backup, followed by the differential backup and finally the incremental backup. Usually, full backup + differential backup is recommended when the backup time window allows. If the incremental data volume for differential backup is larger and the backup operation cannot be completed within the allowed backup time window, then the full backup + incremental backup can be used.

Hot backup is performed when the database is running normally, where read/write operations can be performed on the database during the backup period.

Warm backup means that only database read operations can be performed during the backup period, and no write operation is allowed, where the database availability is weaker than hot backup.

Cold backup means that read/write operations are not available during the backup period, and the backup data is the most reliable.

In the case that the database application does not allow the service to stop, a hot backup solution must be used, but the absolute accuracy of the data cannot be guaranteed. In the case where the read/write service of the application can be stopped and the accuracy of the backup data is required, the cold backup solution is preferred. For example, the hot backup solution should be used as much as possible for routine daily backups, while a cold backup solution is recommended in the case of system migration, so as to ensure data accuracy.

A physical backup is a direct backup of the data files corresponding to the database or even the entire disk. Logical backup refers to exporting data from the database and archiving the exported data for backup. The difference between the two is shown in Table 2.4.

Backup portability means that the backup results of the database can be restored to different database versions and database platforms. In terms of recovery efficiency, the physical backup only needs to directly recover data files of data blocks, which is highly efficient; the logical backup is equivalent to re-executing SQL statements when recovering, so the system overhead is high and inefficient when the data volume is large. Compared with the strong dependence of physical backup on the physical format of logs, the logical backup is only based on logical changes of data, which makes the application more flexible and enables cross-version replication, replication to other heterogeneous databases, and customization support when the table structure of source and target databases are inconsistent.

Logical backups only support backup to SQL script files. Logical backups take up less space in comparison with physical backups, because the latter generate data files. Physical backups also allow backing up only metadata, at which time the backup result takes up the least amount of space.

2.1.4 Security Management

In a broad sense, the database security framework is divided into three levels: network security, operating system security, and DBMS security.

(1) Network security. The main technologies for maintaining network security are encryption technology, digital signature technology, firewall technology, and intrusion detection technology. The security at the network level focuses on the encryption of transmission contents. Before transmission through the network, the transmission content should be encrypted, and the receiver should decrypt the data after receiving it to ensure the security of the data in the transmission process.

(2) Operating system security. Encryption aiming at securing the operating system refers to the encryption of data files stored in the operating system, the core of which is to ensure the security of the server, mainly in terms of the server's user accounts, passwords, access rights, etc. Data security is mainly reflected in the encryption technology, security of data storage, security of data transmission, such as Kerberos, IPsec, SSL and VPN technologies.

注意

Kerberos is a computer network authorization protocol used to authenticate personal communications in a non-secure network by secure means. It was originally designed to provide strong authentication between client and server applications through a key system. In a cluster using Kerberos authentication, the client does not authenticate directly with the server, instead, authenticates with each other through the key distribution center (KDC).

The Internet Protocol Security (IPsec) is a family of network transport protocols (a collection of interconnected protocols) that protect IP addresses by encrypting and authenticating their packets.

The secure sockets layer (SSL) protocol and its successor, transport layer security (TLS), are security protocols that provide security and data integrity for network communications. TLS and SSL encrypt network connections at the transport layer.

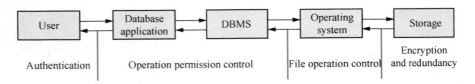

Fig. 2.3 Security control model

(3) DBMS security. The encryption aimed at DBMS security refers to the encryption and decryption of data in the process of reading and writing data by means of custom functions or built-in system functions, involving database encryption, data access control, security auditing, and data backup.

To summarize, all the three levels of security involve encryption. The security at the network level focuses on encryption of the transmission content, where the sender encrypts the transmission content before the network transmission and the receiver decrypts the information after receiving it, thus securing the transmission. The encryption aiming at securing the operating system refers to the encryption of data files stored in the operating system. The encryption aimed at DBMS security refers to the encryption and decryption of data in the process of reading and writing data by means of custom functions or built-in system functions.

Security control is to provide security against intentional and unintentional damage at different levels of the database application system, for example:

(1) Encryption of access data → intentional illegal activities.
(2) User authentication and restriction of operation rights → intentional illegal operations.
(3) Improvement of system reliability and data backup → unintentional damage behavior.

The security control model shown in Fig. 2.3 is only a schematic diagram, while all database products nowadays have their own security control models. When a user needs to access a database, he or she first has to enter the database system. The user provides his identity to the application, and the application submits the user's identity to the DBMS for authentication, after that, only legitimate users can proceed to the next step. When a legitimate user is performing a database operation, the DBMS further verifies that the user has such operation rights. The user can only operate if he or she has operation rights, otherwise the operation will be denied. The operating system also has its own protection measures, such as setting access rights to files and encrypting storage for files stored on disk, so that the data is unreadable even if it is stolen. In addition, it is possible to save multiple copies of data files, thus avoiding data loss when accidents occur.

The authentication of database users is the outermost security protection provided by the DBMS to prevent unauthorized users from accessing.

As database applications now commonly use the "user name + password" authentication mode, it is necessary to enhance the password strength, the main measures for which are as follows.

(1) Longer strings, such as 8–20 characters, should be used.
(2) A mixture of numbers, letters and symbols should be used.
(3) Passwords should be changed regularly.
(4) Passwords should not be used repeatedly.

The security policy mainly involves password complexity, password reuse, password validity, password modification, password verification, and prohibits the explicit display of passwords. In general, it is recommended to use an interactive method and real-time password input method for login; some fixed-running scripts or codes should be deployed on a specific and trusted server side, where the user sets a specific password-free login method to allow the code and scripts executed by a specific server to log in to the database through the password-free method.

GaussDB (for MySQL) sets a password security policy for new database users created on the client side.
    The password length is at least eight characters.
    The password should contain at least one uppercase letter, one lowercase letter, one digit and one special character.
    The password should be changed periodically.

Access control is the most effective method of database security management, and also is the most problematic link. Its basic principle is to assign different rights to different users according to the classification requirements of sensitive data.

(1) The principle of least right. To meet the needs of the minimum right range, the arbitrary expansion of the scope of authority grant is not allowed. For example, a user who needs to query data only needs to be granted SELECT right, and cannot be granted DELETE and UPDATE rights.
(2) Check the key rights. Rights such as DROP, TRUNCATE, UPDATE, and DELETE, which will cause data to disappear or change, should be granted cautiously, and it is also necessary to check whether the users who have obtained the rights continue to use the rights.
(3) Check the rights of key database objects. The access rights of system tables, data dictionaries and sensitive database tables should be strictly checked.

Role based access control (RBAC) is mainly used in right management for large database systems or systems with a large volume of user data.

A database "role" is a collection of operations that one or a group of users can perform in a database. Roles can be created based on different job responsibilities, and then the user is assigned to the corresponding role. Users can easily switch roles or bears multiple roles.

The starting point of RBAC is to exclude direct contact between users and database objects, so that rights are assigned to roles, and users can only obtain the appropriate rights to access the corresponding database objects if they have the corresponding roles.

For example, if User A wants to query the data of Table T, then we can grant User A the right to query Table T directly, or we can create Role R, then grant the right to view Table T to Role R, and finally grant Role R to User A.

Audit can help database administrators to find the vulnerabilities in the existing architecture and its usage. Audit of users and database administrators is to analyze and report on various operations, such as creating, deleting, and modifying instances, resetting passwords, backing up and restoring, creating, modifying, and deleting parameter templates, and other operations.

The levels of database audit are as follows.

(1) Access and authentication audit: analysis of database user's login (log in) and logout (log out) information, such as login and logout time, connection method and parameter information, login path, etc.
(2) User and database administrator audit: analysis and reporting on the activities performed by users and database administrators.
(3) Security activity monitoring: recording of any unauthorized or suspicious activities in the database and generation of audit reports.
(4) Vulnerability and threat audit: identification of possible vulnerabilities in the database and the "users" who intend to exploit them.

The encryption of database is divided into two layers—the encryption of kernel layer and the encryption of outer layer. Kernel-layer encryption means that the data is encrypted or decrypted before physical access, which is transparent to the database users. If encrypted store is used, the encryption operation runs on the server side, which will increase the load on the server to some extent. Outer-layer encryption means developing special encryption and decryption tools, or defining encryption and decryption methods, which can control the encryption object granularity, and encrypt and decrypt at table or field level, and users only need to focus on sensitive information range.

 When enabling kernel-layer encryption for high-load systems, it is important to carefully consider its impact on performance as the functionality is enabled at the entire database management system level.

The outer-layer encryption requires extra development time, the algorithms of encryption and decryption for different data objects and different data types are complicated, and there are also certain business rules that need to be followed after encrypting some business-critical data, for example, the names of tables can be associated after being encrypted, etc. So it is a very large project to implement a good encryption engine.

2.1.5 Performance Management

There are upper limits on the processing capacity of resources. For example, the disk space is limited, and there are also upper limits on CPU frequency, memory size and network bandwidth. Resources are divided into supply resources and concurrency control resources. The supply resources, also called basic resources, are the resources corresponding to computer hardware, including the resources managed by the operating system, whose processing capacity is ordered as "CPU > memory >> disk ≈ network". Concurrency control resources include but are not limited to locks, queues, caches, mutually exclusive signals, etc., which are also resources managed by the database system. The basic principle of performance management is to make full use of resources and not to waste them.

Unlike the even supply of resources, the use of resources is uneven. For example, if a distributed system fails to choose a reasonable data slicing method, the nodes with more data will be heavily loaded and their resources will be strained, but the nodes with less data will be lightly loaded and their resources will be relatively "idle", as shown in Table 2.5.

	$1 \text{ ns} = 10^{-9} \text{ s}$
注意	

Resource bottlenecks can be exchanged. For example, a system with low I/O performance and sufficient memory can be exchanged through high memory and high CPU consumption. A system with limited network bandwidth can also improve the efficiency of data transfer by compressing the transfer, i.e., using the CPU to

Table 2.5 Performance indicators

Indicator	Description	Time (ns)
L1 cache reference	Read the level-1 cache of CPU	0.5
L2 cache reference	Read the level-2 cache of CPU	7
Main Memory reference	Read Memory data	100
Compress 1k bytes with Zippy	Compress 1k bytes with Zippy algorithm	10,000
Send 2k bytes over 1 Gbit/s Network	Send 2k bytes over 1 Gbit/s network	20,000
Read 1 MB sequentially from Memory	Read 1 MB sequentially from Memory	250,000
Disk seek	Disk seek	10,000,000 (10 ms)
Read 1 MB sequentially from Network	Read 1 MB sequentially from Network	10,000,000
Read 1 MB sequentially from Disk	Read 1 MB sequentially from Disk	30,000,000

handle compression and decompression. This is the optimization idea of exchanging space for time and time for space.

For the use of database, the ideal situation is to have infinite resources, CPU with infinite processing speed, infinite amount of memory, infinite disk space, and infinite network bandwidth. But the database is actually always running in a limited environment. The effective management of resources can ensure that the database system can meet the user's performance requirements for the system during the peak period, and the meaning of performance management lies in the efficient use of resources. Real-time system performance monitoring through the logs or tools provided by the database can respond to system problems in a timely manner, analyze existing problems based on historical performance data, identify potential problems, and propose better preventive measures based on development trends. The data collected by performance management is the basis for system capacity planning and other forward planning, because data speaks with facts, not with feelings.

Regarding performance management, the basic indicators of database systems include throughput and response time. OLTP and OLAP performance management goals should actually be treated differently, but the two indicators should be analyzed together. In performance management, one of the indicators cannot be pursued unilaterally. OLTP is to provide the highest possible throughput on top of acceptable response times to reduce consumption per unit of resource, to move quickly through the shared area for concurrency, and to reduce bottleneck constraints. OLAP is to reduce response time as much as possible within limited resources, and a transaction should make full use of resources to accelerate processing time. In the case of SQL, for example, SQL optimization for OLTP should minimize the use of resources by SQL. OLAP systems, on the other hand, require SQL to make the best possible use of resources within a limited range. For OLAP systems, when processing batch jobs, the higher the resource utilization rate, the better (it needs to be within a certain time window).

Some of the main scenarios to which performance optimization applies are as follows.

(1) Performance optimization for go-online scenario or below-expected performance. It may be obvious for OLTP systems that the performance fails to reach the expectation after going online, because the development environment and test environment tend to pay more attention to functional development, and even stress tests are SQL stress tests of some form query types. For batch operations on the OLAP, in the full data or historical data environment, its performance will be very different from the scenario of a small volume of sample data.

(2) Performance optimization for the situation where the response gradually becomes slower after going online for a while. Due to the development of data volume and business, the model and specification of system data have deviated from the original design, and the performance has also changed. In this case, it is basically necessary to analyze and find out which factors are related to this based on the long-term accumulation of performance data.

(3) System optimization for sudden slowdown during system operation (emergency processing). In the emergency processing scenario, performance problems do not happen for any reason. Sudden performance changes are often caused by code changes, such as put-into-production of newly developed business, new requirement changes, DDL changes, unexpected configuration changes, database upgrades, etc. Generally, this kind of problem has a high degree of urgency, which often requires the intervention of experienced personnel and quick response.

(4) Performance optimization for the situation where the system suddenly becomes slow and then returns to normal after a period of time. This is generally due to bottlenecks that limit throughput during peak periods, and capacity expansion is the simplest way to solve it. However, due to the extra investment and time period involved, this method needs to be supported by sufficient resources. A more natural solution is to reduce the number of operations per unit (concurrency control) or to reduce the resource consumption per unit of operation.

(5) System optimization based on the reduction of resource consumption. In this scenario, the whole system generally does not suffer from obvious performance problems, but rather emphasizes the effectiveness of resource usage, which is relatively well-timed and less stressful. For example, to analyze and optimize the top ten jobs that consume the most resources and have the longest response time in system application.

(6) Preventive daily inspection. Inspection work is generally applicable to scenarios where the whole system does not have obvious performance problems.

The data to be collected for performance management include CPU usage data, space utilization, users and roles using the database system, response time of heartbeat queries, performance data submitted to the database with SQL as the basic unit, and job-related performance data submitted by database tools (such as load, unload, backup, restore, etc.). As far as the timing of data collection is concerned, some daily data collection can be arranged, or data collection can be carried out during the time period when users use the system intensively in one day, or during the time period when the system pressure is relatively high.

After data collection is completed, corresponding performance reports need to be generated. For example, periodic performance reports or performance trend analysis reports. There are many monitoring reports that can be extracted in the database system, for example, regular performance reports (daily, weekly and monthly reports) can be established by using performance-related data; the performance trend analysis report can be established by using common indicators to obtain an intuitive display of the current system performance; you can also generate reports of specific trend types, such as reports based on abnormal events, reports of SQL or jobs that consume a lot of resources, reports of resource consumption of specific users and user groups, and reports of resource consumption of specific applications.

| Built-in resource views or monitoring reports are some advanced features provided by the database that are not available in some databases.

2.1.6   O&M Management

1. Database installation

The basic principles adopted by different database products are similar, but each product has its own characteristics and precautions, which users need to understand and learn before installation.

The first is the installation of the database, the process of which is shown in Fig. 2.4.

The premise of database installation is some basic preparations, mainly as follows.

Fig. 2.4 Database installation

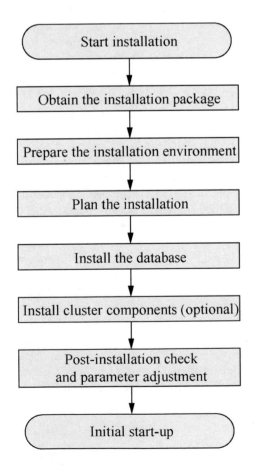

(1) To understand the theory of relational database.

(2) To understand the knowledge of operating system.

(3) To understand the characteristics of database products and server architecture.

　　The software architecture is the composition of the components within the database product. What needs to be understood is which components are basic, major, and must be installed, and which are optional.

　　Generally speaking, the network architecture should ensure that the database server can run and manage the network and the planning of the database network.

　　The database network refers to the intranet used by the database, hosts and spares, and cascading brackets synchronously.

　　Management network generally refers to the communication network used between management module and agent module.

　　To understand the server architecture is to understand the considerations of building the product in single-host mode, master-standby mode, cluster mode or distributed mode.

(4) To know and understand the proper nouns and specific terms of the target database. The meaning of the same word in different database products may vary greatly, cannot be generalized.

(5) To read the installation manual, especially the installation notes.

2. Database uninstallation

　　Before the database is upgraded, it is necessary to uninstall and clean up the old version of the database. The basic steps of traditional database uninstallation are as follows.

(1) (Optional) Make a full backup of the database.

(2) Stop the database service.

(3) Uninstall the database.

　　The basic steps of cloud database uninstallation are as follows.

(1) (Optional) Make a full backup of the database.

(2) Delete the data instance from the cloud platform.

　　The uninstallation approaches are similar for single-host, master-standby, and one-master-multi-standby architectures, and the uninstallation operations to be performed on each node are the same. Uninstallation of distributed clusters generally uses proprietary uninstallation tools. Some users need to destroy the data on the store media after uninstalling the database in order to prevent data leakage.

3. Database migration

　　Database migration needs to design different migration schemes according to different migration scenarios, and the factors to be considered are as follows:

(1) the available time window for migration;

(2) the available tools for migration;

(3) whether the data source system stops writing operations during the migration process;

(4) the network conditions between the data source system and the target system during the migration;

(5) estimated backup recovery time based on the volume of data migrated;

(6) audit the data consistency between the source database system and the target database system after migration.

Judging the network situation during database migration is mainly to provide reference for deciding whether data direct connection can be used. If the network condition is good at both ends, then the direct data migration without landing can be more efficient because it can avoid the large disk I/O overhead generated by the data landing. In the audit of data consistency, a quick comparison method is usually to compare the number of the same table on both sides and confirm that the numbers of records are the same. The method of comparing the results of aggregation operations on specific columns can also be used, such as finding the sum of amount fields and comparing the results, grouping statistics based on date fields, and counting whether the numbers of records for each day are the same.

Data migration often faces the challenge of completing a huge amount of work within a limited time, and designing multiple scenarios and contingency plans is a prerequisite for successful data migration.

4. Database expansion

The capacity of any database system is determined after estimating the volume of data in the future at a certain time point. When determining the capacity, not only the volume of data store should be considered, but also the following shortcomings should be avoided:

(1) Inadequacy of computing power (average daily busy level of CPU of the whole system > 90%).

(2) Insufficient response and concurrency capability (qps and tps are significantly reduced, failing to meet the SLA).

注意   SLA is the abbreviation of Service Level Agreement. When signing a contract with a customer, some performance commitments are generally made to the customer, for example, the database system provided should be able to meet 10,000 queries/s, the response time for a single query should not exceed 30ms, and to meet the database-related service indicators. SLA may also include service commitments such as 7×24 response.

(3) Insufficient data capacity. The definition of insufficient capacity is different between OLTP and OLAP.

The differences between vertical and horizontal capacity expansion are as follows.

(1) Vertical expansion refers to increasing the hardware of the database server, such as increasing memory, increasing store, increasing network bandwidth, and improving the performance configuration of hardware. This method is relatively simple, but it will encounter the bottleneck of single-node hardware performance.

(2) Horizontal expansion refers to increasing the number of servers horizontally, taking advantage of the servers in the cluster to improve the overall system performance.

The differences between Downtime expansion and smooth expansion are as follows:

(1) Downtime expansion is a simple way, but limited by the time window. Once there is a problem, the expansion will fail, and it will take too long to be accepted by customers.

(2) Smooth expansion has no impact on database services, but the technical implementation is relatively complex. Especially, the complexity of expansion will rise sharply with the increase of database servers.

5. Routine maintenance

In order to carry out routine maintenance, a more rigorous work plan should be formulated for each job, and implemented to check the risks and ensure the safe and efficient operation of the database system.

Database troubleshooting mainly involves the following matters.

(1) Configure database monitoring indicators and alarm thresholds.
(2) Set the alarming process for the fault events at each level.
(3) Receive the alarm and locate the fault according to the logs.
(4) Record the original information in detail for the problems encountered.
(5) Strictly abide by the operating procedures and industry safety regulations.
(6) For major operations, the operation feasibility should be confirmed before operation, and the operation personnel with authority should perform them after the corresponding backup, emergency and safety measures are in place.

Database health inspection mainly involves the following matters.

(1) View health inspection tasks.
(2) Manage health inspection reports.
(3) Modify the health inspection configuration.

2.2   Key Concepts of Database

2.2.1   *Database and Database Instance*

Database system is made for managing data, and database is actually a collection of data, which is expressed as a collection of data files, data blocks, physical operating system files or disk data blocks, such as data files, index files and structure files. But not all database systems are file-based, there are also databases that write data directly into memory.

Database instance refers to a series of processes in the operating system and the memory blocks allocated for these processes, which are the channels to access the database. Generally speaking, a database instance corresponds to a database, as shown in Fig. 2.5.

A database is a collection of physically stored data, and a database instance is the collection of software processes, threads and memory that access data. Oracle is process-based, so its instance refers to a series of processes; and a MySQL instance is a series of threads and the memory associated with the threads.

Multi-instance is to build and run multiple database instances on a physical server, each using a different port to listen through a different socket, and each having a separate parameter profile. Multi-instance operation can make full use of hardware resources and maximize the service performance of the database.

Distributed database presents unified instances, and generally does not allow users to directly connect to instances on data nodes. A distributed cluster is a set of mutually independent servers that form a computer system through a high-speed network. Each server may have a complete copy or a partial copy of the database, and all servers are connected to each other through the network, together forming a complete global large-scale database that is logically centralized and physically distributed.

Multi-instance and distributed cluster are shown in Fig. 2.6.

Fig. 2.5 Database instance

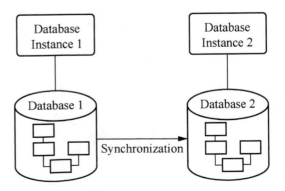

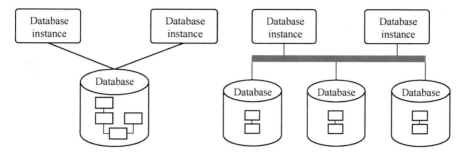

Fig. 2.6 Multi-instance and distributed cluster

2.2.2 Database Connection and Session

Database connection is a physical communication connection, which refers to the network connection between a client and a dedicated server or a shared server established on the same network. When establishing a connection, it is necessary to specify the connection parameters, such as server host name, IP address, port number, and user name and password for the connection, etc.

Database Session refers to the logical connection between the client and the database, which is a context from the beginning throughout the end of communication. This context is located in the memory of the server, recording the client of this connection, the corresponding application process number, the corresponding user login information and other information.

The session and connection are established simultaneously, which are descriptions of the same thing at different levels, as shown in Fig. 2.7. Simply put, the connection is the physical communication link between the client and the server, while the session refers to the logical communication interaction between the user and the server. In a database connection, a proprietary server is an instance on the database server. The scheduling server generally refers to the server on the distributed cluster where the external interface component resides, which in GaussDB (DWS) corresponds to the coordinator node (CN).

Frequent creation and closing of database connections is costly, which makes the allocation and release of connection resources a bottleneck for the database, thus eroding the performance of the database system. The connection pool is used to reuse database connections, responsible for allocating, managing and releasing database connections. It allows an application to reuse an existing database connection instead of creating a new one, allowing efficient and secure reuse of database connections.

The basic idea of connection pool is to store database connections as objects in memory during system initialization. In this way, a user who needs to access the database does not need to establish a new connection, but directly takes out an established idle connection object from the connection pool, as shown in Fig. 2.8. Instead of closing the connection directly after use, the user puts the connection back

Fig. 2.7 Flow chart of
establishing database
connection

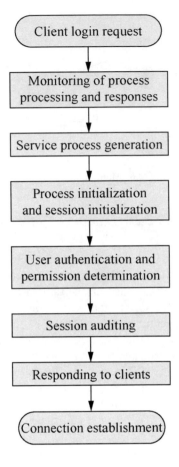

into the connection pool for the next user to request. Connection creation and disconnection are managed by the connection pool itself, and the initial number of connections, the upper and lower limits of number of connections, the maximum times of uses per connection, and the maximum idle time can be controlled by setting the parameters of the connection pool. However, there are alternatives, that is, monitoring the number and usage of database connections through its own management mechanism. Connections also vary by database product. Oracle's connection overhead is large, while MySQL's is relatively small. For highly concurrent service scenarios, if there are many connections accumulated, the overall connection cost of the whole database should also be considered by database administrators.

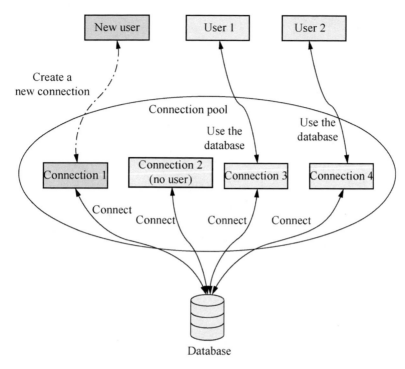

Fig. 2.8 Database connection pool

2.2.3   Schema

Schema is a collection of related database objects that allows multiple users to share the same database without interfering with each other. The schema organizes database objects into logical groups for easier management and form namespaces to avoid object name conflicts. A schema contains tables, other database objects, data types, functions, operators, etc.

"table_a" shown in Fig. 2.9 indicates tables with the same name. Since they belong to different schemas, they are allowed to use the same name, but in fact they may store different data and have different structures. When accessing one of the tables with the same name, it is necessary to specify the schema name to explicitly point to the target table.

Conceptually, a schema is a set of interrelated database objects. Different databases may adopt different concepts to reflect the schema, so database users generally use the English word "schema" to express the concept.

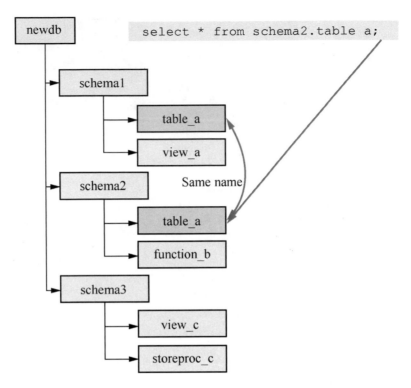

Fig. 2.9 Schema

2.2.4   *Tablespace*

Tablespace is composed of one or more data files, with which you can define where database object files are stored. All objects in the database are logically stored in the tablespace, and physically stored in the data files belonging to the tablespace.

The function of table space is to arrange the physical store location of data according to the usage pattern of database objects, so as to improve the performance of database. It places frequently used indexes on the disk with stable performance and fast computing speed to facilitate data archiving, and place tables that are used less frequently and require lower access performance on the disk with slower computing speed.

You can also specify the physical disk space occupied by data through tablespaces and set the upper limit of physical space usage to avoid running out of disk space.

In view of the fact that tablespaces correspond to physical data files, tablespaces can actually associate data with store, and then the tablespaces themselves specify the store locations of database objects such as tables and indexes in the database. After the database administrator creates a tablespace, he or she can refer to it when creating database objects.

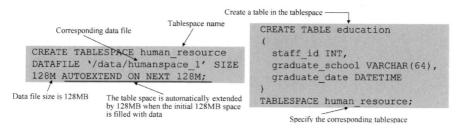

Fig. 2.10 Tablespaces

Table 2.6 Tablespaces within GaussDB (for MySQL)

Tablespace	Description
SYSTEM	Used to store metadata of GaussDB (for MySQL)
TEMP	When a user's SQL statement requires disk space to complete an operation, GaussDB (for MySQL) database will allocate temporary segments from the TEMP tablespace
TEMP2	Used to store NOLOGGING table data
TEMP2-UNDO	Used to store NOLOGGING table's UNDO data
UNDO	Used to store UNDO data
USERS	The default user tablespace, used to carry all the information of a new user when the user is created but no tablespace is specified

Figure 2.10 shows the tablespaces of GaussDB (for MySQL), which are created as the system predefines six tablespaces, including SYSTEM tablespace, TEMP tablespace, TEMP2 tablespace, TEMP2_UNDO tablespace, UNDO tablespace, and USERS tablespace, as shown in Table 2.6.

TEMP tablespaces, as the intermediate result set of SQL statements, are be used by common temporary tables of users. When executing DML (insert, update and delete, etc.) operations, the old data generated before the execution of the operation will be written to the UNDO tablespace, which is mainly used to implement transaction rollback, database instance recovery, read consistency and flashback queries.

2.2.5   Table

In a relational database, a database table is a collection of two-dimensional arrays that represent the relationships between the data objects being stored. Each row in the table is called a record and consists of several fields; each column in the table can be called a field, which has two attributes—column name and data type, as shown in Table 2.7.

Table 2.7 Database table

Author number	Author name	Author's age	Author's address
001	Zhang San	40	×××× City, ×××× Province
002	Li Si	50	×××× City, ×××× Province
...	...	...	...

GaussDB (for MySQL) supports the creation of temporary tables, which are used to hold the data needed for a session or a transaction. When a session exits or a user commits and rolls back a transaction, the data in the temporary table is automatically cleared, but the table structure remains.

The data in a temporary table is temporary and procedural, with no need to be retained permanently like a normal data table.

Temporary tables cannot be displayed using the [SHOW TABLES] command.

To avoid deleting a permanent table with the same table name, you can use the [DROP TEMPORARY TABLE staff_history_session;] command when performing a delete of the table structure.

The data in the temporary table exists only for the life of the session and is automatically cleared when the user exits the session and the session ends, as shown below.

```
CREATE TEMPORARY TABLE staff_history_session
(
startdate DATE,
enddate DATE
);
```

Temporary tables with the same name can be created for different sessions. The name of the temporary table can be the same as the name of the permanent table.

Execute the following command to create a temporary table in GaussDB (for MySQL):

```
CREATE TEMPORARY TABLE test_tpcds (a INT, b VARCHAR (10));
```

2.2.6 How the Table Is Stored

According to the way data is stored, tables are divided into row store and column store, as shown in Fig. 2.11. GaussDB (for MySQL) currently supports only row store, while GaussDB (DWS) supports both row store and column store. The default store mode is row store, which differs from column store only in store mode. From

Work number	Name	Gender	Age	Salary
1001	Zhang San	Male	21	5000.00
1002	Zhao Si	Femal	22	6000.00
1003	Wang Wu	Male	30	15000.00
1004	Li	Femal	18	3500.00

Row store

Column storage

Direction of data storage sequence

Row storage (record order from top to bottom)

Row1	1001	Zhang San	Male	21	5000.00
Row2	1002	Zhao Si	Femal	22	6000.00
Row3	1003	Wang Wu	Male	30	15000.00
Row4	1004	Li	Femal	18	3500.00

Direction of data storage sequence

Column storage (record order from top to bottom)

C1	1001	1002	1003	1004
C2	Zhang San	Zhao Si	Wang Wu	Li
C3	Male	Femal	Male	Femal
C4	21	22	30	18
C5	5000.00	6000.00	15000.00	3500.00

Fig. 2.11 How the table is stored

the presentation form of tables, the tables in the two store modes still hold two-dimensional data, which accord with the relational theory of relational database.

If the table in the form of row store (row store table) stores the same row of data in different columns, records can be written once when performing INSERT and UPDATE operations; But when you choose to query, even if you only query a few columns, all the data will be read.

The table in the form of column store (column store table) first splits the rows when writing data, at which time a row is split into multiple columns, and then the data of the same column is stored in the adjacent physical area. Therefore, in the column store mode, the times of write of a row record is obviously more than that in the row store mode. This increase in the write times leads to higher overhead and poorer performance of the column store table compared with the row store table when performing INSERT and UPDATE operations. However, when querying, column store tables just scan the columns involved and then read them, so the I/O scanning and reading range are much smaller than row store tables. Column-store query can eliminate irrelevant columns. If only a few columns need to be queried, it can greatly reduce the amount of data to be queried, and then speed up the query. In addition, for column store tables, each row hold the data of the same data type, and the data of the same type can be compressed by a lightweight compression algorithm to achieve a good compression ratio, so the space occupied by the column store table is relatively small.

Row store tables, on the other hand, are difficult to compress because the field types of the tables are not uniform and cannot be compressed dynamically unless they are confirmed in advance.

Regarding the choice of store mode, row store is the default store mode. The scenarios for which column store is suitable are mainly queries of statistical analysis type (scenarios with a lot of GROUP and JOIN operations), OLAP, data mining and other application query scenarios that make a lot of query requests. One of the main advantages of column storage is that it can greatly reduce the I/O occupation of the system in the reading process, especially when querying massive data, I/O has always been one of the main bottlenecks of the system. Row store is suitable for scenarios such as point queries (simple queries with fewer returned records and based on indexes), lightweight transactions like OLTP, and scenarios that involves a lot of write operations and more data additions, deletions and changes. Row store is more suitable for OLTP, such as the traditional applications based on addition, deletion, change and check operations. Column store is more suitable for OLAP, and is well suited to play a role in the field of data warehousing, such as data analysis, mass store and business intelligence, which mainly involves infrequently updated data.

2.2.7   Partition

A partitioned table is obtained by dividing the data of a large table into many small subsets of data. The main types of partitioned tables are as follows.

(1) Range-partitioned table: The data is mapped to each partition based on a range determined by the partition key specified when the partition table is created. This is the most commonly used partition method, and the date is often used as the partitioning key, for example, the sales data is partitioned by month.
(2) List-partitioned table: A huge table is partitioned into small manageable blocks.
(3) Hash-partitioned tables: In many cases, users cannot predict the range of data changes on a particular column, and therefore cannot create a fixed number of range partitions or list partitions. In this case, hash-partitioned tables provide a way to divide the data equally among a specified number of partitions, so that the data written to the table is evenly distributed among the partitions; however, the user cannot predict which partition the data will be written to. For example, if the sales cities are spread all over the country, it is difficult to partition the table in a list, and then the table can be hash-partitioned.
(4) Interval-partitioned table: It is a special kind of range-partitioned table. For ordinary range partition, users will pre-create partitions, and if the inserted data is not in the partition, the database will report an error. In this case, the user can add the partition manually or use the interval partition. For example, the user can use the range-partitioned table in the way of one partition per day, and create a batch of partitions (e.g. 3 months) for subsequent use when the service is

deployed, but the partitions need to be created again after 3 months, otherwise the subsequent service data entry will report an error. This approach of range partition increases maintenance costs and requires the kernel to support automatic partition creation. But with interval partition, the user does not need to care about creating subsequent partitions, which reduces partition design and maintenance costs.

Example: The code for range-partitioning a date is as follows.

```
CREATE TABLE tp
(
id INT,
name VARCHAR(50),
purchased DATE
)
    PARTITION BY RANGE ( YEAR (purchased))
(
    PARTITION p0 VALUES LESS THAN (2015),
    PARTITION p1 VALUES LESS THAN (2016),
    PARTITION p2 VALUES LESS THAN (2017),
    PARTITION p3 VALUES LESS THAN (2018),
    PARTITION p4 VALUES LESS THAN (2019),
    PARTITION p5 VALUES LESS THAN (2020)
);
```

The advantages of partitioned tables are as follows.

(1) Improved query performance: When querying partitioned objects, you can search only the partitions you care about (also known as partition pruning), which improves retrieval efficiency.
(2) Enhanced availability: If a partition in a partitioned table fails, the data in other partitions of the table is still available.
(3) Easy maintenance: If a partition of a partitioned table fails and you need to repair the data, you can repair only that partition.
(4) Balanced I/O: Different partitions can be mapped to different disks to balance I/O and improve the performance of the whole system.

The data covered by the query condition is located in a partition, so SQL only needs to scan the data of a partition in the query process, instead of scanning the whole table, as shown in Fig. 2.12. Suppose the table contains 10 years of data, if there is no partitioned table, you have to scan all the data of 10 years to calculate the result, while with a partitioned table, you only need to scan 1 year of data in a partitioned table, thus the amount of scanned data is only 1/10.

Table 2.8 shows the applicable scenarios of partitioning.

Scenario 1 (Row 1 in Table 2.8): Usually this situation occurs in WHERE clause, where the filter condition uses a partition field and the partition field is equal to a partition; or when "BETWEEN...AND..." statement is used, the search condition

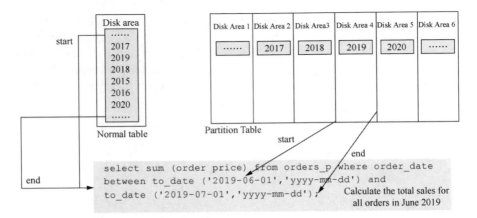

Fig. 2.12 Partition pruning

Table 2.8 Applicable scenarios of partitioning

Scenario description	Advantages
When rows with high access rates in a table are located in a single partition or in a few partitions	Significantly reduces search space, thus improving access performance
When inserting data into an empty partition	Improves the efficiency of inserting data into the empty partition
When the records that need to be loaded or deleted in large quantities are located in a single partition or in a few partitions	Reads or deletes the corresponding partition (s) directly, thus improving the processing performance; at the same time, the fragmentation workload can be reduced because a large number of fragmented deletion operations are avoided

is within several partitions, so when the query statement scans data, it will only search specific partitions instead of scanning the whole table through partition pruning. In general, the I/O overhead of partition scanning is n/m compared to scanning the entire table, where m is the total number of partitions and n is the number of partitions that satisfy the WHERE condition.

Scenario 2 (Row 2 in Table 2.8): Inserting data into an empty partition is similar to loading data into an empty table, and the efficiency of inserting data is higher with this internal implementation.

Scenario 3 (Row 3 in Table 2.8): If data is to be deleted or truncated, the data in some partitioned tables can be processed directly because the quick positioning and deletion function of partition makes the processing much more efficient than the scenario without partition.

Table 2.9 Data distribution

Distribution method	Description
Hash	The table data is hashed to all DNs in the cluster by the Hash method
Replication	Each DN in the cluster has a copy of the full table data
List	Table data is distributed to specified DNs by the List method
Range	Table data is distributed to specified DNs by the Range method

2.2.8 Data Distribution

The data tables of GaussDB (DWS) distributed database are scattered on all data nodes (DNs), so you need to specify the distribution columns when you create the tables, as shown in Table 2.9.

The sample code for the Hash distribution is as follows.

```
CREATE TABLE sales_fact
(
region_id INTEGER,
depart_id INTEGER,
product_id INTEGER,
sale_amt NUMERIC (9,2),
sale_qty INTEGER
)
DISTRIBUTE BY HASH(region_id,depart_id,product_id);
```

The sample code for the Replication distribution is as follows.

```
CREATE TABLE depart_dim
(
depart_id INTEGER,
depart_name VARHCARH2(60)
)
DISTRIBUTE BY REPLICATION;
```

The data policy selection is shown in Fig. 2.13.

It should be noted that GaussDB (DWS) only supports Hash and Replication distribution methods, while database shared storage of GaussDB (for MySQL) is not involved at present.

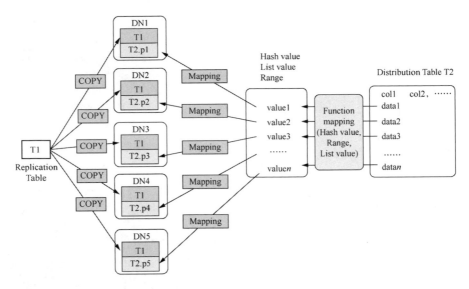

Fig. 2.13 Data policy selection

Table 2.10 Data types

数据类型	说明	数据类型	说明
SMALLINT	2 字节常用整数，取值范围是 -32768~+32767	VARCHAR(n)	变长，有长度限制 n
INTEGER	4 字节常用整数，取值范围是 -2147483648~+2147483647	CHAR(n)	定长，不足补空白
BIGINT	8 字节常用整数，取值范围是 -9223372036854775808~9223372036854775807	TEXT	变长，长文本数据
DECIMAL	精度数字，decimal(m,n) 表示精确到小数点后 n 位、共 m 位的数字	DATE	3 字节，以 YYYY-MM-DD 的格式显示。例如 2009-07-19
NUMERIC	精度数字，等同于 decimal	TIME	3 字节，以 HH:MM:SS 的格式显示。例如 11:22:30
FLOAT	4 字节，单精度浮点型数字	TIMESTAMP	4 字节
DOUBLE	8 字节，双精度浮点型数字	BOOLEAN	1 字节，TRUE 或 FALSE

2.2.9 Data Types

The data in the database is classified into basic data, compound data, serial number data and geometric data. Basic data includes numerical value, character, binary data, date and time, Boolean data, enumeration data, etc., as shown in Table 2.10.

FLOAT and DOUBLE numbers in floating-point numbers are inaccurate, which will sacrifice accuracy. Inaccuracy means that some values cannot be accurately converted into values in an internal format, but are stored in an approximate form, so some missing may occur when the data is stored and then output. Therefore, in applications with strict requirements for precision such as financial calculations, data types with high precision like DECIMAL and NUMERIC should be preferred.

CHAR type is a fixed-length string, which automatically fills the empty digits when the inserted character is less than the set length. For example, under the definition of CHAR(10), when the character "abc" is inserted, it will be supplemented with 7 null digits to ensure that the whole character string is 10 bytes long.

Basic data type is the built-in data type of the database, including INTEGER, CHAR, VARCHAR and other data types.

Regarding the field design, considering the query efficiency, the design suggestions are as follows.

(1) Give priority to the use of efficient data types. Ensure that the specified maximum length is greater than the maximum character number to be stored to avoid truncation of characters when the maximum length is exceeded. In the database, when using SQL statements to insert data, if the characters are truncated, the SQL statement will not report an error. It is recommended to use data types with higher execution efficiency as much as possible. Generally speaking, integer data operations (including $=, >, <, \geq, \leq, \neq$ and other conventional comparison operations, as well as GROUP BY) are more efficient than strings and floating-point numbers. The data type of the short field is also recommended. Data types with shorter lengths not only reduce the size of data files and improve I/O performance, but also reduce memory consumption during related calculations and improve computational performance. For example, for integer data, try not to use INT if you can use SMALLINT, and try not to use BIGINT if you can use INT.

(2) Use consistent data types. Try to use the same data type for the associated columns in the table; otherwise, the database must dynamically convert them into the same data type for comparison, which will bring some performance overhead. When there is a logical relationship between multiple tables, the fields representing the same meaning should use the same data type.

For string data, it is recommended to use the data type of variable-length string and specify the maximum length. Ensure that the specified maximum length is greater than the maximum character number to be stored to avoid truncation of characters when the maximum length is exceeded.

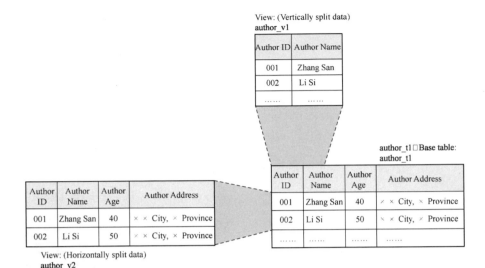

Fig. 2.14 View

2.2.10 View

Unlike the base table, a view is not physically present, but is a dummy table. If the data in the base table changes, then the data queried from the view will also change. In this sense a view is a window through which the data of interest to the user in the database and its changes can be seen, and the view is run once each time it is referenced.

"author_v1" shown in Fig. 2.14 is vertically split data, only two columns in the base table are visible, and other columns are not visible through the view; "author_v2" is horizontally split data, only all data in the table with age values greater than 20 are visible, but all columns are visible. No matter how to split, the data of "author_v1" and "author_v2" views are not really stored in the database. When the user accesses the view through the SELECT statement, the user accesses the data in the underlying base table through the view, so the view is called a "dummy table". To the user, accessing a view is exactly the same as accessing a table.

The main functions of a view are as follows.

(1) Simplifies operations. When querying, we often have to use aggregate functions and display information about other fields, and we may need to associate other tables, thus there is a long statement to write. If this action happens frequently, we can create views, just by executing the SELECT * FROM view statement.
(2) Improves security. Users can only query and modify the data they see, because the view is virtual, not physically present, and it just stores a collection of data. The view is a dynamic collection of data, and the data is updated as the base table

is updated. We can present the important field information in the base table to the user through the view, but the user cannot change and delete the view at will to ensure the security of the data.

(3) Achieves logical independence and shields the impact from the structure of real tables. Views allow the application and database tables to be somewhat independent of each other. Without a view, the application must be built on top of the table; but with a view, the application can be built on top of the view. The application is separated from the database table by the view.

The following sample code encapsulates more complex logic through views.

```
CREATE VIEW stu_class(id,name,class)
AS
SELECT student.s_id,student.name,stu_info.class
FROM student, stu_info
WHERE student.s_id=stu_info.s_id;
```

The user uses the same simplified SQL query statement as the normal table, with the code shown below.

```
SELECT * FROM stu_class WHERE class='Beijing'
```

However, the view also has its limitations, mainly as follows.

(1) Performance issues: The query may be simple, but the statement that encapsulates the view is complex.
(2) Modification restrictions: For complex views, users cannot modify the base table data through the view.

However, if the view is a single table queried directly using the SELECT statement as follows:

```
CREATE v_abc(a,b,c) AS SELECT a,b,c FROM tableA;
```

This form is called a simple view, which enables the modification of the table through the view, for example, using the "UPDATE v_abc SET a='101' WHERE b='xxxx';" statement.

However, if the view has aggregate functions, summary functions, or GROUP BY grouping calculations, or if the view is a result view with multiple table associations, they are complex views that cannot be used to make changes to the base table data.

2.2.11 Index

An index provides pointers to data values stored in specified columns of a table, like a table of contents of a book. It can speed up table queries, but also increase the processing time of insertion, update, and deletion operations.

If you want to add an index to a table, then which fields the index is built on is a question that must be considered before creating the index. It is also necessary to analyze the service processing of the application, data usage, fields that are often used as query conditions or required to be sorted, so as to determine whether to establish an index.

When creating indexes, the following suggestions are used as a reference.

(1) Create indexes on columns that are frequently required to be searched and queried, which can speed up the search and query.
(2) Create an index on a column that used as the primary key, which emphasizes the uniqueness of the column and organizes the arrangement structure of the data in the table.
(3) Create indexes on columns that often need to be searched based on ranges as the ordering of indexes can ensure the continuity of the specified ranges.
(4) Create indexes on columns that need to be ordered frequently as the ordering of indexes can reduce query time.
(5) Create indexes on the columns that often use the WHERE clause to speed up the judgment of the condition.
(6) Create indexes for fields that often follow the keywords ORDER BY, GROUP BY, and DISTINCT.

The created index may not be used, and when to use the index will be automatically judged by the system after the index is successfully created. Indexes are used when the system thinks it is faster to use them than to scan them sequentially. Successfully created indexes must be synchronized with tables to ensure that new data can be found accurately, which increases the load of data operation. We also need to remove useless indexes periodically, and we can query the execution plan by EXPLAIN statement to determine whether to use an index or not.

The indexing methods are shown in Table 2.11.

If a table declares a unique constraint or primary key, a unique index (possibly a multi-field index) is automatically created on the fields that make up the unique constraint or primary key to implement those constraints.

Create a normal index

```
CREATE INDEX index_name ON table_name(col_name);
```

Table 2.11 Indexing methods

Indexing method	Description
Normal index	A basic index type without restriction, allowing to insert duplicate values and null values in the columns that define the index, but only to speed up the query
Unique index	The value in the index column must be unique, but null values are allowed
Primary key index	A special type of unique index, not allowing null values
Combined index	An index created on multiple combined fields in a table, which will only be used if the left field of these fields is used in the query condition
Full-text index	Used primarily to find keywords in the text, rather than comparing directly with the values in the index

Create a unique index

```
CREATE UNIQUE INDEX index_name ON table_name(col_name);
```

Create a normal combined index

```
CREATE INDEX index_name ON table_name(col_name_1,col_name_2);
```

Create a unique combined index

```
    CREATE UNIQUE INDEX index_name ON table_name(col_name_1,
col_name_2);
```

Create a full-text index

```
CREATE FULLTEXT INDEX index_contents ON article(contents);
```

2.2.12 Constraints

Data integrity refers to the correctness and consistency of data. Integrity constraints can be defined at the time of defining a table. Integrity constraint itself is a rule that does not occupy database space. Integrity constraints are stored in the data dictionary together with the table structure definitions.

Figure 2.15 shows the common constraint types, as follows.

Fig. 2.15 Common
constraint types

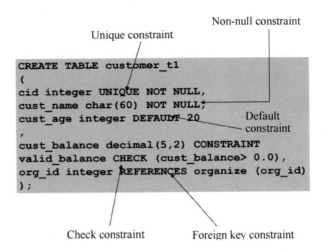

Unique constraint

Non-null constraint

```
CREATE TABLE customer_t1
(
cid integer UNIQUE NOT NULL,
cust_name char(60) NOT NULL,
cust_age integer DEFAULT 20
,
cust_balance decimal(5,2) CONSTRAINT
valid_balance CHECK (cust_balance> 0.0),
org_id integer REFERENCES organize (org_id)
);
```

Default
constraint

Check constraint   Foreign key constraint

(1) Unique (UNIQUE) and primary key (PRIMARY KEY) constraints. When all values in the field will not have duplicate records, you can add unique constraints to the corresponding fields, such as ID card field and employee number field. If a table does not have a unique constraint, then duplicate records can appear in the table. If the fields can be guaranteed to satisfy the unique constraint and not-null constraint, then the primary key constraint can be used, and usually a table can only have one primary key constraint.

(2) References key constraint is used to establish a relationship between two tables, which is necessary to specify which column of the primary table is referenced.

(3) Check constraint is a constraint on the range of legal values in a field. For example, the balance in the savings account table is not allowed to be negative, so a check constraint can be added to the balance field so that the balance field takes a value ≥ 0.

(4) Not-null constraint. If the current field should not have null values or unknown data in service sense, you can add not-null constraints to ensure that the inserted data are all not-null data, such as the ID card field of personal information.

(5) Default constraint. When inserting data, if no specific value is given, then the default constraint will be used to give a default initial value, for example, if the default value of the initial member's rank is 0, when a new member record is added, the member's rank will be 0.

If the field values can be filled in from the service level, then it is recommended that the default constraint not be used to avoid unintended results when the data is loaded. Add a not-null constraint to a field that clearly does not have a null value, and the optimizer will automatically optimize it and explicitly name the constraint that is allowed to be explicitly named. Explicit naming is supported for all types of constraints except not-null and default constraints.

If a default constraint is used, it is actually assigned by default for some unexpected cases. Such default values may hide potential problems. So for OLAP

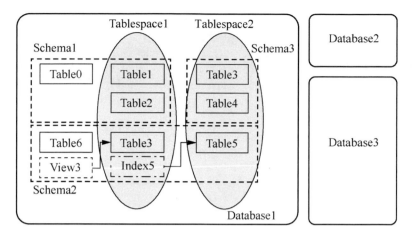

Fig. 2.16 Relationship between database objects

systems, default constraints should be used carefully or sparingly. But in OLTP system, they are relatively more commonly used.

A summary of database objects is shown in Fig. 2.16.

Schema: A database can contain one or more named schemata. A schema is a logical concept, including tables, indexes and other database objects.

Tablespace: A tablespace is used to specify where to store database objects such as tables and indexes in the database, which is a physical concept. After the database administrator creates a tablespace, he or she can refer to it when creating database objects.

Table: A tablespace can contain multiple tables. All the data in the database exist in the form of tables, and the tables are built in the database. The same tables can be stored in different databases or in different modes of the same database.

Schema 1 includes objects Table 0, Table 1 and Table 2.
Schema 2 includes objects Table 3, Table 5, Table 6, View3 and Index5.
Schema 3 includes objects Table 3 and Table 4.

There are two Table3, but they are in Schema2 and Schema3 respectively, so they can have the same name, and are distinguished by Schema2.Table3 and Schema3. Table3.

View3 corresponds to Table3, which is a dummy table that does not occupy actual physical space.

Index5 corresponds to Table5, the table and index can be not in the same tablespace.

The objects of physical data stored in Tablespace1 are Table1, Table2, Table3 and Index5.

The objects stored in Tablespace2 are Table3, Table4, and Table5.

2.2.13   Transaction

Transaction is a user-defined sequence of data operations, these operations are executed as a complete job unit. The data in the database is shared, allowing multiple users to access the same data at the same time. When multiple users add, delete, or change operations on the same piece of data at the same time, it can cause data exceptions if no action is taken.

All statements within a transaction, as a whole, are either all executed or none executed.

For example, when Account A transfers $1000 to Account B, the first operation is to subtract $1000 from Account A, and the second operation is to add $1000 to Account B. All the operations must be successful or failed through transactions.

The ACID characteristics of the transactions are shown below.

(1) Atomicity. The transaction is the logical unit of the database jobs; the operations in the transaction are either all done or none done.
(2) Consistency. The result of transaction execution must be a transition from one consistent state to another.
(3) Isolation. The execution of a transaction in the database cannot be interfered with by other transactions. That is, the internal operation of a transaction and the use of data are isolated from other transactions; multiple transactions subject to concurrent execution cannot interfere with each other. For example, in the process of transferring money from Account A to Account B, if Account C also transfers money to Account A, the transaction of transferring money from Account C to Account A should be isolated from the transaction of transferring from Account A to Account B, without interfering with each other. If the isolation level is not enough, there will be multiple data inconsistencies.
(4) Durability. Once a transaction is committed, the changes to the data in the database are permanent. Post-commit operations or failures will not have any effect on the outcome of the transaction. For example, at the beginning of a transaction, read the value of A as 100, and after calculation, A becomes 200, and then continue to perform subsequent operations after submitting the operation, at this time, the database fails. When the failure is recovered, the value of A should be 200 when it is fetched from the database, not the initial value of 100 or some other value.

There are two markers for the end of a transaction: normal end—COMMIT (commit the transaction); and abnormal end—ROLLBACK (roll back the transaction).

After committing a transaction, all operations of the transaction are physically stored in the database as permanent operations. After rolling back a transaction, all operations in the transaction are undone and the database returns to the state it was in before the transaction started.

There are two types of transaction processing models.

(1) Explicit commit: Transactions have explicit start and end marks.
(2) Implicit commit: Each data operation statement automatically becomes a trans-
    action. GaussDB (for MySQL) adopts implicit COMMIT by default, without
    adding COMMIT statement, and each statement is regarded as an automatic
    commit of transaction.

Implicit commit can be turned off with the SET autocommit = 0 statement.
  The code to set explicit commit is as follows.

```
CREATE TABLE customer (a INT, b CHAR (20), INDEX (a));
START TRANSACTION;
INSERT INTO customer VALUES (10, 'Heikki');
COMMIT;
SET autocommit=0;
INSERT INTO customer VALUES (15, 'John');
INSERT INTO customer VALUES (20, 'Paul');
DELETE FROM customer WHERE b = 'Heikki';
ROLLBACK;
SELECT * FROM customer;
```

Figure 2.17 shows the specific operations of transaction commit and rollback.
  GaussDB (for MySQL) is an OLTP database that adopts an explicit transaction
processing model, but it does not provide a statement that explicitly defines the
transaction start, instead, it takes the first executable SQL as the transaction start.
  You may face a data inconsistency in implicit commit—dirty read, which means
that one transaction reads data that has not been committed (uncommitted) from
another transaction. The uncommitted data is called "dirty" data because of the
possibility of rollback.
  The transaction T1 shown in Fig. 2.18 transfers $200 from Account A to
Account B, where the initial balance of Account A is $1000 and the initial balance
of Account B is $500.

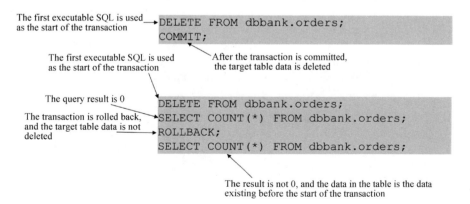

Fig. 2.17 Transaction commit and rollback

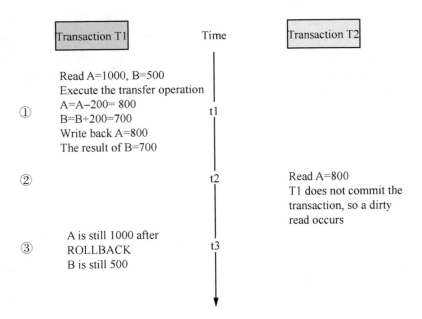

Fig. 2.18 Dirty read. (**a**) Transaction T1 changes the value of A from 1000 to 800 and changes the value of B from 500 to 700, but has not yet committed the transaction. (**b**) At this time, Transaction T2 starts to read the data, and gets *A* of value 800 modified by the transaction T1. (**c**) Transaction T1 is rolled back, but because it is not committed, A recovers to the initial value 1000, while the value of B is 500; at this time, for Transaction T2, the value of A is still 800. This case is dirty read, that is, Transaction T2 reads data that has not been committed by Transaction T1.

There is another kind of data inconsistency—non-repeatable read (NRR), which refers to that a transaction read the data that can be modified by other data. The reason why it is called NRR is that a transaction reads the same data many times during processing (repeated reads), but this data may change, as shown in Fig. 2.19.

Phantom read is a more special scenario of non-repeatable read—after Transaction T1 reads the data based on certain conditions (using the WHERE filter condition), Transaction T2 deletes some records or inserts some new records, after which these changed data are satisfied with the WHERE filter condition. Then when Transaction T1 reads the data based on the same conditions again, it will find that some data is inexplicably missing or increased.

Such missing or increased data is called phantom data.

A. Transaction T1 calculates that the sum of A and B is 300.
B. Transaction T2 reads the value of B, and records calculated result 400.
C. Transaction T1 reads the values of A and B again and sums them up, but this time the calculation result becomes 500. At this time, for transaction T1, the same data source is read many times in one transaction with the result changing. This case is the so-called NRR.

Fig. 2.19 Non-repeatable read (NRR)

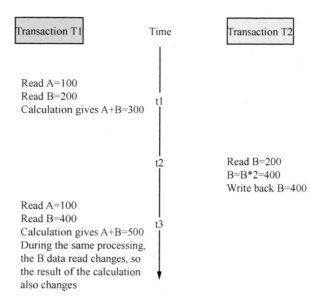

The ANSI SQL standard defines 4 transaction isolation levels to avoid 3 kinds of data inconsistency. The transaction levels, from high to low, are shown below.

(1) Serializable. All transactions in the system are executed one by one in a serial manner, so all data inconsistencies can be avoided. However, this serializable execution method of controlling concurrent transactions in an exclusive manner will lead to queuing of transactions that significantly reduces the concurrency of the system, so should be used with great caution.

Here serialization means that all operations are serially queued, for example:

```
Q1 indicates the insert operation "INSERT INTO TA valules(1,2,3)";
Q2 indicates the query operation "SELECT * FROM TA";
```

Under the serializable transaction isolation mechanism, Q2 must wait for Q1 to complete before getting the returned result. If Q1 is not completed, Q2 is always in the queuing state.

(2) Repeatable read. Once a transaction is started, all data read during the transaction is not allowed to be modified by other transactions. This isolation level has no way to solve the problem of phantom reads. It only "protects" the data it reads from being modified, but other data still can be modified. If other data is modified to meet the current transaction's filter conditions (WHERE statement), then a phantom read will occur.

Table 2.12 Correspondence between 4 transaction isolation levels and problems

Transaction isolation level	Dirty read	Non-repeatable read	Phantom read
Read uncommitted	Possible	Possible	Possible
Read committed	Impossible	Possible	Possible
Repeatable read	Impossible	Impossible	Possble
Serializable	Impossible	Impossible	Impossible

For the Q1 transaction, the "SELECT * FROM TA WHERE order_date='2019-01-01'" statement queries 100 rows for the first time, and then goes to perform query operations on other tables. At this time, the Q2 transaction performs an insert operation "INSERT INTO TA values (1,2,3,'2019-01-01')", adding a record of orderr_date=2019-01-01. Then if the Q1 transaction executes the "SELECT * FROM TA WHERE order_date='2019-01-01'" statement again, the query results become 101 rows. For Q1 transaction, it queries the same transaction in the same range but gets different results. This is the so-called phantom read.

(3) Read committed. A transaction can read data that has been committed by other transactions. If a certain data is read repeatedly in processing, and the read data happens to be modified and committed by other transactions, then the current transaction that reads data repeatedly will encounter data inconsistency.

(4) Read uncommitted. A transaction can read data that has been modified by other transactions but has not yet been committed. Data modified by other transactions but not yet committed may be rolled back. The read of this "uncommitted" data is a dirty read, which may occur at this isolation level.

GaussDB (for MySQL) implements 2 levels of transaction isolation: read committed and repeatable read. The table about the correspondence between the four transaction isolation levels and the problems is shown in Table 2.12.

2.3 Summary

This chapter describes the core objectives of database management, and introduces the scope of database management work, explaining the basic concepts of database object management, backup recovery, and disaster recovery levels, as well as the important concepts of database. Some concepts that tend to be confused are compared and explained, and the important but rather obscure concepts are introduced and analyzed based on scenarios.

2.4 Exercises

1. [Multiple Choice] To migrate data from a database to other heterogeneous databases, you can use the ( ) approach.

   A. Physical backup
   B. Logical backup

2. [Multiple Choice] To improve the speed of table queries, you can create the database object ( ).

   A. View
   B. Function
   C. Index
   D. Sequence

3. [Single Choice] When an organization sets disaster recovery standards, it wants to have the ability to restore the system to an externally serviceable state within 1 h after a disaster occurs. This indicator refers to ( ).

   A. RTO
   B. RPO

4. [Multiple Choice] To add an index to a table, on which fields is it recommended to create the index? ( )

   A. Creating indexes on columns that are frequently required to be searched and queried can speed up the search.
   B. Creating an index on a column that used as the primary key emphasizes the uniqueness of the column and organizes the arrangement structure of the data in the table.
   C. Create indexes on the columns that often use the WHERE clause to speed up the judgment of the condition.
   D. Create indexes for fields that often follow the keywords ORDER BY, GROUP BY, and DISTINCT.

5. [Single choice] Among the following statements about the selection of data types, ( ) is incorrect.

   A. It is recommended to use data types with higher execution efficiency as much as possible.
   B. The data type of the short field is also recommended.
   C. For string data, try to use the fixed-length string and specify the string length.
   D. When there is a logical relationship between multiple tables, the fields representing the same meaning should use the same data type.

6. [Multiple Choice] Among the following options,   ( ) is a transaction characteristic.

    A. Atomicity
    B. Isolation
    C. Durability
    D. Consistency

7. [Multiple Choice] Which of the following situations will not occur under the Repeatable Read? ( )

    A. Dirty read
    B. Non-repeatable read
    C. Phantom read

Chapter 3
Getting Started with SQL Syntax

Huawei GaussDB (for MySQL) is a cloud-based high-performance, high-available relational database that fully supports the syntax and functionality of the open source database MySQL. This chapter introduces GaussDB (for MySQL) data types, system functions and operators to help readers get started with SQL syntax.

After learning this chapter, readers will be able to do the following four things.

(1) Describe the definitions and types of SQL statements and identify the categories to which a given statement belongs, including data definition language (DDL), data manipulation language (DML), data control language (DCL), and data query language (DQL).
(2) List the available data types and learn to select the correct data type for creating a table. For example, when to choose a character data and when to choose numeric value data. The right data type helps improve the efficiency of storing and querying data.
(3) Describe the usage of different system functions and master how to use them correctly in query statements. For example, what numeric processing function should be used in specific numeric processing; what character processing functions should be used in character processing. The correct system functions can improve the use of the database and query efficiency.
(4) List the common operators and master the priority and usage of different operators. For example, when to use the logical operator and when to use the comparison operator. The correct operators can also improve the query efficiency and query accuracy.

© The Author(s) 2023
Huawei Technologies Co., Ltd., *Database Principles and Technologies – Based on Huawei GaussDB*, https://doi.org/10.1007/978-981-19-3032-4_3

3.1   Overview of SQL Statements

3.1.1   What is an SQL Statement

Structured query language (SQL) is a purpose-built programming language used to manage relational DBMS or to perform stream processing in relational data stream management systems. SQL is based on relational algebra and tuple relational algorithms, which includes the DDL and DML. The scope of SQL management covers data insertion, query, update and deletion, as well as database schema creation and modification, and data access control. GaussDB (for MySQL) is a kind of relational database. SQL statements include DDL, DML, DCL and DQL.

DDL is used to define or modify objects in the database, where database objects include tables, indexes, views, databases, stored procedures, triggers, custom functions, etc. The following operations are mainly involved.

(1) Define databases: create a database (CREATE DATABASE), modify a database attribute (ALTER DATABASE), and delete a database (DROP DATABASE).
(2) Define tablespaces: create a tablespace (CREATE TABLESPACE), modify a tablespace (ALTER TABLESPACE), and delete a tablespace (DROP TABLESPACE).
(3) Define tables: create a table (CREATE TABLE), modify a table attribute (ALTER TABLE), delete a table (DROP TABLE), and delete all data in a table (TRUNCATE TABLE).
(4) Define indexes: create an index (CREATE INDEX), modify an index attribute (ALTER INDex), and delete an index (DROP INDEX).
(5) Define roles: create a role (CREATE ROLE), and delete a role (DROP ROLE).
(6) Define users: create a user (CREATE USER), modify a user attribute (ALTER USER), and delete a user (DROP USER).
(7) Define views: create a view (CREATE VIEW), and delete a view (DROP VIEW).
(8) Define events: create an event (CREATE EVENT), modify an event (ALTER EVENT), and delete an event (DROP EVENT).

DML is used to insert, update and delete data in database tables, mainly involving the following operations.

(1) Data operations: insert data (INSERT), update data (UPDATE) and delete data (DELETE).
(2) Import/Export operations: import (LOAD) and export (DUMP).
(3) Other operations: call (CALL), replace (REPLACE), etc.

DCL is used to set or change database transactions, save point operations and permission operations (user or role authorization, permission revoking, role creation, role deletion, etc.), locking tables (two locking modes of shared lock and exclusive lock are supported), locking instances, and shutdown, etc. The following operations are mainly involved.

(1) Transaction management: start a transaction (START TRANSACTION/ BEGIN), commit a transaction (COMMIT), and roll back a transaction (ROLLBACK).
(2) Save point setting: start a save point (SAVEPOINT), roll back a save point (ROLLBACK TO SAVEPOINT), and publish a save point (PUBLISH SAVEPOINT).
(3) Authorization operations: grant a permission (GRANT), revoke a permission (REVOKE), create a role (CREATE ROLE), and delete a role (DROP ROLE).
(4) Locking table: lock a table (LOCK TABLE), and unlock a table (UNLOCK TABLE).
(5) Locking instance (LOCK INSTANCE FOR BACKUP).
(6) Shutdown (SHUTDOWN).

DQL is used to query the data in the database, such as single-table query and multi-table query, which mainly involves the following operations.

(1) Query data (SELECT).
(2) Merge the result sets of multiple SELECT statements.

3.1.2   Comprehensive Application of SQL Statements

The following is a comprehensive application of the operations involved in the above four languages to store a company's employee information.

(1) First of all, you need to create a table to store employee information, which can be realized by the CREATE TABLE statement, i.e. DDL.
(2) To insert specific employee information into the table, it can be achieved by the INSERT statement, i.e. DML.
(3) When you need to commit the inserted information to make it persistent, you can achieve it through the COMMIT statement, i.e. DCL.
(4) It can be done by the SELECT statement, i.e. DQL.

Different SQL statements are applicable to different service scenarios, and the readers have to choose the appropriate SQL statement according to the specific scenario.

3.2   Data Types

Data type is a basic attribute of data. Data are generally divided into common data and uncommon data. Common data types include numeric value, character, date and time, and so on. Uncommon data types include Boolean data, spatial data, JSON data, etc.

注意 | Different data types occupy different storage space, and can perform different operations. The data in the database is stored in the data tables. Each column in the data table is defined with the data type. When storing data, the user must comply with the attributes of these data types, otherwise errors may occur.

3.2.1 Common Data Types

1. Numeric Value
   The numeric value types available in GaussDB (for MySQL) database include integer, floating-point number and fixed-point number, which support basic 32-bit integer and 64-bit integer.

   (1) There are five types of integers, as shown in Table 3.1.
       INTEGER (32-bit signed integer) occupies 4 bytes, with value range from -2^{31} to $2^{31}-1$, which can be expressed by the keywords INT, INTEGER, BINARY_INTERGER, INT SIGNED, INTEGER SINGNED, SHORT, SMALLINT and TINYINT. BIGINT (64-bit signed integer) occupies 8 bytes, with value range from -2^{63} to $2^{63}-1$, which can be expressed by the keywords BIGINT, BINARY_BIGINT and BIGINT SIGNED.
   (2) Floating-point numbers are divided into two types as follows.
       FLOAT: single-precision floating-point number occupying 4 bytes, with 8-bit precision.
       DOUBLE: double-precision floating-point number occupying 8 bytes, with 16-bit precision.
   (3) The fixed-point numbers occupy 4–24 bytes, with actual length related to the effective number it represents, and with value range from -1.0E128 to 1.0E128, which can be expressed by keywords DECIMAL and NUMERIC. They are in the following syntax format, requiring s ≤ p.

   NUMERIC/DECIMAL、NUMERIC/DECIMAL(p) and NUMERIC /DECIMAL(p,s)

       The bytes occupied by DECIMAL/NUMERIC depend on their precision, among which, "p" takes values ranging from 1 to 65, and "s" from 0 to 30.

Table 3.1 Integer types

Integer type	Range (signed)	Range (unsigned)	Space occupied/byte
TINYINT	[-128, 127]	[0, 255]	1
SMALLINT	[-32768, 32767]	[0, 65535]	2
MEDIUMINT	[-8388608, 8388607]	[0, 16777215]	3
INT(INTEGER)	[-2147483648, 2147483647]	[0, 4294967295]	4
BIGINT	$[-2^{63}, 2^{63}-1]$	$[0, 2^{64}-1]$	8

If the values of "p" and "s" are not specified, "p" defaults to 10, meaning that there is no restriction on the value after the decimal point. If the value of "s" is not specified or s = 0, the fixed-point number has no decimal part.

2. Character

The character types supported by GaussDB (for MySQL) are CHAR, VARCHAR, BINARY, VARBINARY, TEXT, BLOB, ENUM, and SET. Under the default encoding set "utf8mb4", Chinese characters occupy 3 bytes, numeric and English characters occupy 1 byte, and other characters occupy up to 4 bytes. The characters are divided into fixed-length strings and variable-length strings.

CHAR(n) is used to store fixed-length bytes or strings, with the n indicating the length of the string, and taking values from 0 to 255. If the length of the input string is less than n, the right end will be made up with spaces. For example, CHAR(4) will occupy 4 bytes no matter how many characters are input.

VARCHAR(n) is used to store variable-length bytes or strings, with the n indicating the length of the string, and taking values from 0 to 65535. If the length of the input string is less than n, there is no need to make up with spaces. The number of bytes occupied by VARCHAR is the actual number of characters input + 1 byte ($n \leq 255$) or 2 bytes ($n > 255$), so VARCHAR(4) occupies 4 bytes when 3 English characters are input.

In the string comparison between CHAR and VARCHAR, the case sensitivity and the spaces at the end are ignored.

BINARY(n) stores binary fixed-length strings, and automatically adds 0x00 bytes to the end of the strings when the length is less than n bytes.

VARBINARY(n) stores binary variable-length strings, but there is no need to add 0x00 bytes to the end of the strings when the length is less than n bytes.

TEXT stores variable-length strings of large objects, which can save character data, such as articles and diaries. Its keywords are mainly TINYTEXT (1 byte), TEXT (2 bytes), MEDIUMTEXT (3 bytes), and LONGTEXT (4 bytes).

BLOB stores binary variable-length strings of large objects, which can save binary data, such as photos. Its keywords are mainly TINYBLOB (1 byte), BLOB (2 bytes), MEDIUMBLOB (3 bytes) and LONGBLOB (4 bytes).

ENUM refers to single-select enumeration, which can contain up to 65535 different elements.

SET refers to multi-select enumeration, which can contain up to 64 different elements.

3. Date

The types of date data are shown in Table 3.2.

Gaussian database supports two date types: timestamp without time zone (8 bytes) and timestamp with time zone. When storing timestamp data without

Table 3.2 Date types

Date type	Range	Format	Space occupied/byte
Year	1901–2155	YYYY/YY	1
Date	1000-01-01 - 9999-12-31	YYYY-MM-DD	3
Time	-838:59:59 - 838:59:59	HH:MM:SS	3
Timestamp	1970-01-01 00:00:00 - 2037-12-31 23:59:59	YYYY-MM-DD HH-MM-SS	4
Datetime	1000-01-01 00:00:00 - 9999-12-31 23:59:59	YYYY-MM-DD HH-MM-SS	8

time zone, you can use DATETIME, DATE and TIMESTAMP types, which can all indicate year, month, day, hour, minute and second information; however, unlike DATE and DATETIME which support up to seconds, TIMESTAMP can support up to microseconds.

YEAR can also be expressed as a two-digit string "YY", ranging from 00 to 99, among which, values of 00–69 and 70–99 are converted to YEAR values of 2000–2069 and 1970–1999.

The value range of DATETIME/DATE is [0001-01-01 00:00:00, 9999-12-31 23:59:59], Expressed as "2019-08-22 17:29:13".

TIMESTAMP[(n)] can specify the precision to be saved through the parameter n, ranging from 0 to 6; or takes no parameter, in which case the default precision of decimals after the second is 6. For example, 2019-08-22 17:29:13.263183 ($n =$ 6), 2019-08-22 17:34:36.383 ($n = 3$). The value range of TIMESTAMP is [0001-01-01 00:00:00.000000, 9999-12-31 23:59:59.999999].

When storing timestamp data with time zone, TIMESTAMP(n) WITH TIME ZONE and TIMESTAMP(n) WITH LOCAL TIME ZONE can be used. The difference between the two is that TIMESTAMP(n) WITH TIME ZONE holds the time and time zone information and therefore occupies 12 bytes, e.g., 2019-08-22 18:41:30.135428 +08:00. TIMESTAMP(n) WITH LOCAL TIME ZONE uses local data information, which only saves time information, not time zone information. It will be converted to the timestamp of the current time zone of the database when stored, and will be displayed with the information of the local time zone when viewed, so it occupies 8 bytes. For example, when stored, it is displayed as 2019-08-22 18: 41:30.135428; when viewed, it is displayed as 2019-08-22 18:41:30. 135428 +08:00.

3.2.2   Uncommon Data Types

Boolean data can be stored by the keywords BOOL and BOOLEAN, occupying 1 byte. For string input, the normal strings TRUE and FALSE are supported, as well as the single characters T and F, and the string values 1 and 0. Boolean data can be converted to and from INT and BIGINT data because Boolean data can be seen as the numbers 0 and 1, so it can be converted to the integers 0 and 1. Integer data can also be converted to Boolean data. The conversion rule is that integer 0 corresponds to the Boolean value FALSE, and other non-zero integers correspond to the Boolean value TRUE. For the output of Boolean data, when Boolean data is displayed, or when converting Boolean data to character data, Gaussian database uniformly outputs 1 as string TRUE and 0 as string FALSE. When the input value is null, the output of the Boolean data is also null.

Spatial data types include GEOMETRY, POINT, LINESTRING, POLYGON, etc.

JSON data (JSON: Javascript Object Notation) support native JSON data, allowing for more efficient storage and management of JSON documents.

3.2.3   Cases of Data Types

To store department information of a company, first create a table with fields for department information. Suppose the department information to be stored includes department number, department level, department name, establishment time, and whether it is an excellent department, etc., we need to determine the data type of the specific information first: if the department number is numeric data, it can be expressed as NUMBER; if the department level is integer data, it can be expressed as INT; if the department name is character data, it can be expressed as VARCHAR; the establishment time can be expressed by date data; whether it is an excellent department can be expressed by Boolean data. This is the CREATE TABLE statements to create a department information table. The code is shown below.

```
SQL>DROP TABLE IFEXITS T_TEST_CASE;
CREATE TABLE T_TEST_CASE(
section_id NUMBER(10) PRIMARY KEY,
section_grade INT,
section_name VARCHAR(100),
section_is_excellent BOOLEAN,
section_date DATE
);
```

After the table is created successfully, if you want to store the department description information in the table, you can add more columns to the table. Suppose the column name is "section_description", if the department description information is expressed by a string, the content may be bulky; and if it is defined as BLOB data, it can be achieved by the following statement.

```
SQL> ALTER TABLE T_TEST_CASE ADD section_description BLOB;
```

Where, "seciton_description" is the department description field and BLOB is the data type of the field information. The department level is now an integer, and if you want to modify it to a decimal number, recorded as a floating point number, you can do so by modifying the data type of the corresponding column. The "section_grade" field can be modified to DOUBLE type by the following code.

```
SQL> ALTER TABLE T_TEST_CASE MODIFY section_grade DOUBLE;
```

3.3 System Functions

A system function is encapsulation for some service logic to accomplish a specific function. System functions can be executed with or without parameters depending on their specific functions, and they return the result after execution.

GaussDB (for MySQL) provides 10 types of system functions. This section introduces five more common system functions: numeric calculation function, character processing function, time and date function, type conversion function, and system information function.

	GaussDB (for MySQL) system functions cannot be modified manually.

3.3.1 Numeric Calculation Functions

The numeric calculation functions are responsible to calculate numeric values, such as absolute value calculation function ABS(x), sine function SIN(x), cosine function COS(x), inverse sine function ASIN(i), and inverse cosine function ACOS(x).

The ABS(x) function is used to calculate the absolute value. The input parameter can be a numeric value or a non-numeric value that can be implicitly converted to a numeric value. The type of the return value is the same as that of the input parameter. x must be an expression that can be converted to a numeric value type. ABS(x) eventually returns the absolute value *of* x (including INT, BIGINT, REAL, NUMBER, and DECIMAL types).

The SIN(x) and COS(x) functions are used to calculate the sine and cosine values, whose input parameter is an expression that can be converted to a numeric value, and the return value is of type NUMBER.

The ASIN(x) and ACOS(x) functions are used to calculate the arc sine and arc cosine values, whose input parameter is an expression that can be converted to a numeric value, with the range of [-1, 1], and the return value is of type NUMBER. The code is shown below.

```
mysql> SELECT ABS(-10),COS(0),SIN(0),ACOS(1),ASIN(0) FROM dual;
+----------+--------+--------+----------+---------+
| ABS(-10) | COS(0) | SIN(0) | ACOS(1)  | ASIN(0) |
+----------+--------+--------+----------+---------+
|    --  10|   -- 1 |  -- 0  |  --    0 | -     0 |
+----------+--------+--------+----------+---------+
1 row in set (0.00 sec)
```

ROUND(X,D) can truncate the numeric value X before and after the decimal point according to the value specified by D, and round it to return the truncated value. The value of D is in the range $[-30, 30]$. If D is ignored, all fractional parts are intercepted and rounded. If D is negative, it means that the left digit from the decimal point is filled with zeros and rounded, and the decimal part is removed. The code is shown below.

```
mysql> SELECT ROUND(1234.5678,-2),ROUND(1234.5678,2) FROM dual;
+---------------------+--------------------+
| ROUND(1234.5678,-2) | ROUND(1234.5678,2) |
+---------------------+--------------------+
|                1200 |            1234.57 |
+---------------------+--------------------+
1 row in set (0.00 sec)
```

POW(X,Y) is equivalent to POWER(X,Y), which means calculate the Yth power of X. The code is shown below.

```
mysql> SELECT POW(3,2),POWER(3,-2) FROM dual;
+----------+----------------------+
| POW(3,2) | POWER(3,-2)          |
+----------+----------------------+
|        9 | 0.1111111111111111   |
+----------+----------------------+
1 row in set (0.00 sec)
```

The CEIL(X) function is used to calculate the smallest integer greater than or equal to the specified expression n, whose input parameter is an expression that can

Table 3.3 Numeric calculation functions

Syntax	Function	Example
CEIL(X)	Returns the smallest integer greater than or equal to the specified expression X	CEIL(15.3) → 16
SIGN(X)	Takes the sign of X result: greater than 0 then return 1, less than 0 then return −1, equal to 0 then return 0	SIGN(2*3) → 1
SQRT(X)	Returns the square root of the non-negative real number X. The input parameter is an expression that can be converted to a non-negative value	SQRT(49) → 7
TRUNCATE (X,D)	Intercepts the input numeric data in the specified format X indicates the data to be intercepted, and D indicates the interception accuracy	TRUNCATE (15.79,1) → 15.7; TRUNCATE (15.79,-1) → 10
FLOOR(X)	Finds the nearest integer less than or equal to the value of the expression X	LOOR(12.8) → 12
PI()	Returns the value of π, with valid number default to 7 digits	PI() → 3.141593
MOD(X,Y)	Modulo operation	MOD(29,3) → 2

be converted to a numeric value, and the return value is an integer. For example, CEIL(15.3) is calculated as 16. Numeric calculation functions are shown in Table 3.3.

The SIGN(X) function is used to take the sign of the numeric value type, which returns 1 if *greater than* 0, returns -1 if less than 0, and returns 0 if equal to 0. The returned value is of the numeric value type. For example, for SIGN(2*3), $2 \times 3 = 6$, if greater than 0, the calculation result is 1.

The SQRT(X) function is used to calculate the square root of a non-negative real number, whose input parameter is an expression that can be converted to a non-negative values, and the return value is of type DECIMAL. For example, SQRT(49) is calculated as 7.

The TRUNCATE (X,D) function is used to intercept the input numeric data in the specified format, without rounding, where X indicates the data to be intercepted, and D for the interception accuracy, and the return value is of type NUMBER. For example, TRUNCATE(15.79,1) is 15.7 after intercepting a decimal to the right; TRUNCATE(15.79,-1) is 10 after intercepting an integer to the left.

The FLOOR(X) function is used to find the nearest integer less than or equal to the value of the expression, whose input parameter is an expression that can be converted to a numeric value, and the return value is of type NUMBER. For example, FLOOR(12.8) is calculated as 12.

The PI() function is used to return the value of π, with valid number default to 7 digits. For example, PI() returns 3.141593.

The MOD(X,Y) function is used for modulo operations, whose input parameter is an expression that can be converted to a NUMBER data, and the return value is of type NUMBER. For example, MOD (29,3) is calculated as 2.

Other numeric calculation functions include the exponentiation function POWER (), etc.

3.3.2   Character Processing Functions

The character splicing functions CONCAT(str[,...]) and CONCAT_WS(separator, str1,str2,...) are used to splice one or more strings. The CONCAT() function splices the strings generated by each parameter without separating them; the input parameters are strings or expressions that can be converted to strings, separated by commas. The CONCAT_WS() function splices the strings and separate them with commas; the first input parameter is the separator, and the subsequent ones are strings or expressions that can be converted to strings. If the parameter is NULL, CONCAT or CONCAT_WS, the parameter will be ignored. If NULL is enclosed in single quotes, NULL will be treated as a string. The CONCAT() and CONCAT_WS () functions can be nested and support return values of up to 8000 bytes.

```
mysql> SELECT CONCAT('11','NULL','22'),CONCAT_WS('-','11',NULL,'22')
  FROM dual;
  +--------------------------+-------------------------------+
  | CONCAT('11','NULL','22') | CONCAT_WS('-','11',NULL,'22') |
  +--------------------------+-------------------------------+
  | 11NULL22                 | 11-22                         |
  +--------------------------+-------------------------------+
  1 row in set (0.00 sec)
```

In the above example, the CONCAT() function splices the strings '11', 'NULL' and '22' to return the string 11NULL22, and the CONCAT_WS() function splices '11', NULL and '22' by the separator '-', where NULL means null, to return 11–22.

The HEX (str) function returns a string of hexadecimal value, whose input parameter is of numeric value type or character type, and the return value is of string type. The HEX2BIN (str) and HEXTORAW (str) functions return strings represented as hexadecimal strings. The difference between the two is that the HEX2BIN() function returns the BINARY type, where the input hexadecimal string must be prefixed with 0x, while the HEXTORAW() function returns the RAW type.

```
mysql> SELECT HEX('ABC');
  +------------+
  | HEX('ABC') |
  +------------+
  | 414243     |
  +------------+
  1 row in set (0.00 sec)
```

In the above example, the HEX('ABC') function returns the hexadecimal string 414243 for ABC. The HEX2BIN('0X28') function returns the string "(" represented by the hexadecimal string 28. The HEXTORAW('ABC') function returns the hexadecimal string ABC of type RAW.

The string insertion function INSERT(str,pos,len,newstr) replaces the string with the length of len with newstr from pos position, and then returns the replaced string. If pos is not within the length of the string str, the original string is returned. If the value of the parameter len is greater than the length of the rest of the strings starting from the parameter pos, then all strings starting from pos are replaced with newstr. Both the input parameters str and newstr are expressions that can be converted to strings, with the maximum value of up to 8000 bytes.

```
mysql> SELECT INSERT('quadratic',5,2,'what'),REPLACE('123456','45',
'abds') FROM dual;
+-------------------------------+-------------------------------+
| INSERT('quadratic',5,2,'what') | REPLACE('123456','45','abds') |
+-------------------------------+-------------------------------+
| quadwhattic                    | 123abds6                      |
+-------------------------------+-------------------------------+
1 row in set (0.00 sec)
```

INSERT('quadratic',5,2,'what') means that replace the two consecutive characters' of the quadratic string from the fifth character with what, which is equal to REPLACE('quadratic','ra','what').

The REPLACE(str,src,dst) function is to replace the corresponding src substring in the string str with the dst substring. The input parameter str indicates the original string, src indicates the string to be replaced, and dst indicates to replace the string. The return value is of string type.

REPLACE('123456','45','abds') means to replace "45" in the string "123456" with "abds", equal to INSERT('123456',4,2,'abds').

The INSTR(str1,str2) function is a string lookup function that returns the first occurrence of the string to be found in the source string, where str1 indicates the source string, and str2 indicates the string to be found.

```
mysql> SELECT INSTR('gaussdb数据库','库');
+-----------------------------------+
| INSTR('gaussdb数据库','库')        |
+-----------------------------------+
|                                10 |
+-----------------------------------+
1 row in set (0.00 sec)
```

In the example above, the INSTR('gaussdb数据库', '库') function returns the first occurrence of the string "库" in the source string to be found, returning 10, indicating the first occurrence of "库". Character processing functions are shown in Table 3.4.

The LEFT(str, length) function returns the left few characters of the specified string. For example, the result after executing LEFT('abcdef',3) is abc. If length is

Table 3.4   Character processing functions

Syntax	Function	Example
LEFT(str, length)	Returns the left few characters of the specified string	LEFT('abcdef',3) → abc LEFT('abcdef',0) or LEFT('abcdef',-1) → null string
LENGTH (str)	A function to get the number of bytes in a string	LENGTH('1234大') → 7
LOWER (str)	Converts a string to the corresponding lowercase form	LOWER('ABCD') → abcd LOWER('1234') → 1234
UPPER (str)	Converts a string to the corresponding uppercase form	UPPER('abcd') → ABCD UPPER('1234') → 1234
SPACE(n)	Generate n spaces	CONCAT('123',space(3),'abc') → 123 abc
RIGHT (str,len)	Returns the right few characters of the specified string	RIGHT('abcdef',3) → def RIGHT('abcdef',0) or right('abcdef',-1) → null string
REVERSE (str)	Returns the reverse order of a string. Only the string type are supported	REVERSE('abcd') → dcba
SUBSTR (str,start, len)	String interception function	SUBSTR('abcdefg',3,4) → cdef Indicates that intercept a string of length 4 from the third character of the abcdefg string

less than or equal to 0, then a null string is returned. The function of RIGHT(str, length) is opposite to that of LEFT(), which returns the right few characters of the specified string. For example, the result after executing RIGHT('abcdef',3) is def. If length is less than or equal to 0, then a null string is returned.

The LEFT () and RIGHT () functions are described as follows. str is the source string from which the substring is to be extracted. length is a positive integer, specifying the number of characters returned from the left or right. If length is 0 or a negative number, then a null string is returned. If length is greater than the length of the str string, the function returns the entire str string. The client currently supports a maximum string of 32767 bytes, so the function returns a maximum value of 32767 bytes.

The LENGTH(str) function is used to get the length of the string function, for example, the result of executing LENGTH('1234大') is 7. The LENGTH () function returns the number of characters in str, whose input parameter is an expression that can be converted to a string, and the return value is of type INT.

The LOWER(str) function is used to convert a string to the corresponding lowercase form. For example, the result of executing LOWER('ABCD') is abcd, without converting the numeric value type. Corresponding to the LOWER() function, the UPPER(str) function is used to convert a string to the corresponding uppercase form. For example, the result of executing UPPER('abcd') is ABCD, without converting the numeric value type. The LOWER() and UPPER() functions have input parameters that can be converted to string expressions and return values that are of string type.

The SPACE (*n*) function is to generate *n* spaces, and the value range of *n* is [0,4000]. For example, the result of CONCAT('123', SPACE(4),'abc') is 123 abc.

The REVERSE(str) function returns the reverse order of the string, only supports the string type. For example, the result of REVERSE('abcd') is dcba.

SUBSTR(str,start,len) is a string interception function. For example, SUBSTR ('abcdefg',3,4) indicates that intercept a string of length 4 from the third character, delivering the result cdef. The SUBstr () function intercepts and returns a substring with len characters from start in str, where the input parameter str must be an expression that can be converted into a string, and the input parameters start and len must be expressions that can be converted into INT type. The return value is of string type.

3.3.3   Time and Date Functions

The DATE_FORMAT(date,format) function is a formatted date function, used to convert to the required format according to the parameter format. The value of format includes: % w (Monday - Sunday); %w (1–7); %Y (YYYY: 4-digit year); %m (1–12); %d (00–31).

```
mysql> SELECT
DATE_FORMAT(SYSDATE(),'%W'),DATE_FORMAT(SYSDATE(),'%w'),
DATE_ FORMAT(SYSDATE(),'%Y-%m-%d');
   +-------------------------------+---------------------------
+-------------------------------+
   |DATE_FORMAT(SYSDATE(),'%W')|DATE_FORMAT(SYSDATE(),'%w')|
DATE_FORMAT(SYSDATE(),'%Y-%m-%d')|
   +-------------------------------+---------------------------
+-------------------------------+
   | Tuesday                | 2           | 2020-05-19
   |
   +-------------------------------+---------------------------
+-------------------------------+
   1 row in set (0.00 sec)
```

The EXTRACT(field from datetime) function extracts the specified time field "field" from the specified datetime, where the values of the field include year, month, day, hour, minute, and second, and the return value is of the numeric value type. If the field value is SECOND, the return value is of the floating-point number type, where the integer part indicates second, and the decimal part indicates microsecond. This function takes any numeric value or any non-numeric value that can be implicitly converted to a numeric value as an parameter and returns the same data type as the parameter.

```
mysql> SELECT EXTRACT(month from date '2019-08-23') FROM dual;
+-------------------------------------------------+
| EXTRACT(month from date '2019-08-23') |
+-------------------------------------------------+
|                                               8 |
+-------------------------------------------------+
1 row in set (0.00 sec)
```

The above code extracts the month from "2019-08-23", and returns the result 8; and intercepts from the system date according to "YY", and the result is 2019-01-01 00:00:00. Time and date functions are shown in Table 3.5.

3.3.4 Type Conversion Functions

IF(cond,p1,p2) function: Cond is taken as the calculation condition, if the condition is true, p1 is returned, otherwise, p2 is returned.

IFNULL(p1,p2) function: P1 is returned if p1 is not NULL, otherwise p2 is returned.

NULLIF(p1,p2) function: If p1 is equal to p2, NULL is returned; otherwise, P1 is returned. It is not supported that both parameters are CLOB type or BLOB type, and the input parameter p1 cannot be NULL, otherwise the verification will report an error.

The specific example is as follows.

```
mysql> SELECT IF(10>13,10,14),IFNULL(10,12),nullif(10,12);
+------------------+---------------+---------------+
| IF(10>13,10,14) | IFNULL(10,12)  | NULLIF(10,12)  |
+------------------+---------------+---------------+
|               14 |            10 |            10 |
+------------------+---------------+---------------+
1 row in set (0.00 sec)
```

Type conversion functions are shown in Table 3.6.

The ASCII(str) function returns the ASCII value corresponding to the first character of the string str, whose input parameter is a string or a single character, which needs to be enclosed by single quotation marks ("), and the return value is the ASCII value.

CHAR(n) returns characters with ASCII value of n, where the value range of n is [0,127], and the input parameter is an expression that can be converted into the numeric value type.

The CAST(value as type) function converts the column name or value to the specified data type, and the expression can be converted to the same type as itself.

Table 3.5 Time and date functions

Syntax	Function	Example
CURRENT_TIMESTAMP (fractional_second_precision)	Gets the timestamp of the current system time	CURRENT_TIMESTAMP (4) → 2019-08-23 16: 10:45.5461
CURRENT_DATE()	Gets the current date	CURRENT_DATE() → 2019-08-23
CURRENT_TIME()	Gets the current time	CURRENT_TIME() → 16: 10:45
FROM_UNIXTIME (unix_timestamp)	Converts the UNIX timestamp to a date	FROM_UNIXTIME (1111885200) → 2005-03-27 09:00:00
NOW (fractional_second_precision)	Gets the current system time	NOW() → 2019-08-23 16: 15:22
SLEEP(n_second)	Sets the hibernation time in seconds	
UNIX_TIMESTAMP() UNIX_TIMESTAMP (datetime)	Gets the UNIX timestamp function, that is, the number of seconds elapsed from the current time to 1970-01-01 00: 00:00 UTC	UNIX_TIMESTAMP() → 1566548122
DATE_ADD(date2,INTERVAL d_value d_type)	Adds the date and time in date2; the d_type values contain second, minute, hour, day, week, month, and year	DATE_ADD(sysdate(),interval 3 h); that is, the current time plus 3 h → 2020-01-20 00:05:48
DATE_SUB(date2,INTERVAL d_value d_type)	Subtracts the date and time from date2; the d_type values contain second, minute, hour, day, week, month, and year	DATE_SUB(sysdate(),interval 3 h); that is, the current time minus 3 h → 2020-01-19 18:07:16
ADD_TIME(date2, time_interval)	Adds the time interval to date2	ADDTIME('1997-12-31 23: 59:59.999999','1 1: 1:1.000002'); → 1998-01-02 01:01:01.000001
SUB_TIME(date2, time_interval)	Subtracts the time interval from date2	SUBTIME('1997-12-31 23: 59:59.999999','1 1: 1:1.000002'); → 1997-12-30 22:58:58.999997
DATEDIFF(date1,date2)	Gets the date difference between date1 and date2	DATEDIFF(sysdate(),'2017-08-04'),DATEDIFF('2017-08-04',sysdate()) → 1019ǀ-1019
TIMEDIFF(time1,time2)	Gets the time difference between date1 and date2	TIMEDIFF(sysdate(),'2020-01-01 20:20:20'),TIMEDIFF ('2020-01-01 20:20:20', sysdate()); → 500:01:59 ǀ -500:01:59

Table 3.6 Type conversion functions

Syntax	Function	Example
ASCII(str)	Returns the ASCII value corresponding to the first character of string str	ASCII('hello') → 104
CHAR(n)	Returns the character whose ASCII value is n. The value of n is in the range [0,127]. The input parameter is an expression that can be converted to a numeric value	CHAR(67) → C
CAST (value as type)	Converts a column name or value to the specified data type. Expressions can be converted to the same type as themselves	CAST('10' as int) → 10
CONVERT (value, type)	Converts value type to type type. The range of values is all data types except LONGBLOB, BLOB, and IMAGE	CONVERT('2018-06-28 13: 14:15', timestamp) → 2018-06-28 13:14:15.000000

When using CAST () function for data type conversion, the following conditions can be met, otherwise an error will be reported.

(1) The two expressions can be converted implicitly.
(2) The data types must be explicitly converted.

The code is shown below.

```
mysql> SELECT CAST('125e342.83' AS signed);
+-----------------------------+
| CAST('125e342.83' AS signed) |
+-----------------------------+
|                         125 |
+-----------------------------+
1 row in set,1 warning (0.00 sec)
```

The function CONVERT(value,type) converts value type into type type, and the value range is all data types except LONGBLOB, BLOB, and IMAGE.
The code is shown below.

```
mysql> SELECT CONVERT((1/3)*100, UNSIGNED) AS percent FROM dual;
+---------+
| percent |
+---------+
|      33 |
+---------+
1 row in set (0.00 sec)
```

3.3.5   System Information Functions

System information functions are used to query the system information of GaussDB (for MySQL). The VERSION() function is used to return the database version number; the CONNECTION_ID() function returns the server connection ID number; the DATABASE() function returns the name of the current database; the SCHEMA() function returns the name of the current Schema; the USER(), SYSTEM_USER(), SESSION _USER(), and CURRENT_USER() functions return the name of the current user; the LAST_INSERT_ID() function returns the value of auto_increment; the CHARSET(str) function returns the character set of the string str; and the COLLATION(str) function returns the character alignment of the string str.

3.4   Operators

An operator can process one or more operands, which may be before, after, or between two operands. It is an important element that makes up an expression, specifying the operation to be performed on the operands. Operators are classified into unary and binary operators depending on the number of operands required. The priority of operators determines the order in which different operators are computed in an expression. Operators of the same priority are computed in left-to-right order.

Common operators can be divided into logical operators, comparison operators, arithmetic operators, test operators, wildcards and other operators according to usage scenarios.

3.4.1   Logical Operators

The logical operators are shown in Table 3.7.

The operand must be a Boolean value, which can be expressed as three types of value - TRUE, FALSE and NULL, where NULL means unknown.

Logical AND (AND) is used to achieve the logical AND operation between conditions. When all operands are TRUE and not NULL, T is returned; when at least

Table 3.7 Logical operators

Operator	Function
Logical AND (AND)	Used to realize the logical AND operation between conditions in the query condition WHERE/ON/HAVING statements
Logical OR (OR)	Used to realize the logical OR operation between conditions in the query condition WHERE/ON/HAVING statements
Logical NOT (NOT)	The NOT keyword is added before the conditional expression after the WHERE/HAVING clause to take the inverse of the conditional result, often used together with relational operators, such as NOT IN and NOT EXISTS

one operand is FALSE, F is returned, otherwise NULL is returned. Logical AND is generally used in query conditions WHERE/ON/HAVING statements.

For Logical OR (OR), when both operands are not NULL, and at least one is TRUE, T is returned, otherwise F is returned; when one operand is NULL, if the other operand is TRUE, then T is returned, otherwise NULL is returned; if both operands are NULL, then NULL is returned. Logical OR is generally used in the query condition WHERE/ON/ HAVING statements.

For logical NOT (NOT), if the operand is TRUE, T is returned, F is returned; if the operand is FALSE, T is returned; if the operand is NULL, NULL is returned. It supports to add the NOT keyword before the conditional expression after the WHERE/HAVING clause to take the inverse of the conditional result, often used together with relational operators, such as NOT IN and NOT EXISTS.

There is a staffs table, which contains information such as employee name, job number, hiredate, salary, etc. To query the information of employees who joined after the year of 2000 and enjoy salary > 5000 from the staffs table, the following statement can be used. Since both conditions need to be satisfied, the two conditions after WHERE should be joined by AND.

```
SELECT * FROM staffs WHERE hire_date>'2000-01-01 00:00:00' AND
salary>5000
```

If you want to query employees who joined after 2000 or whose salary is >5000 from the staffs table, i.e., if one of the two conditions is required to satisfy, the two conditions after WHERE should be joined by OR.

```
SELECT * FROM staffs WHERE hire_date>'2000-01-01 00:00:00' OR
salary>5000
```

If you want to query from staffs table for employees who did not join after 2000 and whose salary is >5000, you can add NOT in front of the condition of joining after 2000; at this time, the relationship between hiredate and salary is AND, so the two conditions after WHERE are joined by AND.

```
SELECT * FROM staffs NOT WHERE hire_date>'2000-01-01 00:00:00' AND
salary>5000
```

3.4.2 Comparison Operators

The comparison operators are shown in Table 3.8.

Table 3.8 Comparison operators

Operator	Description
<	Less than
>	Greater than
<=	Less than or equal to
>=	Greater than or equal to
=	Equal to
<> or !=	Not equal to

All data types can be compared using the comparison operator and return a value of Boolean type. The comparison operators are all binary operators, and the two piece of data being compared must be of the same data type or of a type that can be implicitly converted. GaussDB database provides six comparison operators, including <, >, <=, >=, =, <> or != (not equal to), which should be selected according to the service scenario.

The comparison operator > is used to query the employees whose salary is greater than 5000 from staffs table.

```
SELECT *FROM staffs WHERE salary>5000
```

The comparison operator <> is used to query the employees whose salary is not equal to 5000 from staffs table.

```
SELECT *FROM staffs WHERE salary<>5000
```

3.4.3 Arithmetic Operators

The arithmetic operators are shown in Table 3.9.

The arithmetic operators shown in Table 3.9 are used to perform calculations on numeric operands. GaussDB database provides the following 11 types of arithmetic operators: +, -, *, /, % (modulo operation), ‖ (string concatenation), | (bitwise inclusive OR), & (bitwise AND), ^ (bitwise exclusive OR), << (left shift), and >> (right shift).

Example of arithmetic operator syntax:

```
SELECT operation AS result FROM sys_dummy;SELECT 2+3 FROM dual。
```

Table 3.9 Arithmetic operators

Operator	Description	Operator	Description
+	Add	|	Bitwise inclusive OR
-	Minus	&	Bitwise AND
*	Multiply	^	Bitwise exclusive OR
/	Divide (the division operator does not round up)	<<	Left shift
%	Modulo operation	>>	Right shift
||	String concatenation		

The operations are in the form of +, −, *, /, etc., and the order of priority is four arithmetic operations > left and right shift > bitwise AND > bitwise exclusive OR > bitwise inclusive OR.

When one of the above bitwise operations is executed, if the input parameter has decimal places, the input parameter will be rounded before the bitwise operation is done. A code example is as follows.

```
mysql> SELECT 2+3, 2*3,3<<1 FROM dual;
+----+----+------+
| 2+3| 2*3| 3<<1 |
+----+----+------+
|  5 |  6 |   6  |
+----+----+------+
1 row in set (0.00 sec)
```

3.4.4   Test Operators

The test operators are shown in Table 3.10.

GaussDB database provides 13 test operators, as shown in Table 3.10. IN and NOT IN operators are used to specify the judgment range of a subquery, where IN means that the element is in the specified set, and NOT IN means that the element is not in the specified set.

The sample code is as follows.

```
SELECT * FROM T_TEST_OPERATOR WHERE ID IN(1, 2);
```

EXISTS means that an eligible element exists, and NOT EXISTS means that no eligible element exists. The sample code is as follows.

Table 3.10 Test operators

Operator	Description
IN	The element is in the specified set
NOT IN	The element is not in the specified set
EXISTS	There is an eligible element
NOT EXISTS	No eligible element exists
BETWEEN ...AND ...	Between the two, for example, a BETWEEN x AND y is equivalent to $a >= x$ AND $a <= y$
NOT BETWEEN ... AND ...	Not between the two, for example, a NOT BETWEEN x AND y is equivalent to $a < x$ OR $a > y$
IS NULL	Equal to NULL
IS NOT NULL	Not equal to NULL
LIKE ... [escape CHAR]	Matches ..., only the character type is supported
NOT LIKE ... [escape CHAR]	Does not match ...
REGEXP	String matches a regular expression; only the string type is supported
REGEXP_LIKE	String matches a regular expression; the string type and NUMBER type are supported; the return value of the expression is of the Boolean type
ANY	Any element of the set

```
SELECT   COUNT(1)   FROM   dual   WHERE   EXISTS(SELECT   ID   FROM
T_TEST_OPERATOR WHERE NAME='zhangsan');
SELECT COUNT(1) FROM dual WHERE NOT EXISTS(SELECT ID FROM
T_TEST_OPERATOR WHERE NAME='zhangsan');
```

BETWEEN...AND... means between the two, i.e. a closed interval, e.g. a BETWEEN x AND y is equivalent to $y>=a$ and $a>=x$; while NOT BETWEEN...and... means not between the two, i.e. an open interval, e.g. a NOT BETWEEN x AND y is equivalent to. The sample code is as follows.

```
SELECT * FROM T_TEST_OPERATOR WHERE ID BETWEEN 1 AND 2;
```

IS NULL means the field is equal to NULL; while IS NOT NULL means the field is not equal to NULL. The sample code is as follows.

```
SELECT * FROM T_TEST_OPERATOR WHERE NAME IS NULL;
```

ANY means it is enough that one of the values in the subquery satisfies the condition, which matches with each content in one of the following three forms.

(1) =ANY: The function is exactly the same as that of the IN operator.

```
SELECT * FROM emp WHERE sal IN ( SELECT sal FROM emp WHERE job =
'MANAGER') ;
```

(2) >ANY: Larger than the largest data in the record returned by the subquery.

```
SELECT *FROM emp WHERE sal>ANY(SELECT sal FROM emp WHERE
job='MANAGER')
```

(3) <ANY: Small than the smallest data in the record returned by the subquery.

```
SELECT * FROM emp WHERE sal<ANY(SELECT sal FROM emp WHERE
job='MANAGER')
```

LIKE means matching with the expression; NOT LIKE means no match with the expression. Only character type is supported. The sample code is as follows.

```
SELECT * FROM T_TEST_OPERATOR WHERE NAME LIKE '%an%';
```

REGEXP and REFEXP_LIKE indicate that the string matches the regular expression and the expression return value is of Boolean type. The syntax of REGEXP_LIKE: REGEXP_LIKE(str,pattern[,match_param]). The input parameter "str" is the string subject to regular processing, supporting the string type and NUMBER type; the input parameter "pattern" is the regular expression to be matched; the input parameter "match_param" indicates the pattern ('i' means case-insensitive search; 'c' means case-sensitive search; 'c' is set by default). The sample code is as follows.

```
DROP TABLE IF EXISTS T_TEST_OPERATOR;
CREATE TABLE T_TEST_OPERATOR(ID INT,NAME VARCHAR(36));
SELECT * FROM T_TEST_OPERATOR WHERE NAME REGEXP'[a-z]*';
SELECT * FROM T_TEST_OPERATOR WHERE REGEXP_LIKE(NAME , '[a-z]*');
```

To find information in a table that indicates a row with an ID field of 1 or 2, you can use the ID IN (1, 2) condition after WHERE to perform a conditional query.

```
SELECT * FROM T_TEST_OPERATOR WHERE ID IN (1,2);
```

Require the system to return 1 when there is a string equal to "zhangsan" in the NAME field in the table, and the EXISTS operator can be used for conditional query.

```
SELECT COUNT(1) FROM SYS_DUMMY WHERE EXISTS (SELECT ID FROM
T_TEST_OPERATOR WHERE NAME='zhangsan');
```

To find out the information in the table with ID fields between 1 and 2, you can use BETWEEN 1 AND 2 for conditional query.

```
SELECT * FROM T_TEST_OPERATOR WHERE ID BETWEEN 1 AND 2;
```

To query the information of the rows in the table whose NAME field is NULL, you can use the IS NULL operator for conditional query.

```
SELECT * FROM T_TEST_OPERATOR WHERE NAME IS NULL;
```

To query the information of the rows in the table whose ID field is 1, 3 and 5, you can use the ANY operator for conditional query.

```
SELECT * FROM T_TEST_OPERATOR WHERE ID= ANY(1, 3, 5);
```

To find the information of rows with "an" string in the NAME field, use the LIKE operator with the wildcard %.

```
SELECT * FROM T_TEST_OPERATOR WHERE NAME LIKE '%an%';
```

3.4.5 Other Operators

Wildcard and other operators are shown in Tables 3.11 and 3.12. % indicates any number of characters, including no character. _ indicates an exact unknown character. These two characters are often used in LIKE and NOT LIKE statements to achieve string matching.

Single quotes (') are used to indicate the string type. If a single quotation mark is included in the string text, then two single quotation marks must be used The sample code is as follows.

Table 3.11 Wildcards

Wildcard	Description
%	Indicates any number of characters, including no character, used in LIKE and NOT LIKE statements
_	An underline, indicating an exact unknown character, used in LIKE and NOT LIKE statements

Table 3.12 Other operators

Operator	Description
Single quote (')	Indicates the string type. If a single quote is included in the string text, then two single quotes must be used
Double quotes (") and back quotes (`)	Indicates the name of an object such as a table, field, index, etc. or an alias

```
INSERT INTO tt1 values ('''');
```

Double quotes (") and back quotes (`) are used to indicate the name of an object such as a table, field, index, etc. or an alias. They are case-sensitive and support keywords as names or aliases. If the object name is included in double quotes or back quotes, GaussDB database takes case-insensitive treatment and treats both upper and lower cases as upper case.

3.5   Summary

This chapter is about the data types, system functions, operators and SQL statements involved in Huawei GaussDB (for MySQL) to help readers get a preliminary understanding of GaussDB (for MySQL) and lay a good foundation for the next step of learning.

3.6   Exercises

1. [True or False] The BIGINT type occupies 4 bytes. ( )

    A. True
    B. False

2. [True or False] the BLOB type is used to store the binary data for large objects with variable length. ( )

A. True

B. False

3. [Single Choice] Run

```
CREATE TABLE aaa (name CHAR (5)) ;
INSERT INTO aaa values ('TEST') ;
SELECT name='test' FROM aaa;
```

and you will get the result ( ).

A. 1

B. 0

4. [Multiple Choice] Which of the following are numeric calculation functions? ( )

A. LENGTH(str)

B. SIN(D)

C. TRUNC(X,D)

D. HEX(p1)

5. [Multiple Choice] GaussDB (for MySQL) takes the UNIX timestamp by the function ( ).

A. UNIX_TIMESTAMP()

B. UNIX_TIMESTAMP(datetime)

C. UNIX_TIMESTAMP(datetime_string)

D. FROM_UNIXTIME(unix_timestamp)

6. [Single Choice] When the function if(cond,exp1,exp2) is false in the cond condition, ( ) is returned.

A. exp1

B. exp2

7. [Multiple Choice] Which of the following are logical operators? ( )

A. AND

B. OR

C. NOT

D. NOT OR

8. [True or False] Wildcards are used in LIKE and NOT LIKE statements. ( )

A. True

B. False

9. [True or False] The arithmetic operator with the lowest priority is ^. ( )

A. True

B. False

Chapter 4
SQL Syntax Categories

GaussDB (for MySQL) is a high-performance and highly reliable relational database provided by Huawei Cloud, which provides users with a multi-node cluster architecture with one write node (master node) and multiple read nodes (read-only nodes) in the cluster. All the node shares the underlying storage software architecture—data function virtualization (DFV). This chapter explains SQL statements according to syntax categories, covering database query language, data manipulation language, data definition language and data control language.

4.1 Data Query

Data query is used to query the data within a database, specifically the operation of retrieving data from one or more tables and views. Data query is one of the basic applications of database. GaussDB (for MySQL) database provides rich query methods, including simple query, conditional query, join query, subquery, set operation, data grouping, sorting and restriction, etc. It is necessary to describe the type of data query language and its usage based on the actual usage scenario.

4.1.1 Simple Query

The most common query in daily use is that implemented by the FROM clause, whose syntax format is as follows.

```
SELECT{ , ... } FROM table_reference{ , ... }
```

© The Author(s) 2023
Huawei Technologies Co., Ltd., *Database Principles and Technologies – Based on Huawei GaussDB*, https://doi.org/10.1007/978-981-19-3032-4_4

The expressions that appear after the SELECT keyword and before the FROM clause are called SELECT item, and the SELECT item is used to specify the columns to be queried. If you want to query all columns, you can use the * sign after the SELECT keyword, while if you only query specific columns, you can directly specify the column name after the SELECT keyword, and note that the column names should be separated by commas. The part after the keyword FROM specifies which table(s) to query from, either a table or multiple tables, or a clause. Simple query belongs to the case of FORM keyword specifying a table.

Example: Create a training table "training", insert three rows of data into the table and then view all the columns in the training table.

Create the training table.

```
CREATE TABLE training(staff_id INT NOT NULL,course_name CHAR(50),
exam_date DATETIME,score INT);
```

Insert three rows of data into the table.

```
INSERT    INTO    training(staff_id,course_name,exam_date,score)
VALUES(10,'SQL majorization', '2017-06-2512:00:00',90);
INSERT INTO training(staff_id,course_name,exam_date,score)
VALUES(10,'information safety','2017-06-2612:00:00',95);
INSERT INTO training(staff_id,course_name,exam_date,score)
VALUES(10,'master all kinds of thinking methons','2017-07-25 12:
00:00',97);
```

The above code first creates a table by CREATE TABLE statement, and then inserts data into the table by INSERT statement, where the table name "training" is followed by the field information to be inserted; VALUES is followed by the information of the specific inserted data, which item-by-item corresponds to the field information behind the table name "training". The staff_id field is defined as NOT NULL, which means that the field data cannot be empty, and the field must have data when inserting. If the value in VALUES contains all the columns in the training table, the specific field specified after the training table can be omitted. After that, you can insert three rows of data into the table by the same INSERT statement, and then query the table by SELECT statement after the insertion is completed.

If you want to query all columns in the table, just add the * sign behind the SELECT keyword. The sample code is as follows.

```
SELECT * FROM training;
STAFF_ID   COURSE_NAME                                EXAM_DATE          SCORE

----------------------------------------------------------------------------
--------------
10   SQL majorization                          2017-06-25 12:00:00    90
10   information safety                        2017-06-26 12:00:00    95
10   master all kinds of thinking methods 2017-07-25 12:00:00   97
```

The keyword FROM is followed by the table name "training", so all the data information in the table training can be queried.

4.1.2   Removing Duplicate Values

Sometimes there may be duplicate records in the table, and when retrieving these records, it is necessary to do so by retrieving only unique records, not duplicate ones, which can be achieved by the keyword DISTINCT. The DISTINCT keyword means to remove all duplicate rows from the result set of SELECT, so that each row in the result set is unique, and the range of values is the names of the fields that already exist or the expressions of the fields. The syntax format is as follows.

```
SELECT DISTINCT { , ... } FROM table_reference { , ... }
```

The keyword DISTINCT is added before the SELECT item, and if there is only one column after the DISTINCT keyword, that column will be used to calculate the duplicate value; if there are two or more columns, the combined result of those columns will be used for duplicate checking.

Table 4.1 shows the employee information table of a department. Now let's query the employees' job and bonus information and remove the records with duplicate jobs and bonuses. According to the contents of the query, we can see that the SELECT item includes job and bonus; to remove the records with the same jobs and bonuses, we need to use the keyword DISTINCT. Add the DISTINCT keyword

Table 4.1 Employee information table of a department

Staff_id	Job	Job	Bonus
30	Wangxin	Wangxin	9000
31	Xufeng	Tester	7000
34	Denggui	Tester	7000
35	Caoming	Developer	10,000
37	Lixue	Lixue	9000

in front of job and bond in the SELECT item to achieve de-duplication and get the corresponding results without duplicate values, with the specific code as follows.

```
SELECT DISTINCT job, bonus FROM sections;
JOB                    BONUS
```

```
---
developer            9000
tester               7000
developer           10000
3 rows fetched.
```

4.1.3   Query Column Selection

When selecting query columns, the column names can be represented in the following forms.

(1) Manually enter the column names, separated by English commas (,). For example, to query both the a and b columns of table t1 and the f1 and f2 columns of table t2, use the SELECT a, b, f1, f2 FROM t1, t2 statement, where columns a and b are the columns of table t1, while f1 and f2 are the columns of table t2, and the results are displayed in the form of Cartesian product.

(2) Calculate the fields. For example, to query the sum of the two fields a and b in table t1, perform numerical calculation on the columns a and b, with the statement SELECT a + b FROM t1.

(3) Use table names to qualify the column names. If two or more tables happen to have some common column names, it is recommended to use the table name to qualify the column names. You can also get query results without qualifying the column names, but the use of fully qualified table and column names not only makes the SQL statement clearer and easier to understand, but also reduces the processing workload inside the database, thus improving the return performance of the query. For example, querying column a of table t1 and column f1 of table t2 can be achieved by the SELECT t1.a,t2.f1 FROM t1,t2 statement.

Again, take the training table as an example. To view the number of the staff taking the course and the training course name in the training table, you can specify to query staff_id column and course_name column in the SELECT item, with the SELECT staff_id, course_name FROM training statement. This allows you to query the staff number and course name information directly from the training table. The sample code is as follows.

Table 4.2 Math score table "math"

Sid	Score
10	95
11	87
12	99

Table 4.3 English score table "English"

Sid	Score
10	82
11	87
12	93

```
SELECT staff_id, course_name FROM training;
STAFF_ID   COURSE_NAME

------------------------------------------------------------------
10         SQL majorization
10         information safety
10         master all kinds of thinking methods
```

Another example is about student scores. There are two score tables, Math and English, both of which contain student numbers and corresponding scores, as shown in Tables 4.2 and 4.3.

Now let's find the math and English scores of the student with the student number 10. To make it easier to describe and use, alias the math score table to "a" and the English score table to "b". The score column in the math score table is aliased to "MATH", and that in the English score table is aliased to "ENGLISH". The WHILE conditional statement can be used to query the scores of student 10. The specific approach is to restrict the student number sid in the math score table to be equal to 10, and restrict the student number sid in the English score table to be equal to 10 also, and the relationship between the two conditions is "AND", connected by the logical operator AND. In this way, we can find out the math score and English score of the student whose student number is 10 at one time, with the specific code as follows.

```
SELECT a.sid,a.score AS math, b.score AS english FROM MATH a,
ENGLISH b WHERE a.sid = 10 AND b.sid = 10;
  SID    MATH    ENGLISH
---------------------------------------
  10      95      82
1 rows fetched.
```

The above aliases are set using the clause AS some_name, which allows you to assign another name to a table name or column name for display. Generally aliases are created to make the column names more readable.

The SQL aliases for columns and tables follow the corresponding column or table names, respectively, and can be interspersed with the keyword AS. To replace the staff_id field in the training table with "empno" to display the results, you can do so by using the SELECT staff_id AS empno, course_name FROM training statement. The keyword AS can be omitted. The alias can also be indicated by adding double quotes (SELECT staff_id "empno", course_name FROM training) so that the staff_id field in the table is displayed as empno. In the previous example the math table "math" uses the alias "a", and the English table "english" uses the alias "b". The same is true for aliasing the MATH and ENGLISH columns in the math and English score tables, respectively. The specific code is as follows.

```
SELECT staff_id AS empno, course_name FROM training;
EMPNO      COURSE_NAME

----------------------------------------------------------------

10         SQL majorization
10         information safety
10         master all kinds of thinking methods

SELECT a.sid, a.score math, b.score english FROM math a, english b WHERE
a.sid = 10 AND b.sid = 10;
SID     MATH     ENGLISH
-----------------------------------
10      95       82
```

4.1.4   Conditional Query

The above example uses a conditional query for querying a student's scores. A conditional query is a query that sets conditions in the SELECT statement to get more accurate results. The condition is specified by both the expression and the operator, and the value returned by the conditional query is TRUE, FALSE or UNKNOWN. The query conditions can be applied not only to the WHILE clause but also to the HAVING clause, where the HAVING clause is used for further conditional filtering of the grouped result set.

Its syntax formats include both CONDITION clause and PREDICATE clause.

The CONDITION clause is a conditional query statement, followed by the PREDICATE clause as the query expectation condition, and can be used with other conditions to perform AND, OR and other operations. The syntax format is as follows.

```
SELECT_statement { PREDICATE } [ { AND | OR } CONDITION ] [ , ... n ]
```

The PREDICATE clause expression supports numeric logic calculations such as =, <, >, >, <, etc. It supports nesting with test operators such as LIKE, BETWEEN......AND......, IS NULL, EXISTS, etc. and the SELECT clause. The syntax format is as follows.

```
{expression { = | <> | != | > | >= | < | <= } { ALL | ANY } expression | ( SELECT )
  | string_expression [ NOT ] LIKE string_expression
  | expression [ NOT ] BETWEEN expression AND expression
  | expression IS [ NOT ] NULL
  | expression [ NOT ] IN ( SELECT | expression [ , ... n ] )
  | [ NOT ] EXISTS ( SELECT )
}
```

The query condition is defined by the expression and the operator jointly. The common ways to define conditions are as follows.

(1) Use the comparison operators >, <, >=, <=, ! =, <>, =, etc. to specify the comparison query conditions. When comparing with data of numeric type, single quotes can be used or not at will; but when comparing with data of character and date type, the data must be include in single quotes.

(2) Use the test operator to specify the range query conditions. If you expect the returned results to satisfy more than one condition, you can use the AND logical operator to connect these conditions; if you expect the returned results to satisfy one of several conditions, you can use the OR logical operator to connect these conditions.

Example: To query for information about trainees taking the course SQL majorization. Here you can use the compare operator to specify the query conditions. This is done by specifying that course_name is equal to the course name string "SQL majorization" after the WHILE keyword in the conditional query, as follows.

```
SELECT * FROM training WHERE course_name = 'SQL majorization';
STAFF_ID   COURSE_NAME        XAM_DATE              SCORE
```

```
---------------------------------------------------------------
10          SQL majorization   2017-06-25 12:00:00  90
```

1 rows fetched.

The commonly used logical operators are AND, OR and NOT, which return TRUE, FALSE and NULL, respectively, where NULL stands for unknown. Their operation priority is: NOT > AND > OR.

The operation rules are shown in Table 4.4.

The test operators are also explained in the previous chapters. GaussDB (for MySQL) supports the test operators shown in Table 4.5.

Table 4.4 Operation rules table

a	b	a AND b	a OR b	NOT a
TRUE	TRUE	TRUE	TRUE	FALSE
TRUE	FALSE	FALSE	TRUE	FALSE
TRUE	NULL	NULL	TRUE	FALSE

Table 4.5 Test operators

Operator	Description
IN/NOT IN	The element is/is not in the specified set
EXISTS/NOT EXISTS	Eligible/No eligible element exists
ANY/SOME	A value that satisfies the condition exists. SOME is a synonym for ANY
ALL	All values satisfy the condition
BETWEEN... AND...	Between the two, for example, a BETWEEN x AND y is equivalent to $a >= x$ AND $a <= y$
IS NULL/IS NOT NULL	Equal to/Not equal to NULL
LIKE/NOT LIKE	String pattern matches/does not match
REGEXP	String matches the regular expression
REGEXP_LIKE	String matches the regular expression

Table 4.6 Employee bonus table

staff_id	Name	Job	Bonus
30	Wangxin	Wangxin	9000
31	Xufeng	Document developer	7000
37	Liming	Liming	8000
39	Wanghua	Tester	8000

Example: Query the information from the employee bonus table "bonuses_depa" shown in Table 4.6. Table 4.5 contains four fields: staff_id, name, job, and bonus.

If you need to query from the table the employees as a developer and with bonus greater than 8000, in view of the query information subject to conditions, you can use the conditional query, that is, specify job equal to the string developer and bonus greater than 8000, and use AND to connect the two, because they are of AND relationship. The sample code is as follows.

```
SELECT * FROM bonuses_depa WHERE job = 'developer' AND bonus > 8000;
   STAFF_ID   NAME      JOB          BONUS
   ------------------------------------------------------------------
   30         wangxin  developer   9000
```

If you need to query from the table the employees whose surname is wang and bonus between 8500 and 9500, you should also use the conditional query; since there are many employees with the surname wang, you should use the operator LIKE and the wildcard % together if you want to query all employees with the surname wang. As for the bonus value range, you can use the test operator BETWEEN... AND...; since the two conditions are of AND relationship, they should be connected with AND, with sample code as follows.

```
SELECT * FROM bonuses_depa WHERE name LIKE 'wang%' AND bonus
BETWEEN 8500 AND 9500;
  STAFF_ID   NAME      JOB          BONUS
  --------------------------------------------------------------
  30         wangxin   developer    9000
```

4.1.5   Join Query

In practical applications, when querying the required data, it is often necessary to use two or more tables or views. Such query of two or more data tables or views is called a join query, which is usually built between "parent-child" tables that are related to each other.

The syntax format is as follows.

```
SELECT [ , ... ] FROM table_reference
                [LEFT [OUTER] | RIGHT [OUTER] | FULL [OUTER] | INNER]
                JOIN table_reference
                [ON { PREDICATE } [ { AND | OR } CONDITION ] [ , ... n ]]
```

The table_reference clause can be a table name, view name, query clause, etc., and the join keyword is JOIN. The OUTER represents the outer join, and INNER represents the inner join. The outer join includes the left join, right join, and full join. ON is followed by restrictions and other information.

When more than one table appears in the FROM clause of the query, the database will perform the join operation.

(1) The SELECT column of the query can be any one column of these tables, as in the above-mentioned example of score query. Similarly, the sample code for querying a column value in Tables 1 and 2 is as follows.

```
SELECT table1.column, table2.column FROM table1, table2;
```

(2) Most join queries contain at least one join condition, which can be either in the FROM clause or in the WHERE clause. The sample code is as follows.

```
SELECT table1.column, table2.column FROM table1 JOIN table2 ON
(table1.column1 = table2.column2);
SELECT table1.column, table2.column FROM table1, table2 WHERE
table1.column1 = table2.column2;
```

(3) The WHERE clause can be used to convert the join relationship of a table to an outer join by specifying the + operator, but it is not recommended to use this method because it is not standard SQL syntax.

The keyword for inner join is INNER JOIN, where INNER can be omitted. The join execution order of an inner join necessarily follows the order of the tables written in the statement.

Example: To query employee ID, highest degree and test scores. The query operation is performed using the relevant column (staff_id) in both the training and education tables.

We know that the education table contains the employee ID and highest degree information, while the training table contains the employee ID and test score information. To query the employee ID, highest degree and test scores at one time, you need to use inner join query between the two tables, because the employee ID in the two tables are corresponding. Firstly, the staff_id column of the two tables is conditionally queried to get the corresponding information, and then the same staff_id fields is used as the query condition for the join query, so as to achieve the simultaneous query of employee ID, highest degree and test scores. The sample code is as follows.

```
SELECT * FROM training;
STAFF_ID  COURSE_NAME        EXAM_DATE            SCORE
-----------------------------------------------------------------
10     SQL majorization    2017-06-25 12:00:00   90
11     BIG DATA            2018-06-25 12:00:00   92
12     Performance Turning 2018-06-29 12:00:00   95

SELECT * FROM education;
STAFF_ID  HIGEST_DEGREE GRADUATE_SCHOOL              EDUCATION_NOTE
-----------------------------------------------------------------
-11    master   Northwestern Polytechnical University   211&985
12     doctor   Peking University                       211&985
13     scholar  Peking University                       211&985
```

```
SELECT e.staff_id, e.higest_degree, t.score FROM education e JOIN
training t ON (e.staff_id = t.staff_id);
STAFF_ID   HIGEST_DEGREE SCORE
----------------------------------------
11         master        92
12         doctor        95
```

A join query queries multiple tables for related rows. The result set returned by an inner join query contains only those rows that match the query and join conditions. However, sometimes it is necessary to include data from unrelated rows, i.e., the result set returns not only the rows that match the join condition, but also all the rows in the left table or the right table, or both tables, thus an outer join is required.

The two data sources specified by an inner join are on equal footing, unlike an outer join, which is based on one data source, and conditionally matches another data source to the base data source.

An inner join returns all the data records in both tables that satisfy the join condition. An outer join returns not only the rows that satisfy the join condition, but also the rows that do not satisfy the join condition.

Outer joins are further divided into left outer join, right outer join and full outer join.

Left outer join, also known as left join, refers to querying the left table as the base table, associating the right table according to the specified join conditions, and getting the data of the base table and the right table that matches the conditions; for the records that exist in the base table but cannot be matched in the right table, the corresponding field position of the right table is expressed as NULL, as shown in Fig. 4.1.

In the query statement, the left table is the education table and the right table is the training table, so the left join takes the education table as the base table and matches the right table training by the employee ID. The query result contains two parts. Suppose the employee IDs of the left table are 11, 12 and 13, and the right table has the same employee IDs 11 and 12, according to the specified SELECT item, the result will contain the information of the employee IDs 11 and 12 and the highest degree information in the left table, and the information of the test scores corresponding to these employee IDs in the right table. Since the employee ID 13 in the left table does not match any content in the right table, the result will contain the information of the employee ID 13 and the highest degree information in the left table, and the test scores corresponding to it in the right table is null, as shown in Table 4.7.

The specific code is as follows.

Fig. 4.1 Left outer join

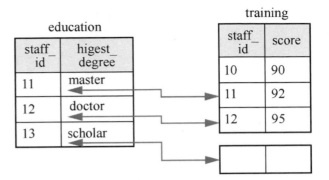

Table 4.7 Staffs table

Staff_id	Higest_degree	score
11	Master	92
12	Master	95
13	Scholar	

```
SELECT e.staff_id, e.higest_degree, t.score FROM education e LEFT
JOIN training t ON (e.staff_id = t.staff_id);
STAFF_ID   HIGEST_DEGREE SCORE
-------------------------------------
11         master        92
12         doctor        95
13         scholar
3 rows fetched.
```

The right outer join, also known as the right join, corresponds to the left join. It means that the right table is the base table and the data in the right table is queried on the basis of the inner join (data not in the left table is filled with NULL), as shown in Fig. 4.2.

The left table is the education table, and the right table is the training table. The right join takes the training table as the base table, and matches the highest degree in the left table by the employee ID. The query results will contain these two parts. If the employee IDs in the right table are 10, 11 and 12, of which the same as those in the left table are 11 and 12, the result will contain information about the employee IDs 11 and 12 in the left table and information about their highest degrees, as well as information about the test scores corresponding to these employee IDs in the right table, according to the SELECT item specified. Since the employee ID 10 in the left table does not match any content in the right table, the result will contain the information of the employee ID 10 and the highest degree information in the left table, and the test scores corresponding to it in the right table is null, as shown in Table 4.8.

The sample code is as follows.

Fig. 4.2 Right outer join

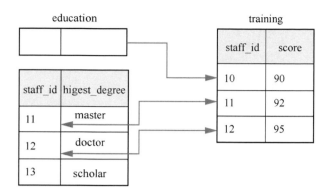

Table 4.8 Staffs table

Staff_id	Higest_degree	Score
		90
11	Master	92
12	Master	95

```
SELECT e.staff_id, e.higest_degree, t.score FROM education e
RIGHT JOIN training t ON (e.staff_id = t.staff_id);
STAFF_ID   HIGEST_DEGREE SCORE
-------------------------------------
                 90
11         master        92
12         doctor        95
```

Semi join is a special type of join that is achieved by adding an IN or EXISTS subquery after WHERE without a specified keyword in SQL. When multiple rows on the right side of IN or EXISTS satisfy the conditions of the subquery, the main query returns only one row that matches the IN or EXISTS subquery, without copying the rows on the left side. That is, after a table finds a matching row in another table, the semi join returns the row in the first table, in contrast to the conditional join. Even if multiple matching rows are found in the right table, only one row is returned from the left table, and none from the right table.

For example, when viewing the education information of employees attending training, even if there are many rows in the training table that match the subquery condition (assuming there are multiple employees under a single employee ID), only one row matching the employee ID is returned from the training table, and multiple rows are returned if multiple employee IDs match the condition. First of all, in the subquery after the keyword EXISTS, find information about the same employee ID in the education table and the training table; then according to the information of the same employee ID, find the employee ID and highest degree information in the education table, and return the query results. The specific code is as follows.

```
SELECT staff_id, higest_degree, education_note FROM education
WHERE EXISTS (SELECT * FROM training WHERE education.staff_id =
training.staff_id);


STAFF_ID   HIGEST_DEGREE EDUCATION_NOTE
---------------------------------------------------------
11             master          211&985
12             doctor          211&985
```

Anti join is a special type of join without a specified keyword in SQL. It is the opposite of a semi join and is implemented by adding a NOT IN or NOT EXISTS subquery after WHERE, returning all rows in the main query that do not satisfy the condition.

For example, if you query the highest degree information of employees who have not attended training, first find information about the same employee ID in the education table and the training table in the subquery after the keyword NOT IN; then find the information with different employee IDs in the education table according to the same employee ID information found; and finally return the employee IDs and highest degree and so on. As you can see, it is the opposite of the above-mentioned semi join. The sample code is as follows.

```
SELECT staff_id, higest_degree, education_note FROM education
WHERE staff_id NOT IN (SELECT staff_id FROM training);
STAFF_ID   HIGEST_DEGREE EDUCATION_NOTE
---------------------------------------------------------
13             scholar         211&985
```

4.1.6   Subquery

A subquery is a query that is embedded inside a query, created table or inserted statement to obtain a temporary result set. Subqueries can be divided into related and unrelated subqueries.

A correlated subquery means that when executing a query, the value of an property of the outer query is obtained first, then the subquery related to this property is executed, and after the execution is finished, the next value of the outer query is obtained, and the subquery is executed repeatedly in turn.

(1) The columns in the outer query table are referenced in the subquery.
(2) The value of the subquery depends on the value of the column in the outer query table.
(3) For each row in the outer query, the subquery is executed once.

An uncorrelated subquery means that the subquery is independent of the outer main query. The execution of the subquery does not need to obtain the value of the main query in advance, but only serves as a query condition of the main query. When the query is executed, the subquery and the main query can be divided into two independent steps, i.e., the subquery is executed first, and then the main query is executed.

The syntax format of a subquery is the same as that of a normal query, and it can appear in the FROM clause, the WHERE clause, and the WITH AS clause. A subquery in the FROM clause is called an inline view, and a subquery in the WHERE clause is called a nested subquery.

The WITH AS clause defines a SQL fragment that will be used by the entire SQL statement, making the SQL statement more readable. The table that stores the SQL fragment is different from the base table in that it is a dummy table. The database does not store the definition and data corresponding to the view, and these data are still stored in the original base table. If the data in the base table changes, the data queried from the table where the SQL fragment is stored also changes. The syntax format is as follows.

```
WITH  {  table_name  AS  select_statement1  }[  ,  ......  ]
select_statement2
```

table_name is the user-defined name of the table where the SQL fragment is stored, i.e., the dummy table's name.

select_ statement1 is the SELECT statement that queries the data from the base table, and the data found is the data information of the dummy table.

select_ statement2 is the SELECT statement to query the data from the user-defined table where the SQL fragment is stored, which is the SQL statement to find the data from the dummy table.

Example: To find the employees in each department whose salary is above the average salary of the department by a correlated subquery.

A staffs table contains information such as names, department IDs and salaries, etc. Now to query the information of employees in each department who have higher-than-average salary in the department, you can do it by subquery. For each row of the staffs table, the main query uses a correlated subquery to calculate the average salary of members of the same department, with the following code.

(continued)

```
SELECT s1.last_name, s1.section_id, s1.salary
  FROM staffs s1
  WHERE salary > (SELECT avg(salary) FROM staffs s2 WHERE s2.
section_id = s1.section_id)
  ORDER BY s1.section_id;
```

For each row of the staffs table, the main query uses a correlated subquery to calculate the average salary of members of the same department. The correlation subquery performs the following steps for each row of the staffs table.

(1) Determine the section_id of the row. The alias of the staffs table is s1 in the main query and s2 in the subquery, and the subquery condition is the section_id in the main query table has the same information as in the subquery table.
(2) Use the average calculation function AVERAGE() to calculate the department average salary and section_id to evaluate the main query.
(3) Compare the salary field with the average salary in the main query and take the results that are greater than the average salary (if the salary in this row is greater than the average salary in the department, the row is returned).

Each row in the staffs table will be calculated once by the subquery.

The following is an example of the WITH AS subquery.

Example: To query information about employees who have attended BIG DATA courses.

```
WITH bigdata_staffs AS (select staff_id, exam_date from training
where course_name = 'BIG DATA' ) SELECT * FROM bigdata_staffs;
  STAFF_ID   EXAM_DATE
--------------------------------------
  11          2018-06-25 12:00:00
```

Example: To create a table with the same structure as the training table by the subquery.

```
CREATE TABLE training_new AS SELECT * FROM training WHERE 1<>1;
```

<> means not equal, so the condition 1<>1 is not valid and the subquery will not return data.

Since the condition following WHILE is not valid, only the table structure is created and no data is inserted into it.

Insert all the data of the training table into the training_new table by subquery.

```
INSERT training_new SELECT * FROM training;
```

Find out all the data in the training table by subquery, and then insert the data into the new table training_new by INSERT statement, where the training_new table already exists, with the table structure same as the training table.

4.1.7   Merging Result Sets

In most databases only one SELECT query statement is used to return a result set. If you want to query multiple SQL statements at once and merge the results of all SELECT queries into a single result set, you need to use the merging result set operator to merge multiple SELECT statements. This type of query is called a merging or compound query, which can be implemented with the UNION operator.

The UNION operator combines the result sets of multiple query blocks into a single result and outputs it. The following should be noted when using it.

(1) Each query block must have the same number of queried columns. For example, if you query a table, the number of fields in both tables must be the same.
(2) The query columns corresponding to each query block must be of the same data type or of the same data type group. For tables, the data types of the columns queried by the two tables should be the same or of the same data type group (interconvertible).
(3) The keyword ALL means keep all duplicate data, and no ALL means delete all duplicate data.

Figure 4.3 shows the tables A and B, where table A has a column, including 1 and 2; table B is also has a column, with the same definition as table A's column field, carrying the contents of 2 and 3. If execute A UNION B, the same content "2" in A and B tables are combined and output, i.e. the result set is 1, 2,

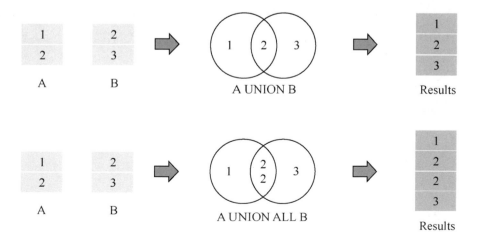

Fig. 4.3 Merging result sets

Table 4.9 Bonuses_depa1 department's staffs table

Staff_id	Name	Job	Bonus
23	Wangxia	Wangxia	5000
24	Limingying	Tester	7000
25	Liulili	Quality control	8000
29	Liuxue	Tester	9000

Table 4.10 Bonuses_depa2 department's staffs table

Staff_id	Name	Job	Bonus
30	Wangxin	Wangxin	9000
31	Xufeng	Document developer	6000
34	Denggui	Quality control	5000
35	Caoming	Tester	10,000

3; if A UNION ALL B, the returned result set outputs both "2" in A and B, i.e. the result set will be 1, 2, 2, 3.

There are employee information of two departments, as shown in Tables 4.9 and 4.10, let's query the information of employees who have received bonuses over 7000. We know the employee information tables of department 1 and department 2, who carry the same number of columns and definitions, so we can merge the result sets to get the information of employees with bonuses over 7000 in the two departments. First, use the SELECT condition to query the IDs, names and bonuses of employees with bonuses over 7000 in department 1; after that, use the same SELECT condition to query such information in department 2; then use UNION ALL to combine the results of the two queries into a result set. This way you can query information from two departments at once. The code is shown below.

```
SELECT staff_id, name, bonus FROM bonuses_depa1 WHERE bonus > 7000
UNION ALL SELECT
staff_id, name, bonus FROM bonuses_depa2 WHERE bonus > 7000 ;
STAFF_ID   STAFF_NAME    BONUS
----------------------------------------------------------------
30         wangxin       9000
35         caoming       10000
25         liulili       8000
29         liuxue        9000
```

4.1.8   Difference Result Sets

What corresponds to the merging result set is difference result set, which can perform subtraction on the query result set to calculate the result that exists in the output of the left query statement but not in the output of the right query statement.

Getting different results in the result sets can be realized by the MINUS and EXCEPT operators. Use A MINUS B C to get the results after removing all records contained in result set A from result set B and result set C, i.e., records that exist in A but not in B and C, with the syntax format as follows.

```
select_statement1 MINUS/EXCEPT select_statement2 { ... }
```

select_statement1 is the SELECT statement that produces the first result set, similar to result set A.

select_statement2 is the SELECT statement that produces the second result set, similar to result set B.

The result returned is the difference result set between result set A and result set B, i.e., the data information that is in result set A but not in result set B.

The contents of result set A are 1, 2, and 3, and the contents of result set B are 2, 3, and 4. Since the column definitions of result set A and result set B are the same, conduct the difference result set calculation for A and B, i.e., A MINUS B yields a difference result of 1, as shown in Fig. 4.4.

The code for querying data using MINUS is as follows.

```
SELECT * FROM education MINUS SELECT * FROM education_disable WHERE
staff_id=13
```

4.1.9   Data Grouping

Grouping is a very important application in database query. Grouping refers to the grouping of records with equal values based on one or some columns in a table,

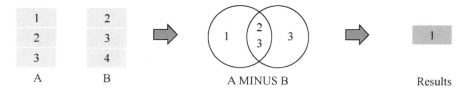

Fig. 4.4 Difference result set

which can be achieved by the keyword GROUP BY with the following syntax format.

```
GROUP BY { column_name } [ , ... ]
```

GROUP BY can be followed by column names (one or more). The specific features of its use are as follows.

(1) The expression in the GROUP BY clause can contain any column of the table or view in the FROM clause, regardless of whether these columns exist in the SELECT list.
(2) The GROUP BY clause groups rows, without guaranteeing the order of the result set. To sort the groups, use the ORDER BY clause. That is, the results returned by GROUP BY are not in order, and to have the results displayed in order, they need to be sorted by the ORDER BY clause.
(3) The expression after GROUP BY can be enclosed in parentheses. For example, two expressions can be enclosed together or separately, but it is not allowed to have one part inside the parentheses and the other part outside. For example, GROUP BY(expr1, expr2) or GROUP BY(expr1), (expr2) is correct, but GROUP BY (expr1, expr2), expr3 is not allowed.

The staffs table is shown in Table 4.11.

Let's group the departments by position and bonus, query the number of employees in each group, and sort the results in ascending order by number. In this regard, first, group by job and bonus, which can be achieved by GROUP BY clause, where GROUP BY followed by the job and bonus column names, respectively job and bonus. Then sort the results in ascending order by number, for which you need to calculate the number of employees in each group. As the employee number field in the table is unique, so you can take the sum of the field by COUNT () function, and then use the ORDER BY clause to sort the sum of the field in ascending order. In this way, you can query the corresponding result information. The specific code is as follows.

Table 4.11 Staffs table

Staff_id	Job	Job	Bonus
30	Wangxin	Wangxin	9000
31	Xufeng	Tester	7000
34	Denggui	Tester	7000
35	Caoming	Developer	10,000
37	Lixue	Lixue	9000
39	Chenjing	Chenjing	9000

```
SELECT job, bonus, COUNT(staff_id) sum FROM bonuses_depa GROUP BY
(job,bonus) ORDER BY sum;
JOB              BONUS  SUM
----------------------------------------------------------
developer        10000  1
tester           7000   2
developer        9000   3
3 rows fetched.
```

The HAVING clause can further filter the data in the result set of the grouping by comparing some properties of the groups with a constant value, where only the groups that meet the conditions of the HAVING clause are extracted. It is often used in conjunction with the GROUP BY clause to select special groups, and the syntax format is as follows.

```
HAVING CONDITION { , ... }
```

HAVING is followed by a restriction, which may not be followed by an alias.

Example: To query the total number of employees for each position with employee number greater than 3 in the sections table.

First, query the number of employees in each position in the table. As the employee number field in the table is unique, so you can group the data by job, and conduct summation on the employee number field by the COUNT() function, so that you can query the employee numbers of jobs in the table. Finally, query the total number of employees for each position with employee number greater than 3. The HAVING clause is used to filter the condition of the sum field of employee number, so that the corresponding information can be queried. The specific code is as follows.

```
SELECT job, COUNT(staff_id) FROM bonuses_depa GROUP BY job HAVING
COUNT(staff_id)>3;
JOB              COUNT(STAFF_ID)
------------------------------------------
developer        4
```

4.1.10   Data Sorting

The ORDER BY clause sorts the rows returned by the query statement according to the specified columns. Without the ORDER BY clause, multiple executions of the same query will not necessarily retrieve rows in the same order. The syntax format of ORDER BY is as follows.

```
ORDER BY { column_name | number | expression} [ ASC | DESC ] [ NULLS
FIRST | NULLS LAST ] [ , ... ]
```

ORDER BY can be followed by a row name, a rank of a column or an expression. The specific usage characteristics are as follows.

(1) The ORDER BY statement sorts the records in ascending order by default. If you want to sort the rows in descending order, you need to use the DESC keyword.
(2) If there are NULL values in the sorted rows, you can specify the sorting position of NULL values in the ORDER BY column by the keyword NULLS FIRST or NULLS LAST. FIRST means that the NULL values will be ranked first, and LAST means be ranked last. If this option is not specified, ASC defaults to NULLS LAST and DESC defaults to NULLS FIRST.

Again, take Table 4.10 as an example, query the bonus information of each job in the staffs table of the department, which requires the query results to be sorted first in ascending order by bonus, and then in descending order by name. This can be achieved by the ORDER BY clause. First, sort the query results in ascending order by bonus, by following the ORDER BY with the bonus field and specifying the ascending keyword as ASC (or leaving it unspecified, because the default is ASC); then sort them in descending order by name, by following the bonus field with the name field, where you must specify the keyword as DESC, as they are sorted in descending order. This will query the corresponding results. The specific code is as follows.

```
SELECT * FROM bonuses_depa2 ORDER BY bonus,name DESC;
STAFF_ID    NAME        JOB                    BONUS

-----------------------------------------------------------------
31          xufeng      document developer  6000
30          wangxin     developer                  9000
34          denggui     quality control     5000
35          caoming     tester              10000
```

4.1.11 Data Restriction

If there are many rows of data in a table, but only a few of them need to be queried, you can use the LIMIT clause to implement the data restriction function. The data restriction consists of two separate clauses, the LIMIT clause and the OFFSET clause.

The LIMIT clause is used to limit the rows allowed to be returned by the query, which can specify the offset and the number of rows or percentage of rows to be returned. This clause can be used to implement top-N statements. To get consistent results, specify the ORDER BY clause to determine the order. The OFFSET clause is used to set the starting position of return. The syntax is shown below.

```
LIMIT [ start, ] count | LIMIT count OFFSET start |OFFSET start
[LIMIT count]
```

start indicates the number of rows to be skipped before the return line, and count is the maximum number of rows to be returned. When both start and count are specified, the start rows will be skipped before the count rows to be returned is counted. To return 20 rows of the result set and skip the first 5 rows, you can do so with the LIMIT 20 OFFSET 5 expression.

In Table 4.10, the query for employee information is limited to a total of 2 rows of data after skipping the first 1 row of the query. Since only 2 rows of data are queried, then the LIMIT clause can be used, where LIMIT 2 can be added after the query statement to limit the query to only 2 rows; to skip the first 1 row, the OFFSET clause can be used, where OFFSET 1 can be added after LIMIT, so that the corresponding data information can be queried. Similarly, the order of LIMIT and OFFSET clauses can be exchanged, or can be realized directly by the LIMIT clause, that is, adding LIMIT 1 2 directly after the query statement. The specific code is as follows.

```
SELECT name, job, bonus FROM bonuses_depa2 LIMIT 2 OFFSET 1;
NAME                    JOB                     BONUS
--------------------------------------------------------------
xufeng                  document developer      6000
denggui                 quality control         5000
```

4.2   Data Update

There are three main ways to update data (data manipulation): data insertion, data modification, and data deletion. These operations are all commonly used by database developers.

4.2.1   *Data Insertion*

At the time of data query, the table must have data, otherwise the data will not be queried. Therefore, data should be inserted into the table first.

The following items should be noted when inserting data.

(1) Only the user with INSERT permission can insert data into the table. SYS user is the system administrator super user. Ordinary users are not allowed to create SYS user objects.
(2) To use the RETURNING clause, the user must have SELECT permission for the table.
(3) If the QUERY clause is used to insert data rows from the query, the user also needs to have the permission to use the SELECT permission of the table in the query.
(4) The commit of INSERT transaction is enabled by default.

The keyword of the data insertion statement is INSERT, and the syntax format presents the following three forms.

(1) Value insertion. Construct a row and insert it into the table with the following syntax.

```
INSERT  [IGNORE]  [INTO]  tbl_name  [PARTION(partion_name[,
partion_name] ...)] [(col_name [, col_name] ...)] [VALUES|
VALUE] (expression [,...])
```

IGNORE means that the INSERT statement ignores errors that occur during execution, and does not support simultaneous use with ON DUPLICATE KEY UPDATE. tbl_name is the name of the table to be inserted; partion_name is one or more partitions or subpartitions (or both) of the table, with the list of names separated by commas; col_name is the name of the table field to be inserted, and expression is the value or expression of the inserted field. If the INSERT statement specifies a field name that contains all the fields in the table, the field name can be omitted.

(2) Query insertion. Use the result set returned by the SELECT clause to construct one or more rows and insert them into the table, with the syntax shown below.

```
INSERT [IGNORE] [INTO] tbl_name [PARTITION (partition_name [,
partition_name] ...)] [(col_name [, col_name] ...)]
[AS row_alias[(col_alias [, col_alias] ...)]] select_ clause
```

select_clause is the SELECT query result set, which will be used as the value in the newly inserted table.

(3) Insert a record, and if a primary key conflict error is reported, then perform the UPDATE operation to update the specified field value, with the syntax below.

```
INSERT [IGNORE] [INTO] tbl_name [PARTITION (partition_name [,
partition_name] ...)] [AS row_alias [(col_alias [, col_ alias]
...) alias] ...)]] [ON DUPLICATE KEY UPDATE] SET
assignment_list
```

Example: To insert data into the training1 table.
The first step is to create training1 table with the CREATE_TABLE statement. Define the column names in the table (which are the same as the fields in the training table), with the following statement.

```
CREATE TABLE training1(staff_id INT NOT NULL,course_name CHAR
(50),exam_date DATETIME,score INT);
```

The second step is to perform the value insertion. Insert a row into the training1 table with the INSERT statement as shown below.

```
INSERT INTO training(staff_id,course_name,exam_date,score)
VALUES(1,'master all kinds of thinking methons','6/26/2017
12:00:00',95);
```

In the third step, a query insertion is performed. Insert all the data of the training table into the training1 table by subquery. This can be achieved by the following statements, using INSERT and SELECT statements to query all the data in the training table and insert it into training1, with the specific statement as follows.

```
INSERT INTO training1 SELECT * FROM training;
```

Step 4, if there is a primary key conflict error, execute the UPDATE operation. First, create the primary key in the training table (achieved by the ALTER TABLE ADD PRIMARYKEY statement), then use the ON DUPLICATE KEY UPDATE statement in the INSERT statement to achieve the record insertion operation, and update the primary key name, exam date and other fields when a primary key conflict occurs. The specific code is shown below.

Create the primary key.

```
ALTER TABLE training1 ADD PRIMARY KEY (staff_id);
```

Insert the record.

```
INSERT INTO training1 VALUES (1, 'master all kinds of thinking
methonds', '2017-07-25 12:00:00',97) ON DUPLICATE KEY UPDATE
course_name = 'master all kinds of thinking methonds',
exam_date ='2017-07-25 12:00:00',score = 97;
```

A primary key is a field that uniquely identifies a row or record in a database table. The primary key cannot be a NULL value and must contain a unique value. When a primary key conflict occurs, the UPDATE operation is required. Here, the UPDATE operation is performed because the primary key staff_id in the training1 table already has the value 1.

4.2.2   Data Modification

Data modification, as the name implies, is to modify the value of the relevant data in the table, in which the following matters should be noted.

(1) The commit of the UPDATE transaction is enabled by default, not requiring the COMMIT clause.
(2) The user who performs the operation needs to have the UPDATE permission of the table.

The data modification keyword is UPDATE, and the syntax format is as follows.

```
UPDATE table_reference SET { [col_name = expression] [ , ... ] |
(col_name[, ...]) = (SELECT expression[, ...]) } [ WHERE
condition ]
```

The table_reference clause is the table or collection of tables to be updated, whose value range is the existing table or collection of tables, with the following example format.

```
{ table_name
 | join_table
 }
```

table_name is the table name to be updated, whose value range is the name of the existing table; col_name is the field name to be modified, whose value range is the name of the existing field; and expression is the value or expression assigned to the field. condition is an expression returning values of Boolean type, only rows returning TRUE under this expression will be updated.

The join_table clause is a set of tables used for linked queries, including inner join, left join, and right join.

```
table_reference [LEFT [OUTER] | RIGHT [OUTER] | INNER ] JOIN
table_reference ON conditional_expr
```

Where, (col_name[,...]) = (expression[,...]) is only supported when using the join_table clause.

Example: To update the records with the same staff_id in the training table and staff_id in the education table, and change first_name to ALAN.

First, create the two tables training and education; as these two tables may already exist, we first delete the tables training and education that may already exist by the DROP TABLE IF EXISTS statement. The code is as follows.

```
DROP TABLE IF EXISTS education;
DROP TABLE IF EXISTS training;
```

Then you can create the tables education and training by the CREATE TABLE statement, with the code as follows.

```
CREATE TABLE education(staff_id INT, first_name VARCHAR(20));
CREATE TABLE training(staff_id INT, first_name VARCHAR(20));
```

Then insert data into the two tables by the INSERT statement, inserting 2 pieces of data into the education table and 4 pieces of data into the training table with the following code.

```
INSERT INTO education VALUES(1, 'ALICE');
INSERT INTO education VALUES(2, 'BROWN');
INSERT INTO training VALUES(1, 'ALICE');
INSERT INTO training VALUES(1, 'ALICE');
INSERT INTO training VALUES(1, 'ALICE');
INSERT INTO training VALUES(3, 'BOB');
```

Now you can update the contents of the table, updating the first_name field that carries the same record on staff_id in the training table and staff_id in the education table. The table to be updated is the training table, so the keyword UPDATE is followed by the table name "training". This update involves two tables, so it can be done with the JOIN clause. The update condition is that the staff_id in the training table and the staff_id in the education table are the same, so the JOIN condition indicates that the staff_id in training table is equal to the staff_id in the education table. The specific record to be updated is the first_name in the training table. Therefore, the keyword SET is followed by the setting information of the first_name in the training table. To set the eligible first_name to ALAN, the following statement can be executed.

```
UPDATE training INNER JOIN education ON training.staff_id =
education.staff_id SET training.first_name = 'ALAN';
```

4.2.3   Data Deletion

Data deletion is to delete data rows from a table, where the following matters should be paid attention to.

(1) The user using this statement must have the DELETE permission of the table.
(2) The commit of the DELETE transaction is enabled by default.

The keyword for data deletion is DELETE, as INSERT as a transaction operation. The specific syntax format is as follows.

```
DELETE FROMtable_name
  [ WHERE condition ]
  [ ORDER BY { column_name [ ASC | DESC ] [ NULLS FIRST | NULLS LAST ] }
[ , ... ] ]
    [ LIMIT [ start, ] count
    | LIMIT count OFFSET start
    | OFFSET start [ LIMIT count ] ]
```

table_name is the name of the table to which the data to be deleted belongs. condition is the condition of the data to be deleted.

The ORDER BY clause specifies the fields of the result set to be sorted.

ASC or DESC specifies whether the ORDER BY clause is to be sorted in ascending or descending order.

NULLS FIRST specifies the sorting position of NULL values in ORDER BY, where FIRST means that rows containing NULL values will be at the top, and LAST means that rows containing NULL values will be at the bottom. If this option is not specified, ASC defaults to NULLS LAST and DESC defaults to NULLS FIRST.

count specifies the number of rows of data to be returned, and start specifies the number of rows to be skipped before the value is returned. When both are specified, it means that the start rows will be skipped before the count rows is returned.

Deleting a row in a table that matches another table can be done in two ways.

The first is achieved by the DELETE FROM statement, where table_ref_list refers to the table to which the data to be deleted belongs, and temporary tables are not supported to appear in this temporary table, join_table is a collection of tables associated with a group of tables, and is used in a similar way to how it is used in data insertion.

```
DELETE table_ref_list FROM join_table
```

The second is achieved by DELETE FROM and USING statements, with the statement contents as the first method. The both methods can achieve the deletion of data.

```
DELETE FROM table_ref_list USING join_table
```

Example: To delete the training record with staff_id of 10 and with username NFORMATION SAFETY from the training table.

First create the training table. This table may already exist, so follow the deletion method introduced in the data insertion to delete the training table that may already exist by the DROP TABLE IE EXISTS statement, with the code as follows.

```
DROP TABLE IF EXISTS training;
```

Then you can create the training table by the CREATE TABLE statement. The code is as follows.

```
CREATE TABLE training(staff_id INT NOT NULL, course_name CHAR(50),
exam_date DATETIME, score INT);
```

Then insert the data into the table by the INSERT statement.

```
INSERT    INTO    training(staff_id,course_name,exam_date,score)
VALUES(10,'SQL majorization','2017-06-25 12:00:00',90);
INSERT INTO training(staff_id,course_name,exam_date,score)
VALUES(10,'INFORMATION SAFETY','2017-06-26 12:00:00',95);
INSERT INTO training(staff_id,course_name,exam_date,score)
VALUES(10,'MASTER ALL KINDS OF THINKING METHONDS','2017-07-25 12:
00:00',97);
```

To delete record where staff_id is 10 and the user name is INFORMATION SAFETY from the training table, firstly delete the table name "training", so add training after DELETE FROM; secondly delete the record with staff_id equal to 10 and course_name of INFORMATION SAFETY, so WHERE should be followed by staff_id = 10 and course_name = 'INFORMATION SAFETY'. The two conditions are of "AND" relationship, so the two conditions are associated with AND, with the specific statement as follows, so that the specified training records are deleted.

```
DELETE FROM training WHERE course_name='INFORMATION SAFETY' AND
staff_id=10;
```

4.3   Data Definition

4.3.1   Database Objects

Data definition is to define the objects in the database. Database objects are the components of the database, mainly including tables, indexes, views, stored procedures, defaults, rules, triggers, functions, etc.

A table is a special data structure in the database for storing data objects and the relationship between objects, consisting of rows and columns.

A index is a structure for sorting the values of one or more columns in a database table, with which the quick access to specific information in a database table is workable.

A view is a dummy table derived from one or several basic tables that can be used to control user access to data.

A stored procedure is a collection of SQL statements designed to accomplish a specific function. It is generally used for report statistics, data migration, etc.

Defaults are pre-determined values assigned to columns or column data items that do not have specific values specified when creating columns or column data to a table.

A rule is a restriction on data information in a database table. It restricts the columns of the table.

Trigger is a special type of stored procedure that triggers execution by a specified event, generally used for data auditing, data backup, etc.

A function is a encapsulation for some service logic to accomplish a specific function. It will return the execution result after it is executed.

DDL is used to define or modify objects in the database, mainly divided into three types of statements—CREATE, ALTER and DROP.

(1) CREATE is used to create database objects.
(2) ALTER is used to modify the properties of the database objects.
(3) DROP is used to delete database objects.

4.3.2 Creating a Table

Database table, also known as a table, is a collection of a series of two-dimensional arrays, used to represent and store database objects and the relationship between objects. The relevant functions of the database table and the corresponding SQL statements are shown in Table 4.12.

A table is the basic structure that constitutes a tablespace, consisting of intervals, involving vertical columns and horizontal rows. For a particular database table, the number of columns is generally fixed in advance, and each column is identified by its name, while the number of rows can change dynamically at any time, and each row can usually be identified by the data in a particular column or columns, involving the SQL statements shown below.

```
CREATE [ TEMPORARY ] TABLE [ IF NOT EXISTS ] [ database_name.]
table_name
 { relational_properties
 | [ ( column_name [ DEFAULT expr [ ON UPDATE expr ] ] [
AUTO_INCREMENT ] [COMMENT 'string'] [COLLATE collation_name]
[inline_constraint] | out_of_line_constraint [ , ...] ) ] AS QUERY}
 [ physical_properties ]
 [ table_properties ]
```

TEMPORARY is to create a temporary table. IF NOT EXISTS means that if the table already exists, it will not be created and will be returned directly; if the table

Table 4.12 Related functions of database tables and corresponding SQL statements

Function	Related SQL statements
Create a table	CREATE TABLE
Modify a table property	ALTER TABLE
Delete a table	DROP TABLE
Delete all data from a table	TRUNCATE TABLE

does not exist, a new table will be created. table_name is the name of the table, which cannot be duplicated with the existing table name. relational_properties is the table properties, including column name, type, row constraint and out-of-row constraint information. DEFAULT is the default value of the column, AUTO_INCREMENT is the specified self-increment, COMENT 'string' is the comment of the specified column, inline_constraint is the column constraint, out_of_line_constraint is the table constraint, and AS QUERY is the specified subquery to insert the rows returned by the subquery into the table when creating the table.

The following items should be noted when creating a table.

(1) To create the current user's table, the user needs to be granted CREATE TABLE system permissions.
(2) The table name and column name (data type and size) must be specified when creating the table.
(3) Self-incrementing columns only support INT and BIGINT types, a table only supports one self-incrementing column, and the self-incrementing column must be a primary key or a unique index.
(4) When creating a foreign key, if no column is specified, the primary key of the parent table is taken by default. If the parent table does not have a primary key, an error is reported.
(5) The partition key must be an integer or an expression whose result is an integer. In some scenarios, you can use columns directly for partitioning.
(6) Current supported partition types: RANGE, LIST, HASH, and KEY.
(7) Up to 1024 partition intervals are supported. If the total number of partitions exceeds 1024, an error is reported.

Partitioning is to divide the data of a table into several smaller parts in some way, but logically it is still a table. Gaussian database supports partitioning by range (RANGE), by hash (HASH), by list (LIST), and by interval (KEY). Take the range partitioning as an example, the syntax format is as follows.

```
PARTITION BY RANGE ( partition_key [, ...] )
( { PARTITION partition_name VALUES LESS THAN
( { partition_value | MAXVALUE } [, ...] )
                    [ TABLESPACE tablespace_name ]
                    [physical_properties_clause]
                    } [, ...]
)
```

PARTITION BY RANGE is the keyword of the range partition table, followed by partition-key indicating the set of columns where the partition keys are located. The length of a single column where a partition key is located cannot exceed 2000. partition_name is the name of the range partition, VALUES LESS THAN is the upper boundary keyword of the range partition, followed by partition_value as the upper boundary of the range partition. Each partition needs to specify an upper boundary. MAXVALUE can be used when creating a range partition, usually for setting the upper boundary of the last partition. TABLESPACE is the tablespace keyword, followed by tablespace_name as the name of the tablespace where the partition is located, and physical_properties_clause which specifies the properties of the page break storage.

Example: To create the education table.

```
CREATE TABLE education(staff_id INT, higest_degree CHAR(8) NOT
NULL,
graduate_school VARCHAR(64), graduate_data DATETIME,
education_note VARCHAR (70)) ;
```

CREATE TABLE is followed by the table name, and the column name and column definition are specified in parentheses after the table name, with the preceding column name and the following column definition are separated by a space. The different columns are separated by commas, where the employee ID is of the integer type; the highest degree is of the fixed-length string type, with the length of 8 bytes, NOT NULL means the value of the column cannot be empty; the school is a variable-length string with the maximum length of 64 bytes; the graduation time is of the time type; and the graduation description is a variable-length string with the maximum length of 70 bytes.

Create a partition table "training".

```
CREATE TABLE training(staff_id INT NOT NULL, course_name CHAR
(20),
  course_period DATETIME,
  exam_date DATETIME, score INT)
  PARTITION BY RANGE(staff_id)
  (
  PARTITION training1 VALUES LESS THAN(100)),
  PARTITION training2 VALUES LESS THAN(200),
  PARTITION training3 VALUES LESS THAN(300),
  PARTITION training4 VALUES LESS THAN(MAXVALUE)
```

CREATE TABLE is followed by the table name, as well as the column name and column definition. The keyword PARTITION BY is followed by RANGE(staff_id) if you create a range partition table with the employee ID as the partition key. The keyword PARTITION is followed by the specific partition name in parentheses. Since it is a range partition, you need to specify the upper boundary keyword for it. The value in parentheses after VALUES LESS THAN is the upper boundary value, and the last value MAXVALUE indicates the upper boundary of the last range partition.

4.3.3   Modifying Table Properties

If, after the table is created, the table properties are found to be inappropriate and need to be modified, the table properties can be modified by the ALTER TABLE statement. The specific operations of modifying table properties include: adding, deleting, modifying and renaming columns, adding, deleting, enabling and disabling constraints, modifying the table name, and modifying the tablespace of the partition. The syntax format is as follows.

```
ALTER TABLE table_name {
| ADD [COLUMN] col_name column_definition
| ADD {INDEX | KEY} [index_name] [index_type] (key_part, ...)
[index_option] ...
| ADD {FULLTEXT | SPATIAL} [INDEX | KEY] [index_name] (key_part, ...)
[index_ option] ...
| ADD [CONSTRAINT [symbol]] PRIMARY KEY |UNIQUE [INDEX | KEY]
| DROP {CHECK | CONSTRAINT} symbol
| ALTER {CHECK | CONSTRAINT} symbol [NOT] ENFORCED
| DROP [COLUMN] col_name
| RENAME COLUMN old_col_name TO new_col_name
}
```

When modifying table properties, the following points should not be overlooked.

(1) When adding column properties to a table, you need to ensure that there are no rows in the table.
(2) When modifying the column properties of the table, make sure that the data types in the table do not conflict, and if there is a conflict, the value of the column needs to be set to NULL.

Commonly used operation examples are as follows.
   Add a column full_masks to the training table.

```
ALTER TABLE training ADD full_masks INT;
```

Delete the course_period column from the training table.

```
ALTER TABLE training DROP course_period;
```

Modify the data type of the course_name column in the training table.

```
ALTER TABLE training MODIFY course_name VARCHAR(20);
```

Add a constraint.

```
ALTER   TABLE   training   ADD   CONSTRAINT   ck_training   CHECK
(staff_id>0);
ALTER TABLE training ADD CONSTRAINT uk_training UNIQUE
(course_name);
```

4.3.4   Deleting a Table

Users can delete tables under their own name. If you need to delete a table under another user name, you need to have the DROP TABLE permission. Ordinary users cannot delete system user objects.

The syntax format of DROP is as follows.

```
DROP [TEMPORARY] TABLE [ IF EXISTS ] [ schema_name. ]table_name
[RESTRICT|CASCADE]
```

IF EXISTS is used to detect the existence of the specified table and delete it if it exists; if not, the deletion operation will not report an error.

4.3.5   Index

A index is a structure for sorting the values of one or more columns in a database table, with which the quick access to specific information in a database table is workable. Indexes can greatly improve the speed of SQL retrieval. Take the directory (index) of Chinese dictionary as an example, we can quickly find the Chinese character we need through a directory sorted by pinyin, strokes, radicals, etc.

For example, to look up the information of the employee with ID 10000 from an employee table with 200,000 pieces of data, if there is no index, you have to go through the whole table until you find the row equal to 10,000. Once an index is built on the ID, you can look it up in the index. Since the index is algorithmically optimized, the lookup is much faster. Therefore, indexes allows fast access to data.

The SQL statements involved in the index are shown in Table 4.13.

Indexes can be classified into single-column indexes and multi-column indexes by number of index columns, and into common indexes, unique indexes, functional indexes, and partitioned indexes by index usage method.

Function	Related SQL statements
Creating an index	CREATE INDEX
Modify index properties	ALTER INDEX
Delete an Index	DROP INDEX

Table 4.13 SQL statements involved in indexing

The index types are described below.

(1) Single-column index: The index is established on one column only.
(2) Multi-column index: Multi-column index is also called combined index; if an index contains more than one column, the index will be used only if the first field specified as the index was created is used in the query condition. Multi-column index of GaussDB (for MySQL) supports up to 16 fields, with a maximum cumulative length of 3900 bytes (whichever is the maximum length of the type).
(3) Common index: B+Tree index is created by default.
(4) Unique index: As the unique index of column values or combinations of column values, an unique index is automatically created on the primary key when the table is created.
(5) Function index: An index based on a function.
(6) Partitioned index: An index created independently on a partition of a table. The deletion of a partitioned index does not affect the use of other partitioned indexes on that table.

Creating an index means creating an index on a specified table. Indexes can be used to improve database query performance, but inappropriate use will lead to a decline in database performance.

(7) Full-text index: Used for word search on CHAR, VARCHAR or TEXT data columns.

The following matters need to be noted when using indexes.

(1) Indexes cannot be created on LONGBLOB and BLOB fields.
(2) The combined index fields cannot be more than 16, and the cumulative length of the fields cannot exceed 3900 bytes, whichever is the maximum length of the type.
(3) Partitioned indexes can only be created with partition tables. The number of partitioned indexes should be the same as the number of partition tables, otherwise an error will be reported.
(4) Creating UPPER() and TO_CHAR() function indexes is supported, with the constraint that the function's argument can only be in one column and that converting the function index to a constraint is not supported.

The keyword to create an index is CREATE INDEX, and the syntax format is as follows.

```
CREATE [ UNIQUE|FULLTEXT|SPATIAL ] INDEXindex_name [index_type]
ON table_name(key_part, ...) [index_option] [algorithm_option|
lock_option]
```

UNIQUE means to create a unique index, which will detect if there are duplicate values in the table each time data is added, and report an error if the inserted or updated values will result in duplicate records.

index_name is the name of the index to be created.

table_name is the name of the table where the index is to be created, which is allowed to have a user modifier.

The sample code for creating an index online on the normal table "posts" is as follows.

(1) Create the normal table "posts".

```
CREATE TABLE posts(post_id CHAR(2) NOT NULL, post_name CHAR
(6) PRIMARY KEY, basic_wage INT, basic_bonus INT);
```

(2) Create the index idx_posts.

```
CREATE INDEX idx_posts ON posts(post_id ASC, post_name);
```

Example code for creating a partitioned index on the partition table "education" is as follows.

(1) Create the partition table "education".

```
CREATE TABLE education(staff_id INT NOT NULL, highest_degree
CHAR(8), graduate_school VARCHAR(64), graduate_date
DATETIME, education_note VARCHAR(70))
 PARTITION BY LIST(highest_degree)
 (
 PARTITION doctor VALURS ('博士'),
 PARTITION master VALURS ('硕士'),
 PARTITION bachelor VALURS ('学士'),
 );
```

(2) Create a partitioned index.

```
CREATE    INDEX    idx_education    ON    education(staff_id,
highest_degree);
```

Create a list partition on the highest degree field, with the doctor partition indicating the highest degree of doctor, master partition indicating master, and bachelor partition indicating bachelor. Create indexes on the employee ID and highest degree fields of the education table, with idx_education as the index name. The indexes are built on three partitions, with the keyword PARTITION followed by the names of the three partitions - doctor, master and bachelor.

An existing index definition can be changed by modifying the index properties, with the following syntax format.

```
ALTER  TABLE  table_name  {ALTER  INDEX  index_name  {VISIBLE  |
INVISIBLE} | RENAME INDEX old_name TO new_name};
```

ALTER INDEX index_name {VISIBLE I INVISIBLE} defaults to the index being available after it is created. Use the command SHOW INDEX FROM posts to see if the index is available.

RENAME INDEX old_name TO new_name is used to rename the index.

A sample operation to modify an index is as follows.

With the following statement you can create the index idx_posts on the posts table.

```
CREATE INDEX idx_posts ON posts(post_id ASC, post_name);
```

To create an index on the posts_id and post_name columns of the posts table, the table name follows ON, the column names are in parentheses, and the default is ascending, ASC can be omitted. Add the keyword ONLINE to create indexes online.

To create an index online, you can use the ALTER INDEX statement, the online rebuild keyword is REBUILD ONLINE, and idx_posts is the index name.

```
ALTER INDEX idx_posts REBUILD;
```

Renaming an index can be done using the ALTER INDEX statement, renaming idx_posts to idx_posts_temp. The specific code is as follows.

```
ALTER INDEX idx_posts RENAME TO idx_posts_temp;
```

The syntax format for deleting an index is as follows.

```
DROP INDEX [ IF EXITSTS ] [ schema_name.]index_name [ ON [schems_
name.]table_name ]
```

The parameters are described as follows.

IF EXISTS: Returns success directly if the index does not exist.

[schema_name.]index_name is the name of the index to be deleted.

ON   [schema_name.]table_name: After   setting   the
ENABLE_IDX_CONFS_NAME_DUPL configuration item, the index names of
different tables are supported to be the same, and the table name must be specified
when deleting the index.

The sample code for deleting an index is as follows.

```
DROP INDEX idx_posts ON posts;
```

4.3.6   View

A view is a dummy table derived from one or several base tables to control user
access to data, where the SQL statements involved are shown in Table 4.14.

A view is different from a base table in that only the definition of the view is
stored in the database, not the data corresponding to the view, which is still stored in
the original base table. The data queried from the view will change as the data in the
base table changes. In this sense, a view is like a window through which you can see
the data of interest to the user in the database and its changes.

The keyword to create a view is CREATE VIEW, and the syntax format is as
follows.

```
CREATE [OR REPLACE] VIEW view_name AS SUBQUERY
```

Table 4.14 SQL statements involved in views

Function	Related SQL statements
Create a view	CREATE VIEW
Delete a view	DROP VIEW

OR REPLACE is used to create a view or update it if it already exists.

view_name is the user name and the view name, which is the current user by default.

AS SUBQUERY is a subquery that looks up the data in the table and then views the found data through the view. Note that the user executing this statement needs to have the CREATE VIEW or CREATE ANY VIEW system permissions. Normal users cannot create a system user object, so they cannot create a view of system object. Examples of view-related operations are as follows.

(1) Create the view training_view, or update the view if it exists.

```
CREATE OR REPLACE VIEW training_view AS SELECT staff_id,score
FROM training;
```

The view can be created by the CREATE VIEW statement; if it exists, you need to update it, so add the keyword OR REPLACE, followed by the view name training_view, and AS is followed by the subquery. If you need to view all the data in the staff_id and score fields of the training table, the subquery is SELECT staff_id,score FROM training.

(2) Create the view training_view and specify the view column alias. As required, the view should be updated if it exists, so the OR REPLACE keyword needs to be added. The keyword is followed by the view name training_view; to specify the view column alias, you can specify the column alias after the view name, and the alias corresponds to the results found in the subquery, with the specific statement as follows.

```
CREATE OR REPLACE VIEW training_view{id,course,date,score} AS
SELECT * FROM training;
```

(3) View the data in the view. The method is the same as querying the data in the table, replacing the table name after the query statement with the view name, with the specific statement as follows.

```
SELECT * FROM training_view;
```

(4) View the view structure. You can view the view structure by the DESCRIBE statement, with the specific syntax as follows.

```
DESCRIBE training_view;
```

The keyword to delete the view is DROP VIEW, and the syntax format is as follows.

```
DROP VIEW [IF EXISTS] view_name
```

If the view exists, IF EXISTS performs the deletion operation, and returns success if the view does not exist.

For example, DROP VIEW IF EXISTS training_view; means if the view training_view exists, then delete the view, and if it does not exist, then return success.

4.4   Data Control

4.4.1   Transaction Control

A transaction is a user-defined sequence of database operations that are either all or nothing, which is an indivisible unit of work. Transaction control provides operations such as transaction initiation, commit, two-stage commit preparation, rollback, and isolation level setting, and supports the creation of save points. The SQL statements involved are shown in Table 4.15.

GaussDB (for MySQL) does not provide a statement that explicitly defines the start of a transaction; the first executable SQL statement (other than a login statement) implicitly starts the transaction. GaussDB (DWS) supports explicit definition statements for transactions, which are started by START TRANSACTION. In the non-explicit definition case, a SQL statement is a transaction by default.

4.4.2   Committing a Transaction

The commit transaction statement "perpetuates" all operations in the current transaction unit of work and ends the transaction.

The syntax format is as follows.

```
COMMIT;
```

Table 4.15 SQL statements involved transaction control

Function	Related SQL statement
Commit a transaction	COMMIT
Roll back a transaction	ROLLBACK

The code to set the commit ban is as follows.

```
SET autocommit=0;
```

(1) Create the training table.

```
CREATE  TABLE  training(staff_id  INT  NOT  NULL,  staff_name
VARCHAR(16), course_name CHAR(20),course_start_date
DATETIME, course_end_date DATETIME, exam_date DATETIME, score
INT);
```

(2) Insert data into the training table.

```
INSERT    INTO    training(staff_id,staff_name,course_name,
course_start_date,course_ end_date,exam_date,score)
  VALUES(10,'LIPENG','JAVA','2017-06-15 12:00:00','2017-06-
20 12:00:00','2017-06- 25 12:00:00',90);
```

(3) Commit a transaction.

```
COMMIT;
```

4.4.3 Rolling Back a Transaction

A rollback transaction is a rollback that undoes all operations in the current unit and ends the transaction. The keyword to roll back a transaction is ROLLBACK, and the syntax format is as follows.

```
ROLLBACK [ TO SAVEPOINT savepoint_name ]
```

TO SAVEPOINT is the rollback to the save point.

savepoint_name is the name of the rollback point.

It is recommended to use the COMMIT or ROLLBACK command to explicitly end the application. If no transaction is committed explicitly and the application terminates abnormally, the last uncommitted unit of work will be rolled back. If implicit auto-commit is required, ROLLBACK is required to turn auto-commit off. The two DDL statements CREATE TABLESPACE and ALTER DATABASE are not rollbackable.

An example of a rollback transaction is as follows.

Create the table posts, insert data into the table and then roll back all operations and end the transaction.

(1) Create the table posts.

```
CREATE TABLE posts(post_id CHAR(2) NOT NULL, post_name CHAR
(16) NOT NULL, basic_wage INT,basic_bonus INT);
```

(2) Insert records into the table posts.

```
INSERT INTO posts(post_id,post_name,basic_wage,basic_bonus)
VALUES('A','general manager',50000,5000);
```

(3) Roll back the transaction.

```
ROLLBACK;
```

After the successful execution, the operation performed in the second step will be undone, that is, the inserted data cannot be found from the table posts. In the above example, if you do not add ROLLBACK, there will be a record in the table; after adding ROLLBACK, the data in the table is null.

4.4.4   Transaction Save Points

Transaction save point is a save point set in the transaction. Transaction save point provides a flexible rollback method, where the transaction can be rolled back to a save point during the execution, the operation before the save point is valid, and the subsequent operations are rolled back. A transaction can set multiple save points.

The syntax format for setting the transaction save point is as follows.

```
SAVEPOINT savepoint_name
```

savepoint_name is the name of the save point. After rolling back to this save point, the transaction state is the same as the transaction state at the time of setting the save point, and the transaction operations of the database after this save point will be rolled back.

An example of setting the transaction save points is as follows.

(1) Create the table bonus_2019.

```
CREATE TABLE bonus_2019(staff_id INT NOT NULL, staff_name CHAR
(50), job VARCHAR(30), bonus NUMBER);
```

(2) Insert record 1 into the bonus_2019 table.

```
INSERT INTO bonus_2019(staff_id, staff_name, job, bonus)
VALUES(23,'limingwang', 'developer',5000);
```

(3) Set the save point S1.

```
SAVEPOINT S1;
```

(4) Insert record 2 into the table bonus_2019.

```
INSERT INTO bonus_2019(staff_id, staff_name, job, bonus)
VALUES(24, 'liyuyu','tester',7000);
```

(5) Set the save point S2.

```
SAVEPOINT S2;
```

(6) Roll back to the save point S2.

```
ROLLBACK TO SAVEPOINT S2;
```

(7) Query the data in the table bonus_2019.

```
SELECT * FROM bonus_2019;
STAFF_ID    STAFF_NAME          JOB             BONUS
23          limingwang          developer       5000
24          liyuyu              tester          7000
```

(8) Roll back to save point S1.

```
ROLLBACK TO SAVEPOINT S1;
```

(9) Query the data in table bonus_2019.

```
SELECT * FROM bonus_2019;
STAFF_ID   STAFF_NAME          JOB            BONUS
23         limingwang          developer      5000
```

4.5   Others

4.5.1   SHOW Command

Function description: This statement has many forms to provide information about the database, tables, columns, and server status, etc.

The syntax format is as follows.

```
SHOW {BINARY | MASTER} LOGS
SHOW CHARACTER SET [like_or_where]
SHOW DATABASES
SHOW TABLES
SHOW CREATE DATABASE db_name
SHOW CREATE TABLE tbl_name
SHOW INDEX FROM tbl_name [FROM db_name]
SHOW WARNINGS [LIMIT [OFFSET,] row_count]
SHOW PRIVILEGES
SHOW PROCESSLIST
```

The parameters are explained below.

[like_or_where] can be followed by a LIKE or WHERE condition for searching.

[FROM db_name] specifies the specific database name.

[LIMIT [OFFSET,] row_count] limits the rows to be displayed.

The code to display the databases under the instance is as follows.

```
SHOW DATABASES;
```

Create the table bonus_ 2019.

```
 CREATE TABLE bonus_ 2019(staff id INT NOT NULL, staff name CHAR
(50), job VARCHAR(30), bonus INT);
 SHOW TABLES;
 SHOW TABLES FROM database name;
```

The result is as follows.

```
# Tables in demo
bonus_ 2019
```

Example: To view the creation statement of the table bonus_ 2019.

```
SHOW CREATE TABLE bonus 2019;
```

The result is as follows.

```
# Table, Create Table
bonus2019, 'CREATE TABLE 'bonus_ 2019 (
staff id' int NOT NULL,
staff name' CHAR(50) DEFAULT NULL,
job' VARCHAR(30) DEFAULT NULL,
bonus' INT DEFAULT NULL
) ENGINE=InnoDB DEFAULT CHARSET- =utf8
```

Example: To display the index in the table.
Create the table bonus_2020 and its index.

```
CREATE  TABLE  bonus_2020(staff_id  INT  NOT  NULL  PRIMARY  KEY
auto_increment, staff_name CHAR(50), job VARCHAR(30), bonus INT);
CREATE INDEX idx_staff ON bonus_2020(staff_name);
```

View the index of the bonus_2020 table.

```
SHOW INDEX FROM bonus_2020;
```

The result of the execution is as follows.

```
#  Table,  Non_unique,  Key_name,  Seq_in_index,  Column_name,
Collation, Cardinality, Sub_part, Packed, Null, Index_type,
Comment, Index_comment, Visible, Expression
bonus_2020, 0, PRIMARY, 1, staff_id, A, 0, , , , BTREE, , , YES,
bonus_2020, 1, idx_staff, 1, staff_name, A, 0, , , YES, BTREE, , ,
YES,
```

4.5.2   SET Command

Function description: This statement enables the user to assign values to different variables, servers or clients.

The syntax format is as follows.

```
SET variable = expr [, variable = expr] ...
variable: {
user_var_name
| param_name
| local_var_name
| {GLOBAL | @@GLOBAL.} system_var_name
| {PERSIST | @@PERSIST.} system_var_name
| {PERSIST_ONLY | @@PERSIST_ONLY.} system_var_name
| [SESSION | @@SESSION. | @@] system_var_name
}
```

The following is an example of using the SET command.
Set the value of the variable name to 43.

```
SET @name = 43;
```

Set the value of the global parameter max_connections to 1000.

```
SET GLOBAL max_connections = 1000;
SET @@GLOBA max_connections = 1000;
```

Set the value of sql_mode for the current session to TRADITIONAL.

```
TRADITIONAL (只影响当前会话)
SET SESSION sql_mode ='TRADITIONAL';
SET LOCAL sql_mode ='TRADITIONAL';
SET @@ SESSION.sql_mode ='TRADITIONAL';
SET @@ LOCAL.sql_mode ='TRADITIONAL';
SET @@ sql_mode ='TRADITIONAL';
SET sql_mode ='TRADITIONAL';
```

4.6   Summary

Upon the study this chapter, readers are expected to master the four languages of SQL statements.

(1) Data query language (DQL): including simple query, conditional query, join query, subquery, merging result set and other query methods.
(2) Data manipulation language (DML): including data insertion, data modification and data deletion, etc.
(3) Data definition language (DDL): including the creation and deletion of tables, indexes, sequences, etc.
(4) Data control language (DCL): including the commit and rollback of transactions.

This chapter introduces the syntax formats, notes, usage scenarios and typical examples of each language.

The next step is to practice and think more in order to perceive how and why and apply flexibly, thus improving the efficiency of database use and development.

4.7   Exercises

1. [Single Choice] The logical expression to find the record whose job is engineer and salary is above 6000 is ( ).

   A. position = 'engineer' or salary > 6000
   B. position = engineer and salary > 6000
   C. position = engineer or salary > 6000
   D. position = 'engineer' and salary > 6000

2. [Single Choice] The expression "age BETWEEN 20 AND 30" in the WHERE clause is equivalent to ( ).

   A. age >= 20 AND age <= 30
   B. age >= 20 OR age <=30

C. age > 20 AND age < 30

D. age > 20 OR age < 30

3. [Multiple Choice] To query students' names, ages and grades from the student table, the results are sorted in descending order of age, and those of the same age are sorted in ascending order of grades. The correct ones in the following SQL statements are ( )

A. SELECT name, age, score FROM student ORDER BY age DESC , score;

B. SELECT name, age, score FROM student ORDER BY age , score ASC;

C. SELECT name, age, score FROM student ORDER BY 2 desc , 3 ASC;

D. SELECT name, age, score FROM student ORDER BY 1 DESC , 2 ;

4. [Single Choice] To increase the value of the AGE field of an employee in the STAFFS table by 5, the SQL statement that should be used is ( ).

A. UPDATE SET AGE WITH AGE+5

B. UPDATE AGE WITH AGE+5

C. UPDATE STAFFS SET AGE = AGE+5

D. UPDATE STAFFS AGE WITH AGE+5

5. [Single Choice] Among the following four groups of SQL commands, all the commands in ( ) are data manipulation language commands.

A. CREATE, DROP, UPDATE

B. INSERT, UPDATE, DELETE

C. INSERT, DROP, ALTER

D. UPDATE, DELETE, ALTER

6. [Single Choice] To delete all the students whose class ID (cid) is 6 in the student table, ( ) among the following SQL statement is correct.

A. DELETE FROM student WHERE cid = 6;

B. DELETE * FROM student WHERE cid = 6;

C. DELETE FROM student ON cid = 6;

D. DELETE * FROM student ON cid = 6;

7. [True or False] When an index is created for a table, if the index is undone, the contents of the corresponding base table are also deleted. ( ).

A. True

B. False

8. [Single Choice] The SQL integrates data query, data manipulation, data definition and data control functions, of which CREATE, DROP and ALTER statements are used to achieve which function? ( )

A. Data query

B. Data manipulation

C. Data definition

D. Data control

9. [Multiple Choice] To create a decreasing sequence seq_1, the starting point is 400, the step length is −4, the minimum value is 100, and the sequence can be looped when it reaches the minimum value. Which of the following statement is correct? ( )

   A. CREATE SEQUENCE seq_1 START WITH 400 MAXVALUE 100 INCREMENT BY -4 CYCLE;
   B. CREATE SEQUENCE seq_1 MAXVALUE 400 MINVALUE 100 INCREMENT BY -4 CYCLE;
   C. CREATE SEQUENCE seq_1 START WITH 400 MINVALUE 100 INCREMENT BY -4 CYCLE;
   D. CREATE SEQUENCE seq_1 START WITH 400 MINVALUE 100 MAXVALUE 400 INCREMENT BY -4 CYCLE;

10. [True or False] The function of the COMMIT command in a SQL statement is to roll back a transaction. ( )

    A. True
    B. False

11. [Multiple Choice] Among the following operations, explicit COMMIT is required for ( ).

    A. INSERT
    B. DELETE
    C. UPDATE
    D. CREATE

12. [Single Choice] There is an empty table t1. Execute the following statement:

```
INSERT INTO t1 values(1,1);
CREATE TABLE t2 AS SELECt * FROM t1;
INSERT INTO t2 values(2,2);
ROLLBACK;
```

Which of the following statement is correct? ( )

    A. The t1 table has 1 piece of data, (1,1), and the t2 table is empty
    B. The t1 table and t2 table are both empty
    C. The t1 table has 1 piece of data, (1,1), and the t2 table has 1 piece of data, (1,1)
    D. The t1 table has 1 piece of data, (1,1), and the t2 table has 2 pieces of data, (1,1) and (2,2)

Chapter 5
Database Security Fundamentals

Database security management aims to protect the data in the database system to prevent data leakage, tampering, and destruction. Database system stores all kinds of important and sensitive data, and as a multi-user system, it is critical to provide appropriate permissions for different users.

This chapter introduces the basic security management techniques used in the database, including access control, user management, permission management, object permissions, and cloud audit services, which will be elaborated in detail from three aspects: basic concepts, usage methods, and application scenarios.

5.1 Overview of Database Security Features

5.1.1 What Is Database Security Management

Database security management is to protect data from unauthorized access, prevent leakage of important information, as well as to avoid the loss of data due to hardware or software errors, including but not limited to network security, system security and data security.

5.1.2 Database Security Framework

In a broad sense, the database security framework can be divided into three levels, as shown in Fig. 5.1.

See Sect. 2.1.4 of this book for a detailed description of the database security framework.

© The Author(s) 2023
Huawei Technologies Co., Ltd., *Database Principles and Technologies – Based on Huawei GaussDB*, https://doi.org/10.1007/978-981-19-3032-4_5

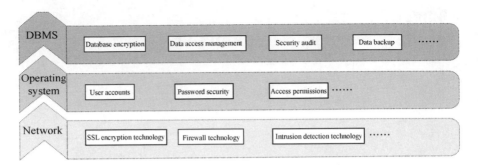

Fig. 5.1 Database security framework

5.1.3   Database Security Features

GaussDB (for MySQL) has the following main security defenses against intentional and unintentional compromises.

(1) The first line of defense is formed through access control and SSL connection to prevent client counterfeiting, information leakage and interactive message tampering.
(2) The second line of defense is formed by user rights management, which mainly reinforces the database server to prevent risks such as permission changes.
(3) The third defense is formed by security audit management, so that all operations on the database can be traced.

GaussDB (for MySQL) also supports anti-DOS attacks to prevent clients from maliciously occupying server-side session resources. If a connection is not authenticated within the set authentication time, the server will forcibly disconnect the connection and release the session resources it occupies to avoid the connection session resources exhaustion caused by malicious TCP connections. This setting can effectively prevent DOS attacks.

This chapter will introduce the main strategies of database security management from three aspects: access control, user rights management and cloud audit service.

5.2   Access Control

5.2.1   What Is IAM

Identity and Access Management (IAM) is a basic service for Huawei Cloud to provide access management, which helps users securely control access rights to Huawei Cloud services and resources.

IAM can be used without payment, and users only need to pay for the resources in the account. After registering Huawei Cloud, the system will automatically create an

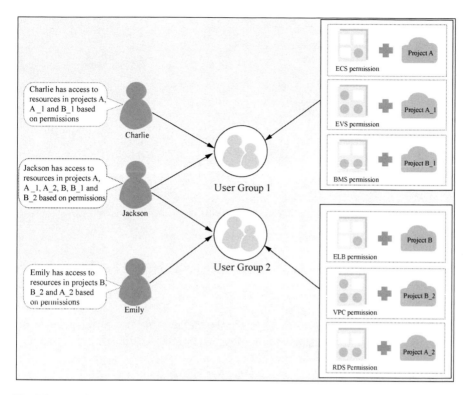

Fig. 5.2   Use of IAM

account, which is the subject of resource attribution and billing. Users have full control over the resources they own and can access all the cloud services of Huawei Cloud. If a user has purchased multiple resources in Huawei Cloud, such as Elastic Cloud Server (ECS), Cloud Hard Disk (Elastic Volume Service, EVS), Bare Metal Server (BMS), etc. for his/her team or application needs, he/she can use the user management function of IAM to create IAM users for employees or applications and grant each IAM user the appropriate permissions according to the job requirements. Newly created IAM users can log in to Huawei Cloud using their individual user names and passwords. IAM users are useful to avoid sharing passwords for accounts when multiple users collaborate to operate the same account. The use of IAM is shown in Fig. 5.2.

5.2.2   IAM Features

IAM features fine-grained permission management, secure access, sensitive operations, bulk management of user permissions through user groups, isolation of resources within a region, joint authentication, delegating resource management to

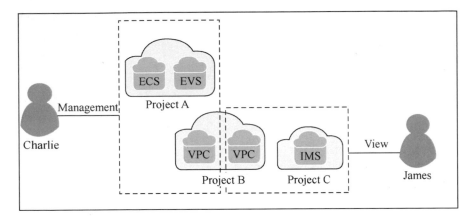

Fig. 5.3 Example of fine-grained permission management

other accounts or cloud services, setting account security policies, and ultimate consistency.

(1) Fine-grained permission management.

Using IAM, different resources within the account can be assigned to the created IAM users on demand to achieve fine-grained permission management, as shown in Fig. 5.3.

For example, control user Charlie has the right to manage the VPCs in Project B, while restricted user James only has the right to view the data of the VPCs in Project B.

(2) Secure access.

You can use IAM to generate identity credentials for users or applications without sharing the account password with other people, and the system will allow users to securely access the resources in the account through the permission information carried in the identity credentials.

(3) Sensitive operations.

IAM provides sensitive operation protections including login protection and operation protection. When logging in to the console or performing sensitive operations, the system will require a second authentication such as a verification code for email, cell phone or virtual MFA, so as to provide a higher level of security protection for the account and resources.

(4) Bulk management of user permissions through user groups.

Instead of individual authorization for each user, just plan the user group and grant the corresponding permission to the user group, then add the user to the user group, thus the user inheriting the permission of the user group. If the user permissions change, just delete the user in the user group or add the user into other user groups to achieve quick user authorization.

(5) Isolation of resources within a region.

Through creating sub-projects in the region, the resources between projects under the same region can be isolated from each other.

(6) Joint authentication.

Users who already have their own authentication system do not need to recreate users in Huawei Cloud, but can directly access Huawei Cloud through the identity provider function, thus achieving single sign-on.

(7) Delegating resource management to other accounts or cloud services.

Through the delegate trust function, users can delegate the operation authority to other Huawei Cloud accounts or cloud services that are more professional and efficient, and these accounts or cloud services will complete daily work instead of users according to the authority.

(8) Setting account security policies.

Improve the security of user information and system data by setting login authentication policies, password policies, and access control lists.

(9) Ultimate consistency.

Final consistency refers to the operations performed by users in the IAM, such as creating users and user groups, giving authorization to user groups, etc. When the IAM replicates data between servers in Huawei Cloud Data Center and realizes data synchronization in multiple regions, it may cause the submitted changes to take effect on a delayed basis. It is recommended that users confirm that the submitted policy changes have taken effect before performing the operation.

5.2.3 IAM Authorization

IAM provides authentication and authorization functions for other Huawei Cloud services. Users created in IAM can use other services in the system according to their permissions after authorization. For services that do not support the use of IAM authorization, the IAM user created in the account must log in with the account to use the cloud services. The explanation of related terms in IAM authorization is shown below.

(1) Service: Cloud services that use IAM authorization, whose service name can be clicked to display the permissions supported by the service and the difference between the different permissions.

(2) Region: The region selected for authorization by the cloud service when using IAM authorization.

(3) Global region: The service is deployed without specifying a physical region, i.e., a global-level service, where the service is authorized in a global project and can be accessed without switching regions.

(4) Other regions: The service is deployed with specifying a physical region, i.e., a project-level service, where authorization is performed in regions other than the global region and takes effect only in the authorized region, and the access to a cloud services requiring switching to the corresponding region.

(5) Console: Whether the cloud service supports permission management in the IAM console.

(6) API: Whether the cloud service supports calling API for permission management.

(7) Delegation: The user delegates operation permissions to the service, and allows the service to use other cloud services as itself, performing daily tasks on behalf of the user.

(8) Policy: Does the cloud service support permission management through policies; a policy is a language that describes a set of permission sets in JSON format, which precisely allows or denies users to perform the specified operations on the resource type of the service.

5.2.4   Relationship Between IAM and GaussDB (for MySQL) usage

If there is a need for fine-grained permission management of the user-owned cloud database GaussDB (for MySQL), IAM can be used, and the following functions can be achieved through IAM.

(1) Enterprises create IAM users in Huawei cloud accounts for employees in different functions in the enterprise according to the business organization structure, so that employees have unique security credentials and can use GaussDB (for MySQL) resources.

(2) According to the functions of enterprise users, set different access rights to achieve the isolation of rights between users.

(3) Delegate GaussDB (for MySQL) resources to other Huawei cloud accounts or cloud services that are more professional and efficient, so that they can be operated and maintained on behalf of the users according to their permissions.

5.2.5   How to Use GaussDB(for MySQL) with IAM

The flow of IAM using GaussDB (for MySQL) is shown in Fig. 5.4.

(1) Create a user group and authorize it. Create a user group in IAM console and grant GaussDB (for MySQL) read-only access "GaussDB ReadOnlyAccess".

> Before authorizing a user group, it is necessary to know the GaussDB(for MySQL) permissions that the user group can get, and select the system permissions supported by the cloud database GaussDB(for MySQL) according to the actual needs.

(2) Create users and join user groups. Create users in the IAM console and add them to the user group created in the previous step.

Fig. 5.4 Flow of IAM
using GaussDB (for
MySQL)

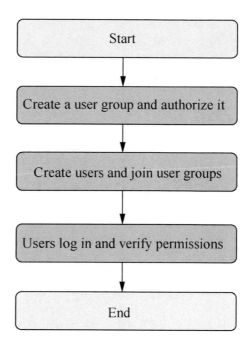

(3) Users log in and verify permissions. Switch to the authorization area in the
    newly created user login console and verify the permissions. Select GaussDB
    (for MySQL) in the "Service List" to display the main interface of GaussDB (for
    MySQL), click the "Purchase a database instance" button in the upper right
    corner, and try to buy an instance of GaussDB (for MySQL). If the purchase
    failed (assuming that the current permission only contains GaussDB
    ReadOnlyAccess), it means that "GaussDB ReadOnlyAccess" is in effect.
         Select any service other than cloud database GaussDB (for MySQL) in the
    "Service List" (assuming the current policy only contains GaussDB
    ReadOnlyAccess), and if it indicates insufficient permissions, it means
    "GaussDB ReadOnlyAccess" is in effect.

5.2.6   Detailed Explanation of SSL

The Secure Sockets Layer (SSL) protocol is a security protocol that provides security
and data integrity to network communications. It is important for the following
reasons.

(1) It is very dangerous to transmit sensitive data (bank data, transaction informa-
    tion, password information, etc.) in clear text in the network, and the purpose of
    SSL protocol is to provide communication security and data integrity guarantee.

(2) In the 7-layer Open System Interconnection (OSI), the SSL protocol is located between the transport layer and the application layer, providing support for secure communication. Many application layer protocols have derived more secure protocols by integrating SSL protocol, such as HTTPS.
(3) Google, Facebook, Taobao and other current mainstream websites and applications all support SSL communication encryption.
(4) GaussDB (for MySQL) supports SSL communication encryption between client and server to ensure the security and integrity of data transmission.

The symmetric encryption algorithm of SSL is to use the same key for encryption and decryption, which is characterized by open algorithm, fast encryption and decryption, and high efficiency. Asymmetric encryption algorithm contains a pair of keys: public key and private key. Encryption and decryption use different keys and are characterized by high algorithm complexity, high security and poor performance compared to symmetric encryption. SSL uses an asymmetric encryption algorithm to negotiate the session key during the handshake phase. After the encryption channel is established, the transmitted data is encrypted and decrypted using a symmetric encryption algorithm.

5.3   User Permission Control

5.3.1   Permission Concept

Permissions are the ability to execute certain a specific SQL statement, and the ability to access or maintain a particular object. As you can imagine, it is easy to manage a village with only a few dozen households, but it would be relatively difficult to manage a large city with several million people. Permission control on users is especially important for database resource and security management.

GaussDB (for MySQL) supports the management of user permissions, which allows you to configure the user's operational access to database objects and the use of database functions.

The permissions granted to GaussDB (for MySQL) accounts determine the operations that the accounts can perform. The different permissions of GaussDB (for MySQL) differ in the contexts and operation levels to which they apply, as shown below.

(1) Administrative permission: enables users to manage GaussDB (for MySQL) server operations; the permission is global, as it is not specific to a particular database.
(2) Database permission: applies to the database and all objects in it; the permission can be granted for a specific database or globally in order to meet different needs.
(3) Object permission: can be granted to specific objects in the database, all objects of a given type in the database (such as all tables in the database), or all objects globally (such as tables, indexes, views, and stored routines).

Table 5.1 An example of permission table

Permission table	Permission description
user	User account, static global permissions and other non-permission columns
global_grants	Dynamic global permissions
db	Database-level permissions
tables_priv	Table-level permissions
columns_priv	Column-level permissions
procs_priv	Stored procedure and function permissions
...	...

GaussDB (for MySQL) supports both static and dynamic permissions, with static permissions built into the server. They can always be granted to user accounts and cannot be unregistered. Dynamic permissions can be registered and deregistered at runtime, but this affects their availability. Dynamic permissions that have not been registered cannot be granted.

The GaussDB (for MySQL) server controls user access to the database through permission tables, which are stored in the GaussDB (for MySQL) database and initialized when the database is initialized. An example of permission table is shown in Table 5.1.

5.3.2   Users

As a database administrator, you should create a database user for each user who needs to connect to the database. The database user connects to the database by user name and password. The user here becomes a database user who can manipulate database objects and access database data after connecting to the database, such as creating tables, accessing tables, executing SQL statements, etc.

By default, users of GaussDB (for MySQL) database can be divided into 3 categories.

System administrator: has the highest permissions of the database (e.g. SYS user, SYSDBA user).

Security administrator: has the CREATE USER permission.

Ordinary user: by default, has PUBLIC object permission and only has the permission of the object they created; if you need other permissions, you need to be empowered by the system administrator through the GRANT statement.

SYSDBA is the user who can login to the database without password, with "zsql/ AS SYSDBA" to connect to the database.

Two points should to be noted here. First, when connecting to a database, the database user must use a database that already exists, and cannot connect to a database that does not exist. Second, a user can establish multiple connections to the database, that is, multiple sessions can be established for operations.

Users can be created by the CREATE USER statement. When using this statement, the following three points should be noted.

(1) The user executing this statement needs to have CREATE USER system permissions, otherwise no new user can be created.
(2) When creating a user, you need to specify the user name and password, the user name and password required when the user connects to the database is specified at this time.
(3) The root user is not allowed to be created, because it is a system-preset user.

The common syntax format for creating users is as follows.

```
CREATE USER user_name IDENTIFIED BY password;
```

user_name is the user name; password is the user password, which needs to be enclosed by single quotes. After the user is successfully created, you can connect to the database with the corresponding user name and password.

The following special characters are not allowed in the user name.

Semicolon (;), vertical line (|), backquote (`), dollar sign ($), bit operator (&), greater than sign (>), less than sign (<), double quote (""), single quote ("), exclamation mark (!) , spaces, and the copyright symbol (©). Double quotes or backquotes are also not allowed. If the user name contains any special characters other than those prohibited above, it must be enclosed in double quotation marks ("") or backquotes (").

When setting a password for a user name, the following requirements must be met.

(1) The length of the password must be greater than or equal to eight characters.
(2) When creating a password, the password must be enclosed in single quotes.

Example: To create a user with the username "smith" and the password "database_123", you can execute the following statement.

```
CREATE USER smith IDENTIFIED BY 'database_123';
```

The user name consists of letters, and the password contains letters, special symbols and numbers, which meet the requirements and can be created successfully. The password in the example satisfies the password requirements.

5.3.3 *Modifying a User*

You can modify users by ALTER USER, during which should pay attention to the following matters.

(1) The user executing this statement needs to have ALTER USER system permissions, similar to CREATE USER permissions.
(2) If the specified user does not exist, an error message will be displayed. Only the user that already exists can be modified.

User modification is mainly applied to the following scenarios.

(1) Modify the user password.
(2) Manually lock the user or unlock the user. For example, if a user has been locked out after a certain number of failed login attempts, the user needs to be unlocked.

The syntax format for changing the user password is as follows.

```
ALTER USER user_name IDENTIFIED BY new_password;
```

user_name is the user name to be changed and new_password is the new user password.

Example: To change user smith's password to "database_456". The administrator can change it directly with the following statement.

```
ALTER USER smith IDENTIFIED BY 'database_456';
```

5.3.4   Deleting a User

When a user is no longer in use, it is necessary to delete the user, and all the objects created by the user will be deleted accordingly. You can delete a user by the DROP USER statement. Note that the user executing the statement needs to have the DROP USER system permission, similar to the CREATE USER permission.

The syntax format for deleting a user is as follows.

```
DROP USER [ IF EXISTS ] user_name;
```

user_name indicates the user name to be deleted. IF EXISTS is used to detect whether the user to be deleted exists. If the IF EXISTS option is not specified, an error message will be displayed if the user to be deleted does not exist; if the IF EXISTS option is specified, when the user to be deleted does not exist, the result of successful execution will be returned directly, and the user will be deleted if the user exists.

Example: To delete user smith, you can use the following statement.

```
DROP USER IF EXISTS smith;
```

5.3.5   Roles

A role is a set of permissions, by which the database can divide permissions at the organization level. The concept of roles was not introduced until MySQL 8. A database may be accessed by multiple users, so for easy management, you can first group permissions and assign them to roles, with each set of permissions corresponding to one role. For users with different permission levels, you can grant different roles to users, equivalent to granting the permissions that users need in bulk, instead of granting them one by one.

For example, a company can have multiple financial roles with permissions such as paying wages and allocating funds. A role does not belong to any user, that is, a role is not private to a user, but can be owned by multiple users. For example, finance is a role that is not private to a single employee, but can be shared by multiple employees. Suppose the user smith creates the role staffs, then smith.staffs is private to smith. Other users can access or operate on smith.staffs if they have the appropriate permissions, but smith.staffs belongs only to the smith user.

Roles can be created through the CREATE ROLE statement. It should be noted that the user executing the statement needs to have the CREATE ROLE system permission. The role neither belongs to any user nor can log in to the database and execute SQL statement operations, and the role must be unique in the system.

GaussDB (for MySQL) contains the following four system-preconfigured roles by default.

(1) Database administrator: has all system permissions, which cannot be deleted.
(2) RESOURCE, the role to create base object: has the permission to create stored procedures, functions, triggers, table sequences.
(3) CONNECT, the role to connect: has the permission to connect to the database.
(4) STATISTICE, statistical role.

The syntax format for creating a role is as follows.

```
CREATE ROLE role_name;
```

role_name indicates the name of the created role.
Example: To create the role teacher.

```
CREATE ROLE teacher;
```

The role can be deleted with the DROP ROLE statement. When deleting a role, the user executing the statement must have the DROP ANY ROLE system permission, or be the creator of the role, or have been granted the role and have the WITH GRANT OPTION attribute. If the role to be deleted does not exist, an error message is displayed. When a role is deleted, the permissions that the role has are recovered from the user or other role to which the role was granted, and the user associated with the role or the role loses the permissions contained in the role.

The syntax format for deleting a role is as follows.

```
DROP ROLE role_name;
```

role_name represents the role name.
Example: To delete the role teacher.

```
DROP ROLE teacher;
```

The relationship between user roles and permissions is as follows.

(1) Users can define roles and grant them multiple permissions, and roles are a collection of multiple permissions.
(2) When the role is granted to a user or another role, the granted object has all the permissions of the role.
(3) The permissions of a role are inheritable.

GaussDB (for MySQL) supports role-based permission management. Users can define roles, and if a role is granted to a user, the user has all the permissions for that role. The financial role shown in Fig. 5.5 only has the rights to pay wages and allocate funds, while the director only has the rights to review the budget and view the income statements. After granting the financial role to the director, the director inherits the permissions of the financial role and gets the rights to audit the budget, view the income statements, and pay wages and allocate funds.

5.3.6   Authorization

The previous sections all mention permissions, which need to be granted. Authorization is the granting of permissions or roles to users or other roles, so that the corresponding users or roles have the appropriate permissions. For example, a newly created user has no permission and cannot perform any operations on the database or

Fig. 5.5 User, role, and
permission

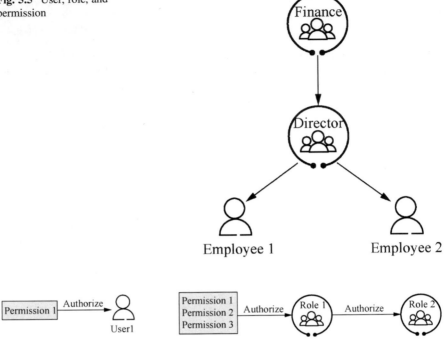

Employee 1   Employee 2

Fig. 5.6 Authorization

even connect to the database. If you grant the CREATE SESSION create connection
permission to the user, and the user has the right to connect to the database. If the
user needs to create a table, he/she needs to have the CREATE TABLE permission
to create a table. The table created by this user belongs to the object of this user, and
this user can add, delete, change, and check the data in the table. Authorization can
be achieved through the GRANT statement, which can grant one permission to a
user or role, or multiple permissions to a user or role at the same time. You can grant
Permission 1 to User 1, or grant permissions 1, 2, and 3 to Role 1, which then granted
by Role 1 to Role 2, and finally you can grant the permissions of Role 2 to the user,
as shown in Fig. 5.6.

The common syntax format for permission granting is as follows.

```
GRANT privilege_name ON db/objects TO grantee [ WITH GRANT OPTION ] ;
```

permission_name: the name of the permission.
db/objects: the database or object that is authorized to be used.
grantee: the user or role to be granted.
WITH GRANT OPTION: optional, means that the granted user or role can grant
the granted permissions to other users or roles again.

> Permissions and roles should be granted following the principle of minimization.

To grant a permission, the user executing the grant statement needs to have been granted the permission and have the WITH GRANT OPTION attribute.

Example: To grant the CREATE USER permission to the user smith, and allow smith to grant this permission to other users or roles.

```
GRANT CREATE USER ON *.* TO smith WITH GRANT OPTION;
```

The syntax format for granting roles is similar to the format for granting permissions, as follows.

```
GRANT role_name TO grantee [WITH GRANT OPTION];
```

role_name is the role name and grantee is the user or role to be granted. WITH GRANT OPTION is optional, if set, the granted user or role can re-grant the granted role to other users or roles.

To grant the role, the user executing the granting role statement needs to meet one of the following conditions.

(1) It has been granted the role and has the WITH GRANT OPTION attribute.
(2) It is the creator of the role.

Example: To grant the role of teacher to smith and allow smith to grant this role to other users or roles.

```
GRANT teacher TO smith WITH GRANT OPTION;
```

Having the WITH GRANT OPTION attribute means that the authorized user can re-grant the acquired permission or role to other users or roles.

5.3.7   Permission Recovery

Permission recovery is the recovery of a permission or role from the authorized person. Once recovered, the user or role in question will no longer have that permission. For example, if you do not want a user to create a table, you can recover the CREATE TABLE system permission from the user. If you do not want the user to access the database, you can recover the CREATE SESSION permission from the user. Permission recovery includes the recovery of system permissions, object permissions and role permissions, all of which can be achieved through the REVOKE statement.

The common syntax format for permission recovery is as follows.

```
REVOKE privilege_name ON db/objects FROM revokee;
```

Where, REVOKE is the authorizer, permission_name is the name of the permission to be recovered, and revokee is the user or role whose permissions are to be recovered. Up to 63 users or roles can be assigned at a time.

To grant a permission, the user executing the grant statement needs to have been granted the permission to be recovered and have the WITH GRANT OPTION attribute. Having the WITH GRANT OPTION attribute means that the authorized user can re-grant the acquired permission or role to other users or roles.

Example: To recover the CREATE USER permission of for the user smith.

```
REVOKE CREATE USER ON *.* FROM smith;
```

When a user who has been granted a role no longer needs to have the permissions contained in the role, the user's role permissions should be recovered. For example, if Employee A is a finance employee that has the right view the company's funds, when he/she is leaving, his/her finance role must be recovered. The system administrator (SYS user, user in the database administrator role) has all system permissions, including the GRANT ANY ROLE system permission, so the system administrator can execute the role recover statement.

If the role is to be recovered, the user who performs the REVOKE operation needs to meet one of the following conditions.

(1) It has been granted the role and has the WITH GRANT OPTION attribute.
(2) It is the creator of the role being recovered.

The common syntax format for recovering a role is as follows.

```
REVOKE role_name FROM revokee;
```

role_name is the name of the role, and revokee is the user or role whose permissions are recovered. Up to 63 users or roles can be assigned at a time. Note that you are not allowed to recover the permissions of the database administrator role. The initial permissions of the database administrator role are determined when the database is created, and you can subsequently grant permissions to the database administrator role, but are not allowed to recover its permissions.

The use of permissions should follow the principle of minimization, and in order to ensure the security of the database, permissions and roles need to be recovered in time when they are not in use.

An example of the application of users, roles and permissions is as follows.

To create the user smith, with the password database_123.

```
CREATE USER smith IDENTIFIED BY 'database_123';
```

Create the role manager, which is implemented by the CREATE ROLE statement.

```
CREATE ROLE manager;
```

Grant the CREATE USER permission to the role manager.

```
GRANT CREATE USER ON *.* TO manager;
```

Grant object query and insertion permissions to manager.

```
GRANT SELECT, INSERT ON mysql.staffs TO manager;
```

5.4   Cloud Audit Services

5.4.1   What Are Cloud Audit Services

The log audit module is the core component of information security audit function, and is an important part of enterprises' and organizations' risk control on information system security. In the context of gradual cloudization of information systems, global information and data security management organizations at all levels, including China's National Standardization Technical Committee, have issued several standards on this, such as ISO IEC27000, GB/T 20945-2013, COSO, COBIT, ITIL, NISTSP800, etc.

Cloud Trace Service (CTS) is a professional log auditing service contained in Huawei's cloud security solution, providing the collection, storage, and query functions for various cloud resource-related operation records, which can be used to support common application scenarios such as security analysis, compliance audit, resource tracking, and problem location, as shown in Fig. 5.7.

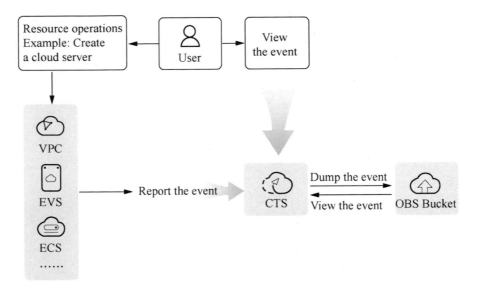

Fig. 5.7 Cloud audit service

The functions of cloud audit service mainly include the following.

Record audit logs: supports recording operations initiated by users through the management console or application programming interface (API), as well as self-triggered operations within each service.

Audit log query: supports querying the operation records within seven days in the management console from multiple dimensions such as event type, event source, resource type, filter type, operation user and event level.

Audit log dumping: supports periodically dumping audit logs to OBS buckets under the object storage service (OBS), which compresses audit logs into event files according to the service dimension.

Event file encryption: supports encrypting the event file with the key in the data encryption workshop (DEW) during the dumping process.

5.4.2   Key Operations to Support Cloud Audit Services

With the cloud audit service, operation events related to GaussDB (for MySQL) instances can be recorded for future queries, audits, and tracebacks. The key operation events supported by the cloud audit service are shown in Table 5.2.

Track event viewing is the operation that the system starts to record cloud service resources after the cloud audit service is started. The cloud audit service management console keeps a record of the last seven days of operations. Log in to the management console and select the "Manage & Deploy > Cloud Audit Service" option in the "All Services" or "Service List" to enter the information page of cloud audit

Table 5.2   Key operation events supported by the cloud audit service

Operation	Resource type	Event
Create an instance	Instance	createInstance
Adds a read-only node	Instance	addNodes
Delete a read-only node	Instance	deleteNode
Restart an instance	Instance	restartinstance
Modify an instance port	Instance	changeInstancePort
Modify an instance security group	Instance	modifySecurityGroup
Upgrade a read-only instance to a primary instance	Instance	instanceFailOver
Bind or unbind a public IP	Instance	setOrResetPublicIP
Remove an instance	Instance	deleteInstance
Rename an instance	Instance	renameInstance
Modify the node priority	Instance	modifyPriority
Modify the specification	Instance	instanceAction
Reset the password	Instance	resetPassword
Back up and restore to a new instance	Instance	restoreInstance
Create a backup	Backup	createManualSnapshot
Delete a backup	Backup	deleteManualSnapshot
Create a parameter template	parameterGroup	createParameterGroup
Modify a parameter template	parameterGroup	updateParameterGroup
Delete a parameter template	parameterGroup	deleteParameterGroup
Copy a parameter template	parameterGroup	copyParameterGroup
Reset a parameter template	parameterGroup	resetParameterGroup
Compare parameter templates	parameterGroup	compareParameterGroup
Apply a parameter template	parameterGroup	applyParameterGroup

service; select the "Event List" option in the left navigation tree to enter the event list information page. The event list supports filtering to query the corresponding operation events. The current event list supports four dimensions of the combined query, with the relevant content described below.

(1) Event source, resource type and filter type. You can select the corresponding query conditions in the drop-down box.

Generally, select "CloudTable" as the event source; select "All Resource Types" as the resource type, or specify a specific resource type; and select "All Filter Types" as the filter type, or select one of "By Event Name", "By Resource ID", "By Resource Name".

(2) Operation user. You can select a specific operation user in the drop-down box, and this operation user is at user level, not at tenant level.

(3) Event Level. The options are "All Event Levels", "Normal", "Warning", "Incident". Only one of them can be selected.

(4) Start time and end time. The operation events can be queried by selecting the time period.

5.5   Summary

This chapter firstly introduces the basic concepts, usage and application scenarios of users, roles and permissions, and the relationship between the three; then elaborates on authorization and permission recovery, including the syntaxes and the conditions that need to be satisfied by users who perform authorization or permission recovery operations.

5.6   Exercises

1. [True or False] The SSL technology can prevent man-in-the-middle from attacking and monitoring the network. ( )

   A. True
   B. False

2. [True or False] The SSL technology can be used only for databases. ( )

   A. True
   B. False

3. [Single Choice] Which of the following syntaxes is used for authorization? ( )

   A. CREATE
   B. ALTER
   C. GRANT
   D. REVOKE

4. [True or False] The names of roles and users can be duplicated. ( )

   A. True
   B. False

5. [True or False] System permissions and object permissions need to be recovered when they are not used. ( )

   A. True
   B. False

6. [Short Answer Question] Why does SSL secure connections?

Chapter 6
Database Development Environment

Huawei's GaussDB (for MySQL) supports the development of applications based on C, Java and other languages. Understanding GaussDB (for MySQL) related system structure and concepts help to develop and use GaussDB (for MySQL) database better.

This chapter explains the use of GaussDB (for MySQL) tools. Before this, readers need to have knowledge of operating systems, as well as C and Java languages, and be familiar with the IDE and SQL syntaxes of C or Java languages.

6.1 GaussDB Database Driver

6.1.1 What Is a Driver

A database driver is an interface between an application and a database store. A driver application is a translator-like program developed by the database vendor to enable a particular development language (e.g. Java and C) to implement database calls. It is able to abstract complex database operations and communications into an access interface for the current development language, as shown in Fig. 6.1.

To meet the requirements, GaussDB (for MySQL) supports database drivers such as JDBC and ODBC.

The data source contains information such as database location and database type, which is actually an abstraction of a data connection. The data source manager shown in Fig. 6.1 is used to manage data sources.

© The Author(s) 2023   189
Huawei Technologies Co., Ltd., *Database Principles and Technologies – Based on Huawei GaussDB*, https://doi.org/10.1007/978-981-19-3032-4_6

Fig. 6.1 Database driver

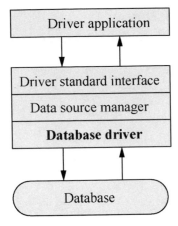

6.1.2   JDBC

Java database connectivity (JDBC) is a Java API for executing SQL statements that provides a unified access interface to a variety of relational databases. Applications manipulate data through JDBC. The flow of JDBC connection to database is shown in Fig. 6.2.

GaussDB (for MySQL) database provides support for JDBC4.0 features. To compile the program code, you need to use JDK1.8.

The installation and configuration steps of JDBC are as follows.

(1) Configure the JDBC package.

Download the driver package from the relevant website, decompress it and configure it in the project.

JDBC package name: com.huawei.gauss.jdbc.ZenithDriver.jar.

(2) Load the driver.

Before creating a database connection, you need to load the database driver class by loading Class.forName("com.huawei.gauss.jdbc.ZenithDriver") implicitly in the code.

(3) Connect to the database.

Before remotely accessing the database, you need to set the IP address and port number for LSNR_IP and LSNR_PORT monitoring in the configuration file zengine.ini.

When creating a database connection using JDBC, the following function is required.

```
DriverManager.getConnection(String url, String user, String
password);
```

Fig. 6.2 Flow of JDBC
connection to database

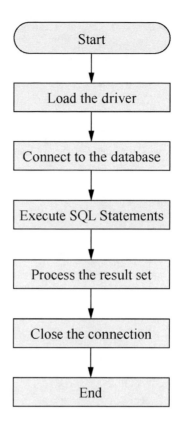

Another way to load the database driver classes is to pass the parameters at the start of the JVM (Java Virtual Machine), where jdbctes is the name of the test case program.

```
java     -Djdbc.drivers=com.huawei.gauss.jdbc.ZenithDriver
jdbctest;
```

This method is not commonly used, so you just need to know about it without going into particular detail.

| Up to 8 monitoring IP addresses can be set at a time, with the IP addresses separated by commas. |

After the database driver class is loaded, you need to connect to the database. Before remote access to the database, set the IP address and port number to be

Table 6.1 Database connection parameters

Parameter	Description
URL	Jdbc:zenith:@ip:port[?key=value[&key=value] ...]
User	Database user
Password	Password of the database user

Table 6.2 JDBC's common interfaces

Interface name	Function
Java.sql.Connection	Database connection interface
Java.sql.DatabaseMetaData	Database object definition interface
Java.sql.Driver	Database driver interface
Java.sql.PrepareStatement	Preprocessing statement interface
Java.sql.ResultSet	Execution result set interface
Java.sql.ResultSetMetaData	A specific description of the information related to the ResultSet object
Java.sql.Statement	SQL statement interface
Java.sql.CallableStatement	SQL statement interface, mainly used to execute stored procedures
Java.sql.Blob	Blob interface, mainly used to bind or get the Blob field of the database
Java.sql.Clob	Clob interface, mainly used to bind or get the Clob fields of the database

monitored by the corresponding parameters in the configuration file, and then use the JDBC to create a database connection. The database connection includes three parameters: url, user, and password, as shown in Table 6.1.

In the url parameter, ip is the database server name, port is the database server port, and the url connection attributes are split by the & symbol. Each property is a key/value pair.

Table 6.2 shows the common interfaces of the JDBC.

The following introduces the development and debugging of JDBC application with the Eclipse environment under Windows operating system as an example.

- Operating system environment: Win10-64bit.
- Compiling and debugging environment: Eclipse SDK version:3.6.1.

The steps of running JDBC application are shown below.

(1) Create a project in Eclipse.
```
New→Project→Java Project→Next→enter ProjectName (such as
test_jdbc)→Finish.
```

(2) Create a class.
```
src→New→Class→enter ClassName (jdbc_test, choose main)→Finish.
```

(3) Load the library.

    `src→build path→configure build path→libraries →add external jars→jdbcjar.`

(4) Run the JDBC application.

    `Write jdbc_test.java document, right click on jdbc_test →run as→Java Application.`

The code for compiling and running the JDBC application is as follows.

```
package com.huawei.gauss.jdbc.executeType;
import java.sql.Connection;
import java.sql.DriverManager;
import java.sql.PreparedStatement;
import com.huawei.gauss.jdbc.inner.GaussConnectionImpl;
public class jdbc_test{
public void test() {
            // 驱动类
            String driver = "com.huawei.gauss.jdbc.ZenithDriver";
            // 数据库连接描述
            String sourceURL = "jdbc:zenith:@10.255.255.1:1888";
        Connection conn = NULL;
        try {
                // 加载数据库驱动类
                Class.forName(driver).newInstance();
        } catch (Exception e) {
                // 抛出异常
                e.printStackTrace();
        }
    try {
            // 数据库连接, test_1为用户名, Gauss_234为密码
            conn = DriverManager.getConnection
                (sourceURL, "test_1", "Gauss_234");
        WHILE(TRUE) {
        // 执行SQL语句, 若在数据库中能查看到此条数据, 说明成功
        PreparedStatement ps = conn.prepareStatement
                                    ("INSERT INTO t1 values (1, 2)");
        ps.execute();
            // 若执行成功, 控制台会输出"Connection succeed!"
            System.out.println("Connection succeed!");
                }
    } catch (Exception e) {
            // 抛出异常
            e.printStackTrace();
        }
    }
}
```

6.1.3   ODBC

Open database connectivity (ODBC) was proposed by Microsoft as an application programming interface for accessing databases. The ODBC connection to database includes the flows of requesting handle resources, setting environment properties, connecting to data sources, executing SQL statements, processing result sets, disconnecting, and releasing handle resources, as shown in Fig. 6.3.

The application interacts with the database through the API provided by ODBC, which enhances the portability, scalability and maintainability of the application while avoiding the application to operate the database system directly.

The steps to install ODBC driver manager are as follows.

(1) Obtain the unixODBC source code package.

Download the file unixODBC-2.3.7.tar.gz or a higher version.
(2) Compile and install unixODBC.

In the process of compiling and installing unixODBC, unixODBC is installed to "/usr/local" directory by default, and the data source file is generated to "/usr/local/etc" directory by default, and the library file is generated in the "/usr/local/lib" directory.

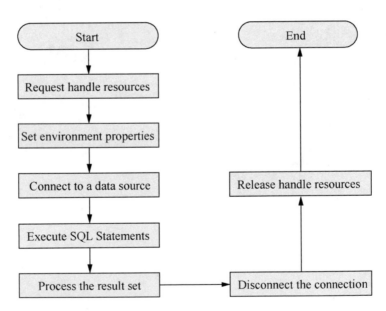

Fig. 6.3 Flow of ODBC connection to database

```
tar -zxvf unixODBC-2.3.7.tar.gz
cd unixODBC-2.3.7
./configure --enable-gui=no
make
make install
```

(3) Configure the ODBC driver file.

The ODBC driver package for GaussDB (for MySQL) is named as GAUSSDB100-VxxxRxxxCxx-CLIENT-ODBC-   SUSE11SP3-64bit.tar.gz. Extract it to the ODBC driver directory "/usr/local/lib".

```
tar   -zxvf   GAUSSDB100-VxxxRxxxCxx-CLIENT-ODBC-SUSE11SP3-
64bit.tar.gz
```

Add the following to the "/usr/local/etc/odbcinst.ini" file.

```
[GaussDB]
Driver64=/usr/local/odbc/lib/libzeodbc.so
setup=/usr/local/lib/libzeodbc.so
```

Explanation	The parameters of odbcinst.ini file are explained as follows. [DriverName]: driver name, corresponding to the driver name in the data source DSN, e.g. [DRIVER_N]. Driver64: path of the dynamic library for the driver, e.g. Driver64=/xxx/odbc/lib/libzeodbc.so. setup: the path of driver installation, same as the path of dynamic library in Driver64, e.g. setup=/xxx/odbc/ lib/libzeodbc.so.

Append the following to the "/usr/local/etc/odbc.ini" file.

```
[zenith]
Driver=DRIVER_N
Servername=192.168.0.1(数据库Server IP)
Port=1888 (数据库监听端口)
```

Explanation	The parameters of odbc.ini file are explained as follows. [DSN]: name of the data source, e.g. [zenith]. Driver: driver name, corresponding to DriverName in odbcinst.ini, e.g. Driver=DRIVER_N. Servername: IP address of the server, e.g. Servername=192.168.0.1. Port: port number of the server, e.g. Port=1888.

Table 6.3 Commonly Used Interfaces of the ODBC

Interface name	Function
SQLAllocHandle	Request environment, link, statement handle
SQLFreeHandle	Release the handle of the ODBC
SQLSetEnvAttr	Set the environment handle property of the ODBC
SQLSetConnectAttr	Set the link handle property of the ODBC
SQLSetStmtAttr	Set the execution handle property of the ODBC
SQLConnect	Use the link handle to link to data sources
SQLDisconnect	Disconnect from data sources
SQLPrepare	Prepare SQL statements for execution
SQLBindParameter	Bind parameters to the execution handle of prepared SQL
SQLBindCol	Bind the result set column to the buffer
SQLExecute	Execute SQL statements
SQLFetch	Get the next result row

(4) Configure environment variables.

```
export LD_LIBRARY_PATH=/usr/local/lib/:$LD_LIBRARY_PATH
export ODBCSYSINI=/usr/local/etc
export ODBCINI=/usr/local/etc/odbc.ini
```

Table 6.3 shows the commonly used interfaces of the ODBC.

Some ODBC interfaces are described as follows.

(1) The interface to allocate ODBC handles.

```
SQLRETURN  SQL_API  SQLAllocHandle(SQLSMALLINT  HandleType,
SQLHANDLE InputHandle, SQLHANDLE *OutputHandle)
```

SQLAllocHandle parameters are introduced as follows.

Input parameters: HandleType, the type of handle to be allocated (SQL_HANDLE_ENV, SQL_HANDLE _DBC, SQL_HANDLE_STMT); InputHandle, the dependent handle.

Output parameter: OutputHandle, the allocated handle.

Return value: SQL_SUCCESS indicates success; !=SQL_SUCCESS indicates failure.

(2) The interface to allocate the ODBC environment handle.

```
SQLRETURN SQL_API SQLAllocEnv(SQLHENV *EnvironmentHandle)
```

SQLAllocEnv parameter is introduced as follows.

Output parameter: EnvironmentHandle, the environment handle assigned to it.

Return value: SQL_SUCCESS indicates success; !=SQL_SUCCESS indicates failure.

(3) The interface to assign the ODBC link handle.

```
SQLRETURN SQL_API SQLAllocConnect(SQLHENV EnvironmentHandle,
SQLHDBC *Connection Handle)
```

SQLAllocConnect parameters are introduced as follows.

Input parameter: EnvironmentHandle, the environment handle.

Output parameter: ConnectionHandle, the link handle assigned to it.

Return value: SQL_SUCCESS indicates success; !=SQL_SUCCESS indicates failure.

(4) The interface to assign the ODBC execution handle.

```
SQLRETURN SQL_API SQLAllocStmt(SQLHDBC ConnectionHandle,
SQLHSTMT *Statement Handle)
```

SQLAllocStmt parameters are introduced as follows.

Input parameter: ConnectionHandle, the link handle.

Output parameter: StatementHandle, the execution handle assigned to it.

Return value: SQL_SUCCESS indicates success; !=SQL_SUCCESS indicates failure.

(5) The interface to release ODBC handles.

```
SQLRETURN SQL_API SQLFreeHandle(SQLSMALLINT HandleType,
SQLHANDLE Handle)
```

SQLFreeHandle parameters are introduced as follows.

Input parameters: HandleType, the type of handle to be released (SQL_HANDLE_ENV, SQL_HANDLE_DBC, SQL_HANDLE_STMT); Handle, the handle.

Return value: SQL_SUCCESS indicates success; !=SQL_SUCCESS indicates failure.

(6) The interface to release ODBC environment handle.

```
SQLRETURN SQL_API SQLFreeEnv(SQLHENV EnvironmentHandle)
```

SQLFreeEnv parameters are introduced as follows.

Input parameter: EnvironmentHandle, the environment handle to be released.

Return value: SQL_SUCCESS indicates success; !=SQL_SUCCESS indicates failure.

(7) The interface to release ODBC link handle.

```
SQLRETURN SQL_API SQLFreeConnect(SQLHDBC ConnectionHandle)
```

SQLFreeConnect parameters are introduced as follows.

Input parameter: ConnectionHandle, the link handle to be released.

Return value: SQL_SUCCESS indicates success; !=SQL_SUCCESS indicates failure.

(8) The interface to release ODBC execution handle.

```
SQLRETURN  SQL_API  SQLFreeStmt(SQLHSTMT  StatementHandle,
SQLUSMALLINT Option)
```

SQLFreeStmt parameters are introduced as follows.

Input parameters: StatementHandle, the execution handle to be released; Option, the type to be released (SQL_DROP).

Return value: SQL_SUCCESS indicates success; !=SQL_SUCCESS indicates failure.

ODBC application debugging under Windows operating system can be performed using the common VC (Visual C++) compilation environment. The following is an example of the debugging process of ODBC application for Linux platform.

- Operating system environment: Linux.
- Compiler: GCC 4.3.4.
- Debugger: CGDB 0.6.6/GDB 7.6.
  The steps of running and debugging JDBC application are shown below.

(1) Write the JDBC application.

Write the corresponding code and name the document as test_odbc.c.

(2) Compile.

Use the gcc -o test -g test_odbc.c -L/home/test/ -lzeodbc -lodbc -lodbcinst command to compile the test_odbc.c file into a test binary program. This compilation requires the GCC compiler.

(3) Run.

Execute the ./test command to run the binary program.

(4) Debug.

Use the gdb/cgdb test command for debugging.

The code for compiling and running the ODBC application is as follows.

```
#if WIN32
#include <windows.h>
#endif
#include <stdlib.h>
#include <stdio.h>
#include "sql.h"
#include "sqlext.h"
int main()
{
    SQLHANDLE  h_env, h_conn, h_stmt;
    SQLINTEGER  ret;
    SQLCHAR  *dsn = (SQLCHAR *)"myzenith";/*数据源名称*/
    SQLCHAR  *username = (SQLCHAR *)"sys";/*用户名*/
    SQLCHAR  *password = (SQLCHAR *)"sys";/*密码*/
    SQLSMALLINT dsn_len = (SQLSMALLINT)strlen((const CHAR *)dsn);
    SQLSMALLINT username_len = (SQLSMALLINT)strlen((const CHAR *)
    username);
    SQLSMALLINT password_len = (SQLSMALLINT)strlen((const CHAR *)
    password);
    h_env = h_conn = h_stmt = NULL;
    //申请句柄资源
    ret = SQLAllocHandle(SQL_HANDLE_ENV, SQL_NULL_HANDLE, &h_env);
    if ((ret != SQL_SUCCESS) && (ret != SQL_SUCCESS_WITH_INFO)) {
        return SQL_ERROR;
    }
    //设置环境句柄属性
    if (SQL_SUCCESS != SQLSetEnvAttr(h_env,
    SQL_ATTR_ODBC_VERSION, (void*)SQL_OV_ODBC3, 0)) {
        SQLFreeHandle(SQL_HANDLE_ENV, h_env);
        return SQL_ERROR;
    }
    //分配链接句柄
    if (SQL_SUCCESS != SQLAllocHandle(SQL_HANDLE_DBC, h_env, &
    h_conn)) {
        return SQL_ERROR; }
    //设置链接句柄自动提交属性
    if (SQL_SUCCESS != SQLSetConnectAttr(h_conn,
    SQL_ATTR_AUTOCOMMIT, (void *)1, 0)) {
        SQLFreeHandle(SQL_HANDLE_DBC, h_conn); // 用于释放ODBC的句柄
        SQLFreeHandle(SQL_HANDLE_ENV, h_env);
        return SQL_ERROR; }
    //链接数据源
    if (SQL_SUCCESS != SQLConnect(h_conn, dsn, dsn_len, username,
    username_len, password,
        password_len)){
        SQLFreeHandle(SQL_HANDLE_DBC, h_conn);
        SQLFreeHandle(SQL_HANDLE_ENV, h_env);
        return SQL_ERROR; }
    //申请执行句柄
    if (SQL_SUCCESS != SQLAllocHandle(SQL_HANDLE_STMT, h_conn,
```

(continued)

```
&h_stmt)) {
    SQLFreeHandle(SQL_HANDLE_DBC, h_conn);
    SQLFreeHandle(SQL_HANDLE_ENV, h_env);
    return SQL_ERROR; }
  //创建表并插入一条记录
  SQLCHAR* create_table_sql = (SQLCHAR*)"CREATE TABLE test(col INT)";
  SQLExecDirect(h_stmt, create_table_sql, strlen
  (create_table_sql));
  // 直接执行SQL语句
  SQLCHAR* insert_sql = (SQLCHAR*)"INSERT INTO test (col) values
  (:col)";
  SQLPrepare(h_stmt, insert_sql, strlen(insert_sql)); // 准备要
  执行的SQL语句
  int col = 1;
  SQLBindParameter(h_stmt, 1, SQL_PARAM_INPUT, SQL_C_SSHORT,
  SQL_INTEGER, sizeof(int), 0,
      &col, 0, NULL); // 往准备好SQL的执行句柄上绑定参数
  SQLExecute(h_stmt); // 执行SQL语句
  printf("Connection succeed!\n");
  //断开数据库链接
  SQLDisconnect(h_conn);
  //释放句柄资源
  SQLFreeHandle(SQL_HANDLE_DBC, h_conn);
  SQLFreeHandle(SQL_HANDLE_ENV, h_env);
  return SQL_SUCCESS;
}
```

6.1.4 Others

In addition to supporting development based on JDBC and ODBC drivers, GaussDB (for MySQL) also supports development based on GSC (C-API), Python and Go drivers.

(1) GSC (C-API) driver: the dependent library is libzeclient.so and the header file is gsc.h.

When creating a database connection using the GSC (C-API), the following function is required.

```
int gsc_connect(gsc_conn_t conn, const CHAR * url, const CHAR *
user, const CHAR * password);
```

The code to create a connection object using the GSC (C-API) is as follows.

```
int test_conn_db(CHAR * url, CHAR * user, CHAR * password)
{
gsc_conn_t conn;
if (gsc_alloc_conn(&conn) != GSC_SUCCESS)
{
return GSC_ERROR;
}
if (gsc_connect(conn, url, user, password) != GSC_SUCCESS)
{
return GSC_ERROR;
}
gsc_free_conn(conn);
conn = NULL;
//to avoid using wild pointer, user should set conn NULL after
free
return GSC_SUCCESS;
}
```

(2) Go driver. The Go driver is released as source code, and the upper-level application brings the code into the application project and compiles it with the application for use. From the file level, Go driver is divided into three parts: Go API, C driver library and C header file. The Zenith Go driver is based on the Zenith C driver, which is obtained through cgo technology packaging. The lib subdirectory is the dynamic library for C driver, and the include subdirectory is the C driver cgo involved in the header files. The Go driver relies on GCC 5.4 and above, and use the GO 1.12.1 or an higher version.

(3) Dynamic library of the Python driver: pyzenith.so. When using the Python driver to connect to a database, get the Connection and establish the connection by calling pyzenith.connect. GaussDB (for MySQL) uses Python, on the basis of the Linux operating system. Python supports time objects, using the following functions to get the time.

Date(year,month,day)—constructs an object containing the date.
Time(hour,minute,second)—constructs an object containing the time.
Timestamp(year,month,day,hour,minute,second,usec)—constructs an object containing the timestamp.
DateFromTicks(ticks)—construct the date value given with ticks value.
TimeFromTicks(ticks)—constructs the time value given with ticks value.
TimestampFromTicks(ticks)—constructs the timestamp value given with ticks value.
The sample code to execute the SQL statement and get all the tuples is as follows.

```
import pyzenith
conn=pyzenith.connect
('192.168.0.1','gaussdba','database_123','1888')
c=conn.cursor()
c.execute("CREATE TABLE testexecute(a INT,b CHAR(10),c
DATE)")
c.execute("INSERT INTO testexecute values(1,'s','2012-12-
13')")
c.execute("SELECT * FROM testexecute")
row =c.fetchall()
c.close()
conn.close()
```

6.2   Database Tools

6.2.1   DDM

Distributed database middleware (DDM) service is a middleware service for distributed relational databases provided by Huawei Public Cloud. It provides applications with distributed and transparent access to multiple database instances in the form of a service, which completely solves the database scalability problem and realizes storage of massive data and high concurrent access; it features easy-to-use, unlimited expansion and excellent performance. Easy-to-use refers to compatibility with MySQL protocol and zero changes to application code; unlimited expansion refers to supporting automatic horizontal splitting, completely solving the database problem of single machine restriction and realizing smooth expansion of service department terminals; excellent performance refers to the combination of high-performance cluster networking (unipolar during public beta) and horizontal expansion functions, thus realizing the linear improvement of performance. The DDM service flow is shown in Fig. 6.4.

DDM service puts all data into one database in the primary stage, whether it is small-, medium- or large-scale database or above. Small-scale (<500 qps or 100 tps, <100 read users, <10 write users): the performance of concurrent reads is improved by read/write separation in a single database. Medium-scale (<5000 qps or 1000 tps, <5000 read users, <100 write users): vertical splitting, distributing different services to different databases. Large-scale and above (10k+ qps, 10k+ tps, 10k+ read users, 1k+ write users): data sharding, dividing the data set into mutually independent and orthogonal data subsets according to certain rules, and then distributing the data subsets to different nodes.

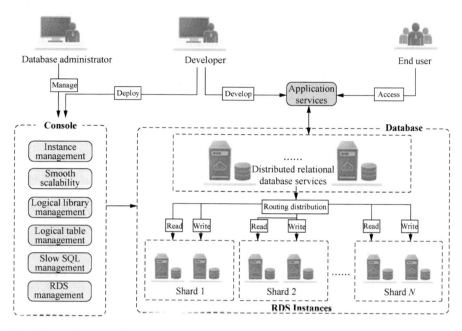

Fig. 6.4 DDM service flow

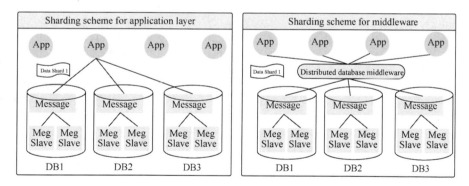

Fig. 6.5 Common data sharding solutions

Data sharding is used to solve the bottlenecks of database scaling. Commonly used data sharding solutions are application-layer sharding solution and middleware sharding solution, as shown in Fig. 6.5.

The advantage of application-level sharding solutions (such as Dangdang's Sharding-JDBC, Taobao's distributed data framework, etc.) is that they are directly connected to the database and have less additional overhead. Its disadvantages are the inability to achieve convergence in the number of connections, the application intrusion approach used leading to a large number of subsequent upgrades and updates and the high cost of operation and maintenance, and the fact that only Java is supported in most cases. The advantages of middleware sharding solutions (e.g., open source Mycat, Cobar, commercial software Ekoson, etc.) are zero changes to the application, language-independence, full transparency to the application for database scaling, and effective convergence of the number of connections through connection sharing. The disadvantage is the possibility of additional latency (<4%).

The key features of DDM are read/write separation, data sharding, and smooth database scaling. In the past, the read/write separation was controlled by the application itself, including configuring all database information in the client and realizing the read/write separation; database adjustment requires synchronous modification of the application, and database failure requires modification of the application, at which time the operation and maintenance and development need to synchronize the adjustment configuration. Nowadays, DDM achieves read/write separation, including: plug-and-play—automatic read/write separation and support for configuring performance weights for different nodes; application transparency— the application still operates a single node and database adjustments are not application-aware; and high availability—master-slave switchover or slave node failure is transparent to the application, as shown in Fig. 6.6.

The sharding application logic implemented by the application itself is complex: the application rewrites SQL statements, routes the SQL to different databases, and aggregates the results; database failure and adjustment require synchronous adjustment by the application, which makes operation and maintenance more difficult dramatically; the application upgrade and update maintenance workload is large and unacceptable for large systems. Today, data sharding is implemented by DDM with zero application changes: large table sharding, which supports automatic sharding by hash and other algorithms; automatic routing, which routes SQL to the real data source according to the sharding rules; connection multiplexing, which is used to substantially improve concurrent database access through connection pool multiplexing of MySQL instances. A comparison of data sharding is shown in in Fig. 6.7.

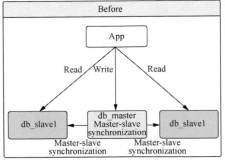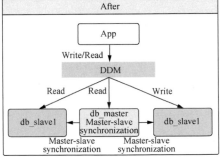

Fig. 6.6 Comparison of read/write separation

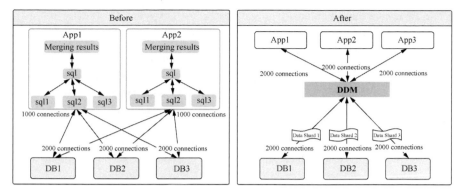

Fig. 6.7 A comparison of data sharding

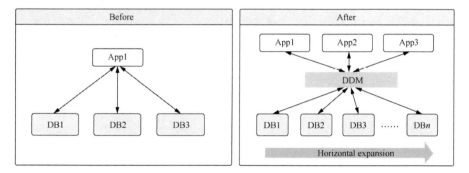

Fig. 6.8 A comparison of database horizontal scaling

If the application itself implements the horizontal expansion of the database, the expansion is prone to application downtime and service interruption, so tools for data migration are required. Nowadays, horizontal expansion of database by DDM can automatically balance data, achieve unlimited expansion (unlimited number of supported shards, ease coping with massive data), full automation (one-click expansion, automatic rollback of abnormalities), and small impact on services (second-level interruption, no service awareness at other times). A comparison of database horizontal scaling is shown in Fig. 6.8.

The applicable scenarios of DMM are as follows.

(1) High-frequency transactions on large applications: e-commerce, finance, O2O, retail, and social applications. Characteristics: large user base, frequent marketing activities, and increasingly slow response of the core database. Countermeasures: The linear horizontal scaling function provided by DDM can easily cope with the high concurrent real-time transaction scenarios.

(2) IoT massive sensors: industrial monitoring, smart city, and Internet of Vehicles. Characteristics: many sensing devices, high sampling frequency, large data scale, breakthrough of single database bottleneck. Countermeasures: The capacity horizontal expansion function provided by DDM can help users to store massive data at low cost.

(3) Massive video and picture data index: Internet, social applications, etc. Characteristics: billions pieces of picture, document, video and other data, and extremely high performance requirements for indexing these files and providing real-time addition, deletion, change and query operations. Countermeasures: The ultra-high performance and distributed expansion function provided by DDM can effectively improve the search efficiency of the index.

(4) Traditional program, hardware and government agencies: large enterprises and banks. Characteristics: Traditional solutions rely on commercial solutions with high hardware cost such as minicomputers and high-end storage. Countermeasures: The linear horizontal scaling function provided by DDM can easily cope with highly concurrent real-time transaction scenarios.

How to use DDM - buy a database middleware.

Step 1: Console > Database > Distributed Database Middleware (DDM) Instance Management.

Step 2: Click the "Buy Database Middleware Instance" button, as shown in Fig. 6.9.

Step 3: Select "Pay As You Go" for the billing mode. Leave the default settings for region, available partitions and instance specifications if there are no special needs, as shown in Fig. 6.10.

Step 4: Enter the instance name, select the corresponding virtual private cloud, subnet and security group (the virtual private cloud must be consistent with the database instance), and then click the "Buy Now" button, as shown in Fig. 6.11.

Step 5: Confirm the specification, check the check box to agree to the service agreement, and click the "Submit" button, as shown in Fig. 6.12.

Multi-instance and distributed cluster are shown in Fig. 6.13.

How to use DDM - data sharding.

Fig. 6.9 Steps of instance purchase (1)

Fig. 6.10 Steps of instance purchase (2)

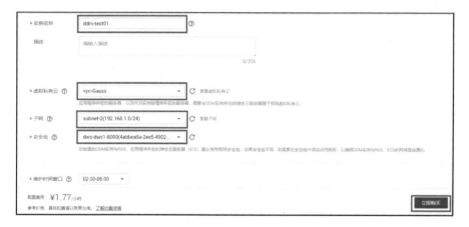

Fig. 6.11 Steps of instance purchase (3)

Step 1: Console > Database > Distributed Database Middleware (DDM) Instance Management.

Step 2: Select the instance that needs to be sharded, and click the "Create Logical Library" text hyperlink, as shown in Fig. 6.14.

Step 3: Select the split mode, set the logical library name and transaction model, and select the associated RDS instance, as shown in Fig. 6.15.

Step 4: Select the RDS instance where the logical library can be created (same as the case of virtual private cloud), and click the "Create" button, as shown in Fig. 6.16.

The data is successfully sharded, as shown in Fig. 6.17.

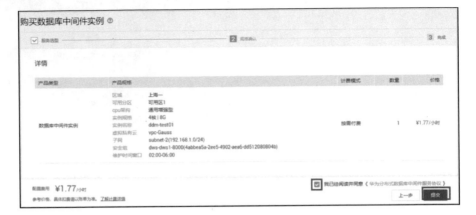

Fig. 6.12 Example purchase step diagram (4)

Fig. 6.13 The instance is purchased successfully

Fig. 6.14 Data sharding (1)

6.2.2 DRS

Data replication service (DRS) is an easy-to-use, stable, and efficient cloud service for online database migration and real-time database synchronization. DRS targets cloud databases, reducing the complexity of data flow between databases and effectively reducing the cost of data transfer.

It features the following capabilities. Online migration: It supports a variety of service scenarios such as cross-cloud platform database migration, under-cloud database migration to the cloud or cross-region database migration on the cloud

Fig. 6.15 Data sharding (2)

Fig. 6.16 Data sharding (3)

Fig. 6.17 Data sharding succeeded

through various network links. It is characterized by incremental migration technology that allows continuous service during migration to the maximum extent, effectively minimizing service system interruption time and impact on service, and realizing smooth migration of database to the cloud. Data synchronization: Realizes the real-time flow of key service data between distinctly different systems. Database

Fig. 6.18 Operation flow of guided migration

migration is aimed at overall relocation, while synchronization is to maintain the continuous flow of data between different service systems. Common scenarios are real-time analysis, reporting system, and data warehouse environment. It is characterized by focusing on tables and data to meet the need for multiple synchronization flexibility, such as many-to-one, one-to-many, which synchronizes data between different tables. Multi-live disaster recovery: Through off-site near-real-time data synchronization, it enables the establishment of database disaster recovery relationships cross regions, cross clouds, between local and cloud, and between hybrid clouds, providing disaster recovery features such as one-key master-standby reversal, data comparison, delay monitoring, data replenishment, supporting disaster recovery rehearsal, real disaster recovery and other scenarios, and supporting various disaster recovery architectures such as master-slave disaster recovery and master-master disaster recovery. It features offsite long-distance transmission optimization and provides features around disaster recovery, unlike the solutions formed based on simple data synchronization. Data subscription: It obtains data change information of key service \ (often needed by downstream service) in the database and caches such information and provides a unified SDK interface to facilitate downstream service subscription, acquisition and consumption, thus decoupling the database from downstream systems and sesrvice processes. Common scenarios include Kafka's subscription to MySQL incremental data.

DRS's key features—guided migration. The operation flow of guided migration is shown in Fig. 6.18.

Figure 6.19 shows how to use DRS—scenario-based selection.

Figure. 6.20 shows how to use DRS—network and security.

DRS contains multiple migration modes. If service interruption is acceptable, select the full migration mode. This mode is a one-time database migration, suitable for database migration scenarios where service is allowed to interrupt. Full migration migrates all database objects and data from a non-system database to the target database at one time, including tables, views, stored procedures, triggers, etc.

If service interruption is required to keep minimal, select the full + incremental migration mode. This mode is a continuous migration of database, which is suitable for scenarios sensitive to service interruption. After completing the migration of historical data to the target database through full migration, the incremental migration phase keeps the source database and target database data consistent through techniques such as catch logs and application logs.

The migration objects that can be selected include databases, tables, views, stored procedures, and triggers, as shown in Fig. 6.21.

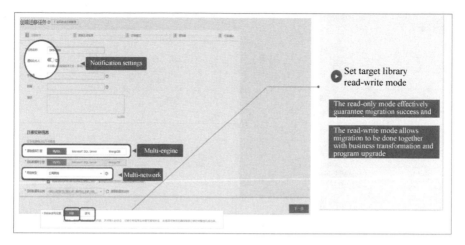

Fig. 6.19 Scenario-based selection

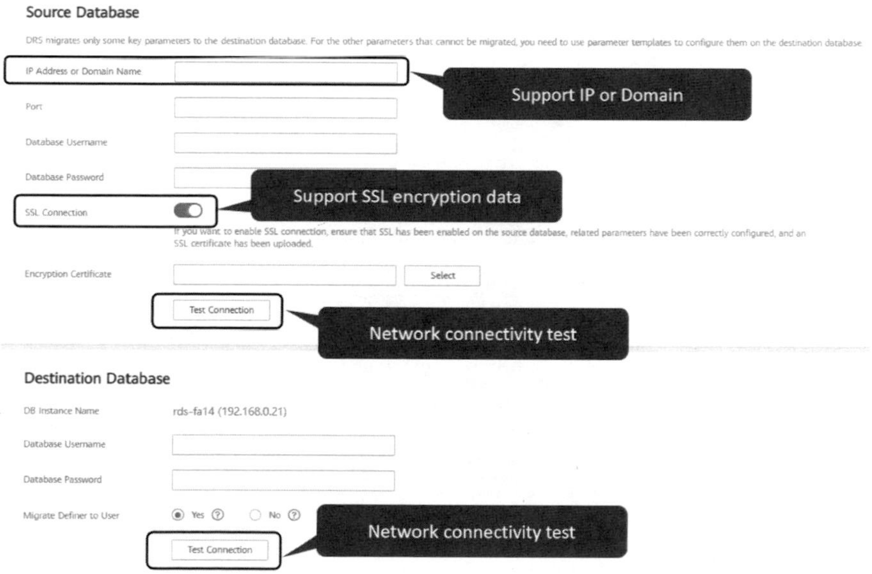

Source Database

DRS migrates only some key parameters to the destination database. For the other parameters that cannot be migrated, you need to use parameter templates to configure them on the destination database

IP Address or Domain Name

Port   **Support IP or Domain**

Database Username

Database Password   **Support SSL encryption data**

SSL Connection

If you want to enable SSL connection, ensure that SSL has been enabled on the source database, related parameters have been correctly configured, and an SSL certificate has been uploaded.

Encryption Certificate   Select

Test Connection

                                              Network connectivity test

Destination Database

DB Instance Name   rds-fa14 (192.168.0.21)

Database Username

Database Password

Migrate Definer to User   ● Yes ⑦   ○ No ⑦

                                              Network connectivity test
Test Connection

Fig. 6.20 Network and security

DRS classifies users who need to be migrated into three categories, i.e. users who can be migrated completely, users who need to be downgraded and users who cannot be migrated, as shown in Fig. 6.22.

In DRS parameter migration, most of the parameters that are not migrated do not cause the migration to fail, but they often have a direct impact on the operation and performance of the service. DRS supports parameter migration to make the service

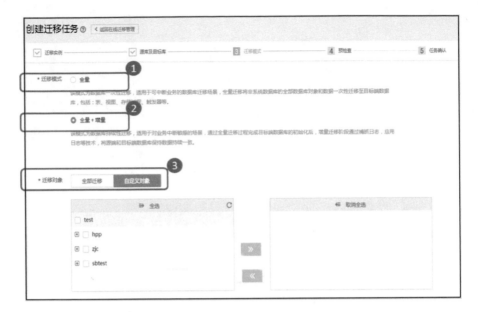

Fig. 6.21 Multiple migration modes

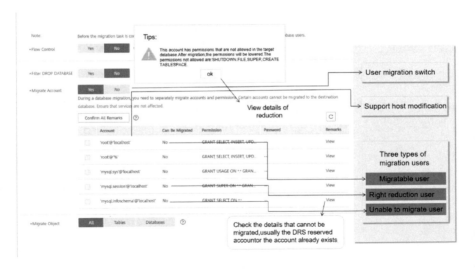

Fig. 6.22 User migration

and application run more smoothly and worry-free after database migration. Service parameters include character set settings, maximum number of connections, scheduling related settings, lock wait time, Timestamp default behavior and connection wait time. The performance parameters include *_buffer size and -_cache size, as shown in Fig. 6.23.

Fig. 6.23 Parameter migration

Fig. 6.24 Precheck

Figure 6.24 shows how to use DRS - precheck.

Migration monitoring of DRS: You can understand the migration progress in real time by observing the macro display, and view the percentage progress of the full migration objects, such as table data, table structure, table indexes, etc. with long migration time. You can view the migration progress of specific migration objects

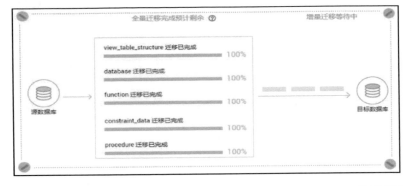

Fig. 6.25 Migration monitoring

through the table, and when the "number of objects" and "number of migrated objects" are equal, the migration of the object is complete. You can view the migration progress of each object through the "View Details" hyperlink, and when the progress is 100%, the migration is complete, as shown in Fig. 6.25.

The macro comparison at object level is used to determine whether data objects are missing; the data is proofread in detail by data-level comparison. The comparison of rows and contents at different levels is shown in Fig. 6.26.

Fig. 6.26 Migration comparison

6.2.3   DAS

Data Admin Service (DAS) is a professional tool to simplify database management. It provides a good visual operation interface, which can greatly improve the efficiency and make data management both secure and simple. DAS features the following characteristics.

(1) Realizes managing database on the cloud, and visual interface to connect and manage database.
(2) Manages data through a dedicated channel in the cloud, where Huawei Cloud strictly controls access to the database with high security.
(3) Accesses to data simply and conveniently, and manage operations via visual objects, easy to use.
(4) Realizes cloud R&D testing, fast deployment, fast access to the database, and improved R&D efficiency.

The DAS includes console, standard version and enterprise version. The console (for database administrators and operation and maintenance personnel) provides basic host and instance performance data, slow SQL and full SQL analysis, covering from real-time performance analysis and diagnosis to comprehensive analysis of historical operation data, and can quickly find out every problem in database operation and potential risk points in advance. Standard version (for developers) is the best database client with advantages of no local client installation, WYSIWYG visual operation experience, synchronization of data and table structure, online editing, intelligent prompt of SQL input, and rich database development functions. Enterprise version (enterprise DevOPS platform) provides database DevOPS platforms for data protection, change auditing, operation auditing and R&D self-service based on permission minimization control and approval process mechanism, helping enterprises to realize standardized, efficient and ultra-secure management means for large-scale database.

DAS can help users build tables like filling out tables, and view, edit, insert and delete table data like editing Excel files; automated SQL input prompts can help users write SQL statements, while chain dependency diagrams show real-time lock waiting session relationships, so users can also be a professional database manager; automatical generation of table data make development work more convenient; when the data is modified or deleted by mistake, a rollback task can be initiated to help users retrieve the data; the automatic timeout mechanism allows users not to worry about bringing down the database due to the long execution time of SQL statements.

DAS application scenario: standard version, as shown in Figs. 6.27 and 6.28.

The Console in Fig. 6.27 is further divided into Conn Console and DAS Console. Conn Console is the console for DAS connection management, and DAS Console is the unified portal for data administration services. API-for-DAS is the unified entrance of external API, responsible for conversion of internal and external API protocols, as well as permission control and API audit. DAS provides database maintenance and management services, including addition, deletion, change and check of database, tables, indexes, fields, views and other objects.

DAS application scenario: enterprise version.

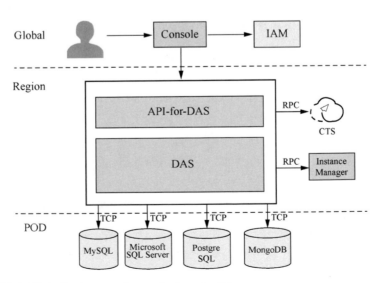

Fig. 6.27 DAS application scenario: standard version (1)

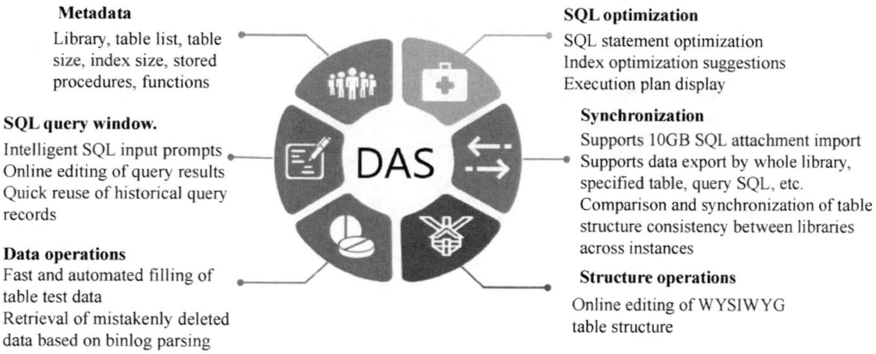

Metadata
Library, table list, table size, index size, stored procedures, functions

SQL query window.
Intelligent SQL input prompts
Online editing of query results
Quick reuse of historical query records

Data operations
Fast and automated filling of table test data
Retrieval of mistakenly deleted data based on binlog parsing

SQL optimization
SQL statement optimization
Index optimization suggestions
Execution plan display

Synchronization
Supports 10GB SQL attachment import
Supports data export by whole library, specified table, query SQL, etc.
Comparison and synchronization of table structure consistency between libraries across instances

Structure operations
Online editing of WYSIWYG table structure

Fig. 6.28 DAS application scenario: standard version (2)

Data is the core asset of the enterprise. How to control the access rights of sensitive data, realize the security of database changes, audit the operation retroactively and reduce the labor cost of DBA is an important demand of enterprises when the number of database instances reaches a certain scale.

The advantages of DAS enterprise version are as follows.

(1) Secure data access: Employees do not have access to database login name and password, and need to apply for permission first for querying the library; it supports multi-dimensional query control on total number of queries per day, total data rows, maximum number of rows returned per query, etc.

(2) Sensitive data protection: Sensitive fields are automatically identified and marked; sensitive data will be desensitized and displayed when employees perform query and export operations.

(3) Change security: All operations on the library are recorded in audit logs, and the database operation behavior is traceable.

(4) Operation audit: It features risk identification of SQL change, service audit control; automatic detection of database water level when change is executed; and data cleaning for large data tables.

(5) Improved efficiency and reduced cost: It features flexible security risk and approval process customization; the empowerment of the roles of service head and database administrator on the library delegates the low-risk library change operations to the service supervisor, reducing the labor cost of the database administrator in the enterprise.

How to use DAS—add a database connection. The steps are as follows.

Step 1: Console > Database > Data Admin Service (DAS).
Step 2: Click the "Add Database Login" button, as shown in Fig. 6.29.
Step 3: Select the database type as GaussDB (for MySQL).
Step 4: Select the database source (RDS instance), and select the instance under the corresponding source, as shown in Fig. 6.30.

Fig. 6.29 Add a database connection (1)

Fig. 6.30 Add a database connection (2)

Fig. 6.31 Add a database connection (3)

Step 5: Fill in the login user name and password under the selected instance, and it is recommended to check the "Remember Password" checkbox, as shown in Fig. 6.31.

Step 6: Click the "Add Now" button, as shown in Fig. 6.32.

Step 7: Select the database instance to log in, and click the "Login" hyperlink, as shown in Fig. 6.33.

Step 8: Log in to the DAS Administration page successfully, as shown in Fig. 6.34.

How to use DAS—create an object.

In the Library Management page, we can create and manage database objects, diagnose SQL, and collect metadata, following the steps as follows.

Fig. 6.32 Add Now

Fig. 6.33 Add a database connection (4)

Fig. 6.34 Add a database connection (5)

Step 1: Click "New Database" on the homepage, fill in the database name and click "OK", as shown in Fig. 6.35.

Step 2: After successful login, you can enter the Library Management page, as shown in Fig. 6.36.

Step 3: Click the "New Table" button, as shown in Fig. 6.37.

Step 4: Enter the New Table page, set the table's basic information, fields, indexes and other information, as shown in Fig. 6.38.

Step 5: After setting up, click the "Create Now" button., as shown in Fig. 6.39.

Step 6: In addition to tables, we can also create new views, stored procedures, events and other objects, as shown in Fig. 6.40.

How to use DAS—create an object.

Open the SQL Operations page, there will be automatic SQL input prompt for assisting to finish the SQL statement.

Fig. 6.35 Create an object (1)

Fig. 6.36 Create an object (2)

Fig. 6.37 Create an object (3)

Step 1: Click the "SQL Window" button at the top of the page, or the "SQL Query" hyperlink at the bottom to open the SQL Operations page, as shown in Fig. 6.41. On the SQL Operations page, we can perform SQL operations, such as query, etc.

Step 2: Write SQL statements. DAS provides SQL prompt function to facilitate writing SQL statements, as shown in Fig. 6.42.

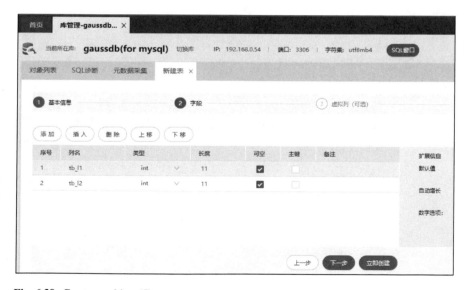

Fig. 6.38 Create an object (4)

Fig. 6.39 Create an object (5)

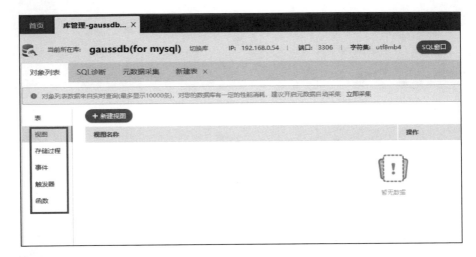

Fig. 6.40 Create an object (6)

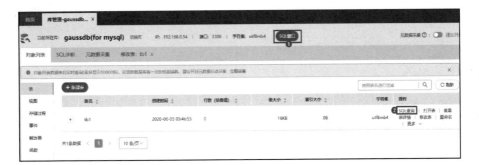

Fig. 6.41 SQL operation (1)

Fig. 6.42 SQL operation (2)

Fig. 6.43 SQL operation (3)

Step 3: After the execution of SQL statement, you can check the operation result and execution record at the bottom, as shown in Fig. 6.43.

How to use DAS—import and export.

In the Import and Export page, we can import the existing SQL statements into the database for execution, and export the database file or SQL result set for saving.

Step 1: Create a new import task. You can import an SQL file or CSV file.

Step 2: Select the file source, either imported locally or from the OBS.

Step 3: Select the database. The imported file will be executed within the corresponding database, as shown in Fig. 6.44.

Step 4: Create a new export task and select the database file to be exported, or choose to export the SQL result set, as shown in Fig. 6.45.

How to use DAS - compare the table structures.

In the Structure Scheme page, we can compare the structures of the tables within the two databases and choose whether to synchronize after the comparison, as shown in Fig. 6.46.

Step 1: Create a table structure comparison and synchronization tasks.

Step 2: Select benchmark database and target database.

Step 3: Select the synchronization type.

Step 4: Start the comparison task.

Step 5: Start the synchronization task.

6.3 Client Tools

Client tools are mainly for users to connect, operate and debug databases more conveniently.

Fig. 6.44 Import and export (1)

Fig. 6.45 Import and export (2)

(1) gsql is an interactive database connection tool run by GaussDB (DWS) at the command line.
(2) Data Studio is a graphical interface tool that allows users to connect to GaussDB (for MySQL) and debug and execute SQL statements and stored procedures through Data Studio.

Fig. 6.46 Compare the table structures

6.3.1   *zsql*

The prerequisites for installing zsql are as follows.

(1) Linux operating system is supported.
(2) Python 2.7 needs to be deployed on the host where the client is located, and Python 2.7.x is mandatory for the host.
(3) zsql client user and user group are created with permissions ≤0750.
(4) The client installation package has been obtained and the integrity check of the zsql client installation package has been completed.

For example, create the user group dbgrp and user omm, and add a password for omm.

```
groupadd dbgrp
useradd -g dbgrp -d /home/omm -m -s /bin/bash omm
passwd omm
```

The method of integrity check of the zsql client installation package is as follows.

(1) Execute the following command to output the check value of the installation package.

```
sha256sum GAUSSDB100-V300R001C00-ZSQL-EULER20SP8-64bit.tar.gz
```

(2) Check the contents of the sha256 file GAUSSDB100-V300R001C00-ZSQL-EULER20SP8-64bit.sha256.
(3) Compare the check value with the contents of the check file. If they are consistent, the check passes, otherwise the check fails.

It should be noted that if you reinstall GaussDB100 zsql client program, you need to make sure the zsql client directory has been deleted, otherwise it will lead to reinstallation failure. It is not allowed to install the client program under the server program directory. For example, if the GaussDB100 database server program is already stored in the "/home/omm/app" directory, you cannot install the zsql client program in this directory, but need to plan the zsql client program to another directory for independent installation. After installation, you need to execute the su command to switch to the client user again.

If you need to uninstall the zsql client program, delete the files in the installation directory first. For example, if the client installer directory is "/home/omm/app", you can delete this directory. Configure the user environment variable, open "~/.bashrc" environment variable (the command is "vi ~/.bashrc"), and delete the following contents.

```
export PATH=/home/omm/app/bin:$PATH
export LD_LIBRARY_PATH=/home/omm/app/lib:/home/omm/app/add-
ons:$LD_LIBRARY_PATH
```

After completing the installation of zsql, you need to log in to the server where GaussDB100 is located as the root user, i.e. the zsql client user. Take omm as an example, put the client installation package under the directory "/home/omm", and modify the installation package user group.

```
cd /home/omm
chown omm:dbgrp GAUSSDB100-V300R001C00-ZSQL-EULER20SP8-64bit.
tar.gz
```

Next, make changes to the user group and execute the su command to switch to the user under which the zsql client is running.

```
su - omm
```

Unpack the installation package accordingly.

```
cd /home/omm
tar -zxvf GAUSSDB100-V300R001C00-ZSQL-EULER20SP8-64bit.tar.gz
```

 If the database user's password contains the special character $, you must escape it with the escape character \ when connecting to the database via zsql, otherwise the login will fail.

Go to the directory where the host was unziped.

```
cd GAUSSDB100-V300R001C00-ZSQL-EULER20SP8-64bit
```

Run the install_zsql.py script to install the zsql client.

```
python install_zsql.py -U omm:dbgrp -R /home/omm/app
```

Here -U is the user running the zsql client, e.g. omm. -R is the directory where the zsql client is installed.

After completing the installation of the zsql client, use zsql to connect.

Log in as the database administrator with the following code format.

```
zsql { CONNECT | CONN } / AS SYSDBA [ip:port] [-D /home/gaussdba/
data1] [-q] [-s "silent_file"] [-w connect_timeout]
```

The sample code is as follows.

```
[gaussdba@plat1~]$ zsql / AS sysdba -q
  Connected
```

CONNECT|CONN: Connects to the database; where [ip:port] is optional, if not specified, the local host is connected by default.

When the database system administrator creates multiple database instances, the −D parameter is required to specify the database directory in order to connect to the specified database. The −D parameter is only required when the database system administrator creates multiple database instances; if it is not specified, the host does not know which database to connect to. Usually users create only one database instance so do not need to specify it. Therefore, the −D parameters are only for HCIA users to understand, no need to learn it in depth.

(1) −q: This parameter is used to cancel SSL login authentication view, which can be used together with the -w parameter.

(2) −s: This parameter is used to set the prompt-free mode to execute SQL statement.

(3) −w: This parameter indicates the waiting timeout time when the client connects to the database, currently 10s by default; can be used with the −q parameter. The value meanings of waiting timeout are as follows.

- −1: means wait for the server response, no timeout.
- 0: means do not wait for the timeout, and return the result directly.
- *n*: means wait for *n* seconds.

After using the -w parameter, when zsql starts to connect to the database, the waiting timeout is set to the specified value. After starting, the waiting response timeout for the currently established connection, the waiting response timeout for the new connection re-established and the query timeout are all specified values; the setting expires after exiting the zsql process.

When logging in as a normal database user, the following three types of logins are available.

(1) Interactive Login Method 1.

```
zsql  user@ip:port  [-D  /home/gaussdba/data1]  [-q]  [-s
"silent_file"] [-w connect_timeout]
Please enter password:
```

(2) Interactive Login Method 2.

```
zsql  conn  user/user_password@ip:port  [-D /home/gaussdba/
data1] [-q] [-s "silent_file"] [-w connect_timeout]
```

(3) Non-Interactive Login Method.

```
zsql user/user_password@ip:port  [-D /home/gaussdba/data1]
[-q] [-s "silent_file"] [-w connect_timeout]
```

user is the database user name and user_password is the database user password. ip:port is the IP address and port number of the host where the database is located, which is 1888 by default.

Interactive Login Method 1 has no conn, where you need to connect and then enter the password. Interactive Login Method 2 has conn, where you can enter the password as connect. Non-Interactive Login Method has no conn, where you can enter the password as connect in a different manner. The most commonly used is the

Non-Interactive Login Method, while for the interactive login methods, you just
need to know about them, because they all have the same result.

Example: User gaussdba logs in locally to the database.

```
[gaussdba@plat1~]$ zsql
SQL> CONN gaussdba/Changeme_123@127.0.0.1:1611
connected.
//启动zsql进程时设置等待响应超时时间
[gaussdba@plat1~]$ zsql gaussdba/Changeme_123@127.0.0.1:1611
-w 20
connected.
//创建新用户jim, 并赋予新用户CREATE SESSION权限
SQL> DROP USER IF EXISTS jim;
CREATE USER jim IDENTIFIED BY database_123;
GRANT CREATE SESSION TO jim;
//切换用户, 再次建立的新连接的等待响应超时时间也是20s
CONN jim/Changeme_123@127.0.0.1:1611
connected.
EXIT
```

When starting the zsql process, set the response timeout to 20s. After starting,
the response timeout for the current connection is 20s. After exiting the zsql process,
the setting expires and the waiting response timeout for new connections remains at
the default value of 20s.

When connecting to zsql, you can set the parameters to meet your specific
functional requirements. If you set the -s parameter to execute SQL statements in
promptless mode, the results will be output to the specified file instead of being
displayed back on the current screen. This parameter should be placed at the end of
the command.

Example: User hr connects to the database in the silent mode, specifying the
output log name as silent.log.

```
[gaussdba@plat1~]$ zsql hr@127.0.0.1:1611 -s silent.log
//创建表training
CREATE TABLE training(staff_id INT NOT NULL, course_name CHAR
(50), course_start_ date DATETIME, course_end_date DATETIME,
exam_date DATETIME, score INT);
INSERT INTO training(staff_id, course_name, course_start_date,
course_end_date, exam_date, score) values(10, 'SQL
majorization', '2017-06-15 12:00:00', '2017-06-20 12:
00:00', '2017-06-25 12:00:00', 90);
//退出数据库系统
EXIT
//查看日志silent.log
cat silent.log
Succeed.
```

The -c parameter refers to the execution of a single SQL statement at startup, which needs to be placed at the end of the command.

```
zsql user/password@ip:port -c "SQL_Statement"
```

Multiple normal SQL statements can be entered in the -c parameter, but the statements need to be separated by a semicolon (;). When entering procedure statements in the -c parameter, only a single entry is supported, and the procedure needs to be ended with a slash /.

The sample code is as follows.

```
[gaussdba@plat1~]$ zsql gaussdba/Changeme_123@127.0.0.1:1611
-c "SELECT ABS(-10) FROM dual;"
connected.
SQL>
ABS(-10)
----------------------------------------
10
1 rows fetched.
```

Objects with $ in their names need to add the escape character \. The maximum length of a single executable SQL statement should be no longer than 1MB.

-f refers to the execution of SQL scripts, which cannot be used with the -c or -s parameters. The setting of the -f parameter is the same as that of the -c and -s parameters, which are placed at the end of the command.

```
zsql user@ip:port [-a] -f sql_script_file
```

Or as follows.

```
zsql user@ip:port [-a] -f "sql_script_file"
```

The -a parameter is used to output the executed SQL statement, which can be used together with the -f parameter, and must be in front of the -f parameter. This means output and execute the SQL statement in the SQL script. If the -a parameter is not set then output the execution result of the statement in the SQL script directly, and no SQL script will be output.

```
[gaussdba@plat1~]$ zsql gaussdba/Changeme_123@127.0.0.1:1611 -a
connected.
SQL> SELECT ABS (-10);
SELECT ABS (-10);          /* 打印SQL脚本*/
ABS (-10)
-----------------------------------------
10
1 rows fetched.
```

Execute the file test.sql.

```
SELECT ABS (-10) FROM dual;
SELECT * FROM dual;
SELECT 123;
COMMIT;
```

Execute the -f "test.sql" command

```
[gaussdba@plat1~]$ zsql gaussdba/Changeme_123@127.0.0.1:1611 -f
"test.sql"
```

Execute the -a -f "test.sql" command.

```
[gaussdba@plat1~]$ zsql gaussdba/Changeme_123@127.0.0.1:1611 -a
-f "test.sql"
```

The result of the -f "test.sql" command is as follows.

```
[gaussdba@plat1~]$ zsql gaussdba/Changeme_123@127.0.0.1:1611 -f
"test.sql"
 connected.
 SQL>
 ABS (-10)
 -----------------------------------------
 10
 1 rows fetched.
 SQL>
 DUMMY
 ----
 X
 1 rows fetched.
```

(continued)

```
SQL>
123
------------
123
1 rows fetched.
SQL>
Succeed.
```

The result of the -a-f "test.sql" command is as follows.

```
[gaussdba@plat1~]$ zsql gaussdba/Changeme_123@127.0.0.1:1611 -a
-f "test.sql"
connected.
SQL> SELECT ABS(-10) FROM dual;
ABS(-10)
-----------------------------------------
10
1 rows fetched.
SQL> SELECT * FROM dual;
DUMMY
----
X
1 rows fetched.
SQL> SELECT 123;
123
------------
123
1 rows fetched.
SQL> COMMIT;
Succeed.
```

The format of the statement to view the database object definition information is as follows.

```
DESCRIBE [-o | -O] object
```

Or as follows.

```
DESC [-o | -O] object
```

-o or -O indicates the object, which is optional.

The SQL statement of query: DESC -q SELECT expression (just know it).

Displays column description information when querying with the SELECT statement, including name, nullable, type, and size(char or byte).

The DESC column size shows the derived value (maximum derived value) at the time of SQL parsing, and the execution returns column data values that do not exceed that size.

expression is a query statement.

Query the definition information of the table privilege.

```
SQL> DROP TABLE IF EXISTS privilege;
SQL> CREATE TABLE privilege(staff_id INT PRIMARY KEY,
privilege_name VARCHAR(64) NOT NULL,privilege_description
VARCHAR(64), privilege_approver VARCHAR(10));
  SQL> DESC privilege;
  Name                      Null?  Type
  -----------------------------------

  ------- --------------------------------
  STAFF_ID                  NOT NULL BINARY_INTEGER
  PRIVILEGE_NAME            NOT NULL VARCHAR(64 BYTE)
  PRIVILEGE_DESCRIPTION              VARCHAR(64 BYTE)
  PRIVILEGE_APPROVER                 VARCHAR(10 BYTE)
```

Execute the SPOOL command to output the execution results to an operating system file.

Specify the output file, either in a relative path or an absolute path.

```
SPOOL file_path
```

Save the execution result and close the current output file stream.

```
SPOOL off
```

Execute the SPOOL command.

```
SQL> SPOOL ./spool.txt
SQL> CREATE TABLE COUNTRY(Code INT,Name VARCHAR(20),Population
INT);
  SQL> SELECT Code, Name, Population
  FROM COUNTRY
  WHERE Population > 100000;
  SQL> SELECT 'This SQL will be output into ./spool.txt' FROM
SYS_DUMMY;
  SQL> SPOOL OFF;
  SQL> SELECT 'This SQL will not be output into ./spool.txt' FROM
SYS_DUMMY;
```

When the SPOOL file is specified, zsql results are output to a file. The contents of the file are approximately the same as those displayed on the zsql command line, and the output is closed only after SPOOL OFF is specified.

If the file specified by the SPOOL command does not exist, zsql will create a file. If the specified file already exists, zsql appends the execution result to the original result.

Exit zsql and enter cat spool.txt to view the contents of the spool.txt file, as follows.

```
SQL> CREATE TABLE COUNTRY(Code int,Name varchar(20),Population
int);
  Succeed.
  SQL> SELECT Code, Name, Population
   2 FROM COUNTRY
   3 WHERE Population > 100000;
  CODE      NAME              POPULATION
  ------------ --------------------- ------------

  0 rows fetched.
  SQL> SELECT 'This SQL will be output into ./spool.txt' FROM
SYS_DUMMY;
   'THIS SQL WILL BE OUTPUT INTO ./SPOOL.TXT'
  ------------------------------------------------

  This SQL will be output into ./spool.txt
  1 rows fetched.
  SQL> SPOOL OFF;
```

Note that spool.txt does not have the SELECT 'This SQL will not be output into ./spool.txt' FROM SYS_DUMMY; statement, because the SPOOL OFF statement has been executed before the execution of this statement.

Logical import IMP and logical export EXP.

```
{EXP | EXPORT}[ keyword =param [ , ... ] ] [ ... ];
{IMP | IMPORT} [ keyword =param [ , ... ] ] [ ... ];
```

(1) Logical import and logical export do not support the export of SYS user data.
(2) During the logical import and logical export of data, you need to have the corresponding operation permission for the object to be exported.
(3) If execute FILETYPE=BIN during logical import and logical export, three types of files are exported: metadata files (user-specified files), data files (.D files), and LOB files (.L files).
(4) If there is a file with the same name existing in the directory during logical import and logical export, the file will be overwritten directly without any prompt.

(5) When logically exporting data, a metadata file and a subdirectory named data will be generated under the specified export file path. If no export file path is specified, a metadata file and a subdirectory named data will be generated under the current path by default. When executing FILETYPE=BIN, the generated subfiles (data file, LOB file) will be placed under the secondary directory data; if the specified metadata file and the generated subfiles already exist, an error will be reported.

Generate the analysis report WSR.

WSR (Workload Statistics Report) is used to generate the performance analysis report. By default, only SYS users have permission to perform the related operations. If an ordinary user needs to use it, he/she needs the SYS user permission—grant statistics to user, which means that the statistics role is granted to the ordinary user. After authorization, the ordinary user has the permissions to create snapshots, delete snapshots, view snapshots, and generate WSR reports, but does not have the permission to change WSR parameters. When an ordinary user performs an operation, he/she needs to carry the SYS name to execute the corresponding stored procedure, such as CALL SYS.WSR$CREATE_SNAPSHOT.

Other functions include SHOW (query parameter information), SET (set parameters), DUMP (export data), LOAD (import data), COL (set column width), WHENEVER (set whether to continue or exit the connection operation when the script runs abnormally), etc.

6.3.2 gsql

To configure the database server using gsql, and log in to any node in the GaussDB (DWS) cluster as the omm user, execute the related command source ${BIGDATA_HOME}/mppdb/.mppdbgs_profile to start the environment variables.

Execute the following command to add the IP address or host name (separated by a comma) of the external service, where NodeName is the current node name and 10.11.12.13 is the IP address of the network card of the server where CN is located.

```
gs_guc   reload   -Z   coordinator   -N   NodeName   -I   all   -c
"listen_addresses='localhost, 192.168.0.100,10.11.12.13'"
```

listen_addresses can also be configured as *. This configuration will monitor all NICs, but there are security risks, so it is not recommended for users. It is recommended that users configure IP address or host name to open the monitoring as needed.

Add the client IP address authentication information (please replace the client_ip/mask below with the real client IP address).

```
gs_guc SET -Z coordinator -N all -I all -h "host all client_ip/mask
sha256"
```

Unzip   the   GaussDB-Kernel-VXXXRXXXCXX-XXXX-64bit-gsql.tar.gz
archive, and you will get the following files.

bin: The location where the gsql executable is stored.

gsql_env.sh: environment variable file.

lib: the dynamic database that gsql depends on.

Load the environment variable file source gsql_env.sh that you just extracted, and
you can use gsql normally.

```
gsql –d postgres –h 10.11.12.13 –U username –W password –p 25308
```

The -d parameter specifies the database name.

The -h parameter specifies the database CN address.

The -U parameter specifies the database user name.

The -W parameter specifies the password of the database user

The -p parameter specifies the port of the database CN.

Download gsql: Visit the https://console.huaweicloud.com/dws to log in to the
GaussDB (for DWS) administration console; in the left navigation bar, click the
"Connection Management" button; in the "gsql Command Line Client" drop-down
box, select the corresponding version of GaussDB (DWS) client; click the "Download" button to download the gsql matching the existing cluster version.

Configure the server: Log in to the ECS (cloud server) using PuTTY. In the
PuTTY login page, Host Name is the ECS public IP address, Port is 22, Connection
type is SSH. Click the "Open" button and click the "YES" button in the pop-up box,
where login as is root, and password is the root user password (the password is not
explicitly displayed, so make sure it is entered correctly and press Enter). Execute
the command cd <client path> (please replace <client path> with the actual client
path).   The   execution   command   punzip   dws_client_1.5.x_redhat_x64.zip
(dws_client_redhat_ x64.tar.gz is the client toolkit name corresponding to "RedHat
x64", which should be replaced with the actual downloaded package name). Execute
the command source gsql_env.sh; if the command line information shown in
Fig. 6.47 is prompted, it means that the client has been successfully configured.

Connect to database: Use gsql client to connect to the database in GaussDB
(DWS) cluster, where the execution statement format is gsql -d <database name> -h
<cluster address> -U <database user> -p <database port> -r. The database name is
the name of the database to be connected. When connecting to the cluster for the first
time using a client, please specify the default database of the cluster as "postgres". If
you connect via public address, please specify the cluster address as the public
access address or public access domain name; if you connect via intranet address,
please specify the cluster address as the intranet access address or intranet access

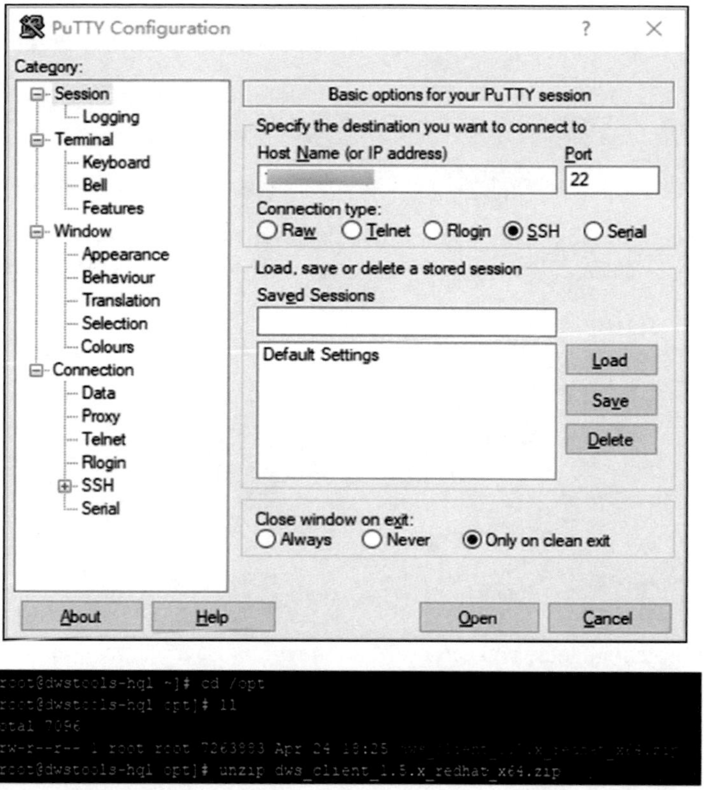

Fig. 6.47 Configure the server

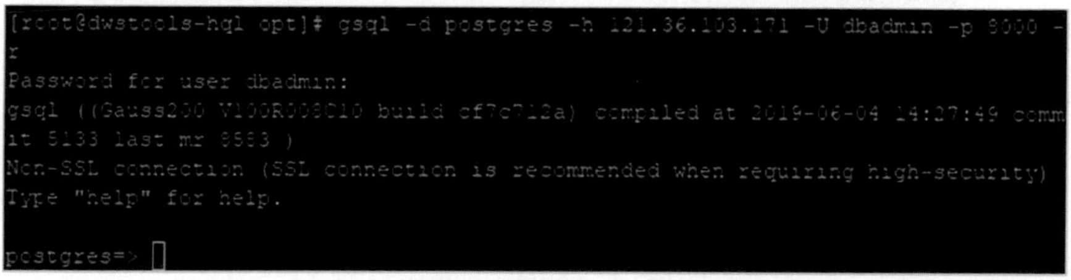

Fig. 6.48 Connect to the database

domain name. Database user is the user name of the cluster database. When you connect to the cluster for the first time using the client, please specify the default administrator user set when creating the cluster, such as "dbadmin". The database port is the "database port" set when creating the cluster, as shown in Fig. 6.48.

Usage: gsql can directly send query statements to the database for execution, and return the execution results.

```
postgres=# SELECT * FROM dual;
 dummy
 -------
 X
 (1 row)
```

The gsql tool also provides some more useful meta-commands for quick interaction with the database. For example, to quickly view the object definition, the code is as follows.

```
postgres=# \d dual
  View "pg_catalog.dual"
 Column | Type | Modifiers
 -------+------+----------
 dummy | text |
 Column:字段名;
 Type:字段类型;
 Modifiers:约束信息;
```

For more commands, you can use \? to view the usage instructions.

6.3.3   Data Studio

Data Studio is a graphical user interface (GUI) tool that can be used to connect to GaussDB databases, execute SQL statements, manage stored procedures, and manage database objects. Data Studio currently supports most of the basic features of GaussDB, providing database developers with a user-friendly graphical interface that simplifies database development and application development tasks, and can significantly improve the efficiency of building programs.

Let's download, install and run Data Studio.

(1) Download and install Data Studio under Windows.

Download: Login to Huawei support website, go to "Technical Support > Cloud Computing > FusionInsight >FusionInsight Tool" page, and select the corresponding version of Data Studio to download.

Installation: After downloading, unzip the Data Studio installation package.

(2) Set the Data Studio profile (optional).

You can modify the configuration file "Data Studio.ini" to personalize the Data Studio operating parameters. The modified parameters will take effect after restarting the Data Studio.

The Data Studio user's manual teaches how to use each parameter.

Fig. 6.49 Connect to GaussDB (for MySQL) database using Data Studio

(3) Run Data Studio.

Double-click the "Data Studio.exe" file to run it (Note: Java 1.8.0_141 or higher is required).

When using Data Studio to connect to GaussDB (for MySQL) database, select the type of database to connect to. Enter a custom name, the IP address of the database, the port of the database, the user name, and the password, as shown in Fig. 6.49.

The connection to GaussDB (DWS) is similar, but you must select the database type as GaussDB (DWS).

The main interface of Data Studio is divided into five sections, as shown in Fig. 6.50.

Area 1 is the top menu bar, Area 2 is the object browser, Area 3 is the editing window for SQL, Area 4 is the query window for SQL statement execution results, and Area 5 is the syntax assistant area for SQL.

The object browser takes database connection as the root node and uses a tree-like hierarchy to display database objects; it provides entrances to various object management operations in the form of right-click menus, such as creating database, disconnecting, creating objects, editing table data, viewing object property information, executing stored procedures, etc.

The SQL editing window provides a window for users to edit, format and execute various SQL statements. After executing SQL statements, users can query the results returned by the statements in the query window, and also sort, filter, copy, and export the results. The syntax assistant automatically associates and provides complementary suggestions based on user input during SQL edition.

The query window is used to display the results returned by the query statement, and users can sort, dynamically filter, copy, export, and edit the results.

The SQL syntax assistant dynamically matches and displays the corresponding SQL statements based on the user input in the SQL edition window.

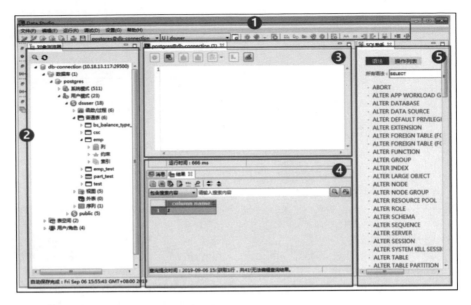

Fig. 6.50 The main interface of Data Studio

Stored procedure management includes viewing, modifying and compiling stored procedure code, executing or debugging stored procedures, and providing templates for creating stored procedures for GaussDB syntax.

Preferences configuration allows users to personalize some of the features of the data source according to their own habits, such as the time interval for automatic saving, the number of records loaded per query result, SQL statement highlighting rules, custom shortcuts, etc.

6.3.4 MySQL Workbench

MySQL Workbench is a GUI tool for designing and creating new database icons, building database documentation, and performing complex MySQL migrations. As a next-generation tool for visual database design and management, it is available in both open source and commercial versions. This software supports Windows and Linux operating systems. MySQL Workbench provides database developers with a user-friendly graphical interface that simplifies database development and application development tasks, and can significantly improve the efficiency of building programs.

It comes with the MySQL Workbench client for Windows-based platforms.

MySQL Workbench download: Log in to the MySQL official website and select MySQL MySQL Workbench from the DOWNLOADS option at the bottom of the page; unzip the downloaded client installation package (32-bit or 64-bit) to the path

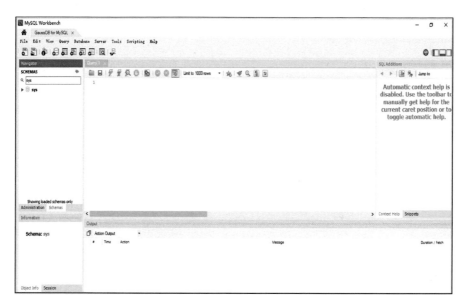

Fig. 6.51   The main interface of MySQL Workbench

you need to install (e.g. D:\MySQL Workbench); open the installation directory and double-click MySQL Workbench.exe (or click the right mouse button and run as administrator).

Connection to the database using MySQL Workbench: Enter the connection information in MySQL Workbench.

The main interface of MySQL Workbench includes: navigation bar, SQL edition window, query result window, and basic database information, as shown in Fig. 6.51.

The basic functions of MySQL Workbench mainly comes in the following aspects. Navigation bar: Shows the management functions of the database, such as status check, connection management, user management, data import and export; provides the entrance of various object management operations, such as starting and stopping instances, querying logs, viewing operation files; shows the performance of the database, where reports can be set or generated. SQL edition window: Edits, formats and executes various SQL statements; in the process of editing SQL statements, grammar assistant will automatically associate according to user input and provide suggestions for completion. Query result window: Displays the results returned by the query statements, where users can sort, dynamically filter, copy, export, and edit the results. Database basic situation: Shows the existing database and the basic situation of objects at all levels under the database. Database backup: According to customer's demand, provides enterprise-level online backup and backup recovery functions. Audit check: The search field provides narrow-displayed operation events, including exhibition activity acquisition of inclusion type and display events of query type, and all activities are displayed by default. Custom filters are also available.

6.4 Summary

This chapter introduces GaussDB database related tools, including JDBC, ODBC, gsql. The drivers in GaussDB database include JDBC, ODBC, etc. GaussDB database provides some related connection tools, including zsql, gsql, Data Studio.

6.5 Exercises

1. [Multiple Choice] Which of the following functions can be implemented by the JDBC common interface? ( )

   A. Executes SQL statements
   B. Executes stored procedures
   C. Unloads database
   D. Deletes database

2. [Single Choice] Through ODBC interaction, while avoiding the direct operation of the database system by the application program, what characteristics of the application program are enhanced? ( )

   A. Portability, compatibility and maintainability
   B. Portability, compatibility and scalability
   C. Maintainability, scalability, and portability
   D. Compatibility, maintainability and scalability

3. [Multiple Choice] The key features of DDM include ( ).

   A. Smooth scalability
   B. Read/write separation
   C. Intelligent management
   D. Data sharding

4. [True or False] When DDM database middleware is purchased, the virtual private cloud can be different from the database virtual private cloud it uses. ( )

   A. True
   B. False

5. [Single Choice] Which of the following is not a capability of DRS? ( )

   A. Online migration
   B. Data synchronization

    C. Multi-live disaster recovery

    D. Smooth scalability

6. [True or False] The migration function provided by DRS does not support the service interruption function. ( )

    A. True

    B. False

7. [Multiple Choice] The gsql connection command contains the ( ) parameters.

    A. Database name

    B. Cluster address

    C. Database user

    D. Database port

8. [True or False] gsql is an interactive database connection tool provided by GaussDB (DWS) that runs at the command line. ( )

    A. True

    B. False

9. [Multiple Choice] The basic features of MySQL Workbench include ( ).

    A. Navigation bar

    B. Database situation display

    C. Data backup

    D. Audit check

10. [Multiple Choice] Which of the following functions does Data Studio support? ( )

    A. Browses database objects

    B. Creates and manages database objects

    C. Manages stored procedures

    D. Edits SQL statements

11. [Short Answer Question] Briefly describe the process of developing applications with ODBC.

12. [Short Answer Question] Briefly describe the process of DDM data sharding.

13. [Short Answer Question] Briefly describe the process of DRS data migration.

14. [Short Answer Question] Briefly describe the process of connecting to a database using gsql and explain what are the important parameters involved.

Chapter 7
Database Design Fundamentals

Database design refers to constructing a suitable database schema for specific application objects according to the characteristics of database system, establishing database and corresponding applications, so that the whole system can effectively collect, store, process and manage data to meet the usage requirements of various users.

This chapter introduces the relevant concepts, overall objectives and problems to be solved in database design, and details the specific work in stages including requirement analysis, conceptual design, logical design and physical design according to the New Orleans design methodology. Finally, the specific means of implementation of database design are introduced with relevant cases.

Through this chapter, the reader is able to describe the characteristics and uses of the data models, enumerate the types of data models, describe the criteria of the third normal form (NF) data model, describe the common concepts in the logical model, distinguish the corresponding concepts in the logical and physical models, and enumerate the common means of anti-NF in the physical design process.

7.1 Database Design Overview

Database design refers to the construction of an optimized database logical model and physical structure for a given application environment, and the establishment of the database and its application system accordingly, so that it can effectively store and manage data to meet the application needs of various users. It is worth noting that there is no "optimal" standard for database design, and different designs and optimizations need to be made for different applications. The OLTP and OLAP scenarios are very different, and there are corresponding differences in the methods and optimization tools for database design.

Readers need to first understand what the most common methods and techniques are, and then use them in conjunction with different practical scenarios.

© The Author(s) 2023
Huawei Technologies Co., Ltd., *Database Principles and Technologies – Based on Huawei GaussDB*, https://doi.org/10.1007/978-981-19-3032-4_7

7.1.1 Difficulties of Database Design

In practical applications, database design will encounter many difficulties, mainly the following.

(1) The lack of service knowledge and industry knowledge of technical staff familiar with the database.

Database design needs to be flexibly adjusted for different applications, which requires the relevant personnel to have a good understanding of the application usage scenario and service background, while the technical personnel familiar with the database often lack service knowledge and industry knowledge.

(2) People who are familiar with service knowledge often lack understanding of database products.

Relatively speaking, people familiar with service knowledge and service process often lack understanding of database products and are not familiar with database design process. Therefore, in the process of data model design, the two party need to fully communicate with each other in order to do a good job of database design.

(3) There is no way to clarify the scope of service requirements of the database system for the application service in the initial stage.

In the initial stage of the project, the application service is not particularly clear, and the users' requirements are not established. And the database system is gradually improved along with the users' requirements, which is also a difficult point in database design.

(4) User requirements are constantly adjusted and modified during the design process, and even after the database model is landed, new requirements will appear, which will have an impact on the existing database structure.

Because of the uncertainty of the requirements, database adjustment is frequent, these will cause some trouble to the database design, so the database design is a spiral forward work, which needs to be constantly adjusted, improved and optimized to better meet the needs of the application.

7.1.2 Goal of Database Design

Database design is the technology of establishing database and its application system, which is the core technology in the development and construction of information system. The goal of database design is to provide information infrastructure and efficient operation environment for users and various application systems. Efficient operation environment means to achieve high efficiency in database data access, database storage space utilization, and database system operation and management. The goal of database design must set the time range and target boundary range, and the design goal without restrictive conditions will fail because of the too large range. Reasonable development of database system goals is a very difficult thing. The goals that are too large or too high will result in unachievable goals, and targets that are too small will be unacceptable to the customer. Therefore, the goals should be planned reasonably in stages and levels so as to form sustainable solutions for the construction process, ultimately meeting the needs of the users and achieving the goals.

7.1.3   Methods of Database Design

In October 1978, database experts from more than 30 countries have dedicated their time to discussing database design methods in New Orleans, USA. They applied the ideas and methods of software engineering to propose a database design specification, which is the famous New Orleans design methodology, currently recognized as a more complete and authoritative design method for database specification. The New Orleans design methodology divides the database design into four phases, as shown in Fig. 7.1.

These four phases are requirement analysis, conceptual design, logical design, and physical design. The requirement analysis phase mainly analyzes user requirements and produces requirement statements; the conceptual design phase mainly analyzes and defines information and produces conceptual models; the logical design phase mainly designs based on entity connections and produces logical models; and the physical design phase mainly designs physical structures based on physical characteristics of database products and produces physical models.

In addition to the New Orleans design methodology, there are also database design methods based on E-R diagrams, and design methods based on the 3NF. They are all specific techniques and methods used in different phases of database design, which will be described in detail in later chapters.

7.2   Requirements Analysis

7.2.1   Significance of Requirement Analysis

In real life, the whole building without a good foundation is crooked. Experience has proven that poor requirement analysis can directly lead to incorrect design. If many

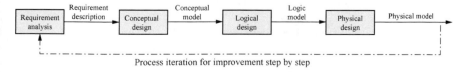

Process iteration for improvement step by step

Fig. 7.1 The four phases in the New Orleans design methodology

problems are not discovered until the system testing stage and then go back to correct them, it will be costly, so the requirement analysis stage must be given high priority.

The requirement analysis phase mainly collects information and analyzes and organizes it to provide sufficient information for the subsequent phases. This stage is the most difficult and time-consuming stage, but is also the basis of the whole database design. If the requirement analysis is not done well, the whole database design may be reworked.

The following points should be done in the requirement analysis phase.

(1) Understand the operation of the existing system, such as the service carried by the existing system, the service process and the deficiencies.
(2) Determine the functional requirements of the new system, that is, to understand the end-user's ideas, functional requirements and the desired results.
(3) Collect the basic data and related service processes that can achieve the objectives, so as to prepare for a better understanding of service processes and user requirements.

7.2.2   Tasks of the Requirement Analysis Stage

The main task of the requirement analysis phase is first to investigate user service behaviors and processes, then to conduct system research, collect and analyze requirements, determine the scope of system development, and finally prepare a requirement analysis report.

The phase of investigation of user service behaviors and processes requires understanding of user expectations and goals for the new system and the main problems of the existing system. In the stage of system research, collecting and analyzing requirements, determine the scope of system development, with the main tasks being divided into the following three parts.

(1) Information research. It is necessary to determine all the information to be used in the designed database system and to clarify the sources, methods, data formats and contents of the information. The main goal of the requirement analysis phase is to clarify what data is to be stored in the designed database, what data needs to be processed, and what data needs to be used for the next system.
(2) Processing requirements. Translate the user's service functional requirements into a requirement statement that defines the functional points of the database system to be designed. That is, convert the requirements described by users in service language into design requirements that can be understood by computer systems or developers; it is necessary to describe the operational functions of data processing, the sequence of operations, the frequency and occasion of execution of operations, and the connection between operations and data, as well as to specify the response time and processing methods required by users. These contents form the necessary part of the user requirement specification.

(3) Understand and record user requirements in terms of security and integrity. In the stage of writing requirement analysis report, it needs to go through the process of system research, collection and processing, and generally the output product in this stage is the requirement analysis report, including user requirement specification and data dictionary. The data dictionary here is a summary document of the data items and data of the existing services, not the data dictionary inside the database product.

7.2.3   Methods of Requirement Analysis

The focus of requirement analysis is to sort out the "information flow" and "service flow" of users. The "service flow" refers to the current status of the service, including service policies, organization, service processes, etc. The "information flow" refers to the data flow, including the source, flow and focus of data, the process and frequency of data generation and modification, and the relation between data and service processing. External requirements should be clarified during the requirement analysis phase, including but not limited to data confidentiality requirements, query response time requirements, output report requirements, etc.

According to the actual situation and the possible support from users, the requirement investigation can be done by a combination of means, for example, viewing the design documents and reports of existing systems, talking with service personnel, and questionnaire surveys. If conditions permit, sample data from existing service systems should also be collected as part of the design process to verify some service rules and understand the quality of data.

| During the requirement analysis process, do not make assumptions or guesses about the user's ideas. Always check with the user for assumptions or unclear areas. |

7.2.4   Data Dictionary

The data dictionary is the result obtained after the introduction of requirement analysis, data collection and data analysis. Unlike the data dictionary in the database, the data dictionary here mainly refers to the description of the data, not the data itself, and includes the following contents.

(1) Data items: They mainly includes data item name, meaning, data type, length, value range, unit and logical relation with other data items, which are the basis of model optimization in logic design stage.

(2) Data structure: Data structure reflects the combination relation between data items, and a data structure can be composed of several data items and data structures.
(3) Data flow: The data dictionary is required to represent the data flow, that is, the transmission path of data in the system, including data source, flow direction, average flow, peak flow, etc.
(4) Data storage: This includes data access frequency, retention time duration, and data access methods.
(5) Processing process: This includes the function of the data processing process and processing requirements. Function refers to what the processing process is used to do, and the requirements include how many transactions are processed per unit of time, how much data volume involved, time response requirements, etc.

There is no fixed document specification for the format of data dictionary, in practice, it can refer to the above content items and can be reflected through different descriptive documents or in the model file. So the data dictionary is a concept at the abstract level, a collection of documents. And in the requirement analysis phase, the most important output is the user requirement specification, where the data dictionary often exists as an annex or appendix to provide a reference for the model designers in their subsequent work.

7.3   Conceptual Design

7.3.1   Conceptual Design and Conceptual Model

The task of the conceptual design phase is to analyze the requirements proposed by the users, synthesize, summarize and abstract the user requirements, and form a conceptual-level abstract model independent of the concrete DBMS, i.e., the conceptual data model (hereinafter referred to as the conceptual model). The conceptual model is a high level abstract model, independent of any specific database product, not be bound by any database product characteristics. At this stage, the conceptual model is independent of the physical attributes of any particular database product.
    The conceptual model has developed the following four main features.

(1) It can truly and fully reflect the real world, including the connection between things and things, as a real model of the real world.
(2) It is easy to understand, enabling discussion with users who are not familiar with the database.
(3) It is easy to change, when the application environment and application requirements change, the conceptual model can be modified and expanded.
(4) It is easy to convert to a relational data model.

The latter two are the basic conditions for the smooth progress of the next stage of work.

7.3.2   E-R Approach

The conceptual model is a conceptual-level abstract model that is independent of the concrete database management system, generated by analyzing the requirements proposed by users and synthesizing, summarizing and abstracting the user requirements. The model can directly organize the real world according to the concrete data model, but many factors must be considered at the same time, and the design work is complicated with unsatisfactory effect, so an approach is needed to describe the information structure of the real world.

In 1976 E-R (Entity-Relation) approach was proposed. This approach quickly became one of the commonly used methods in conceptual models because of its simplicity and practicality, and is now a common approach to describing information structures. The tool used in the E-R approach is called E-R diagram, which mainly consists of three elements - entity, attribute and linkage, which is widely used in the conceptual design stage. The database concept represented by E-R diagram is very intuitive and easy to understand by users.

An entity is a collection of real-world objects that have common attributes and can be distinguished from each other. For example, teachers, students, and courses are all entities, as shown in Fig. 7.2. In an E-R diagram, specific entities are generally represented by rectangular boxes. Each specific record value in an entity, such as each specific student in the student entity, is called an instance of the entity.

Attributes are data items that describe the nature or characteristics of an entity, and all instances belonging to the same entity have the same attributes. For example, the student number, name and gender shown in Fig. 7.3 are all attributes. In the conceptual model, attributes are generally represented by rectangular boxes with rounded corners.

| | In practice, the conceptual model can also be designed not to the attribute level in detail, but to the entity level. If the conceptual model will increase the workload is all the attributes are planned out in detail. The E-R diagram of the conceptual model should delineate the linkages between entities clearly and express them clearly in the practical application project. So it is sufficient that the general conceptual model reaches the level that reflects the linkages between entities. |

Fig. 7.2 Entities

Fig. 7.3 Attributes

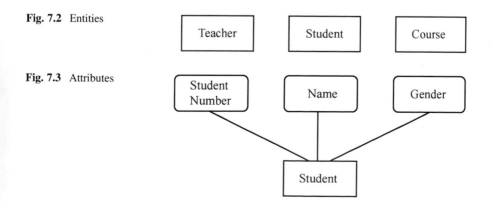

The linkages within and between entities are usually represented by diamond-shaped boxes. In most cases, the data model is concerned with the linkages between entities. The linkages between entities are usually divided into three categories.

(1) One-to-one linkage (1:1): Each instance in entity A has at most one instance linked to it in entity B, and vice versa. For example, a class has a Class Advisor, this linkage is recorded in the form of 1:1.
(2) One-to-many linkage (1:n): Each instance in entity A has n instances linked to it in entity B, while each instance in entity B has at most 1 instance linked to it in entity A, which is recorded as 1:n. For example, there are n students in a class.
(3) Many-to-many linkage (m:n): Each instance in entity A has n instances linked to it in entity B, while each instance in entity B has m instance linked to it in entity A, which is recorded as m:n. Take for example the linkage between students and elective courses. A student can take more than one course, and a course can be taken by more than one student.

Simply put, conceptual design is the conversion of realistic conceptual abstractions and linkages into the form of an E-R diagram, as shown in Fig. 7.4.

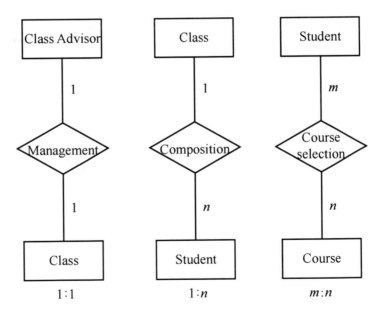

Fig. 7.4 Linkages

7.4   Logical Design

7.4.1   *Logical Design and Logical Models*

Logical design is the process of converting a conceptual model into a concrete data model. According to the basic E-R diagram established in the conceptual design phase, the selected target data model (hierarchical, mesh, relational, or object-oriented) is converted into the corresponding logical-layer target data model, and what is obtained is the logical data model (hereinafter referred to as logical model). For relational databases, this conversion has to conform to the principles of the relational data model.

The most important work in the logical design phase is to determine the attributes and primary keys of the logical model. The primary key identifies the unique primary keyword in the table, also known as a code. A primary key can consist of a single field or multiple fields. The more common way of logical design work is to use E-R design tool and IDEF1X method for logical model building. Commonly used E-R diagram representations include IDEF1X, Crow's Foot for IE models, Unified Modeling Language (UML) class diagrams, etc.

7.4.2   *IDEF1X Method*

The logical model of this book adopts the IDEF1X (Integration DEFinition for Information Modeling) method. IDEF, which stands for Integration DEFinition method, was established in the US Air Force ICAM (Integrated Computer Aided Manufacturing) project, and three methods were initially developed - functional modeling (IDEF0), information modeling (IDEF1), and dynamic modeling (IDEF2). Later, as information systems were developed one after another, IDEF cluster methods were introduced, such as data modeling method (IDEF1X), process description acquisition method (IDEF3), object-oriented design method (IDEF4), OO design method using C++ (IDEF4C++), entity description acquisition method (IDEF5), design theory acquisition method (IDEF6), and Human-system interaction design method (IDEF8), service constraint discovery method (IDEF9), network design method (IDEF14), etc. IDEF1X is an extended version of IDEF1 in the IDEF family of methods, which adds some rules to the E-R method to make the semantics richer.

The IDEF1X method has several features when used for logic modeling.

(1) It supports the semantic structure necessary for the development of conceptual and logical models, and has good scalability.
(2) It has concise and consistent structure in semantic concept representation.
(3) It is easy to understand, enabling service personnel, IT technicians, database administrators and designers to communicate based on the same language.

(4) It can be generated automatically. Commercial modeling software supports the IDEF1X model design methodology and can be quickly converted to and from models at all levels.

7.4.3   Entities and Attributes in the Logic Model

According to the characteristics of entities, they can be divided into two categories.

(1) Independent entity, which is usually represented by a rectangular box with right-angle corners. An independent entity is an entity that exists independently that does not depend on other entities.
(2) Dependent entity, which is usually represented by a rectangular box with round corners. Dependent entities must depend on other entities, and the primary key in a dependent entity must be part or all of the primary key of an independent entity.

The primary key of the independent entity will appear in and become part of the primary key of the dependent entity, as shown in Fig. 7.5, where the chapter entity depends on the book entity. For example, many books have Chap. 2. If there is no book as one of the ID primary keys to distinguish the Chap. 2 of different books, only one record of Chap. 2 will appear in the chapter entity. But in fact, the title, page number and word count of Chap. 2 of different books are different, so the chapter entity depends on the book entity in order to function.

Attributes are the characteristics of the entity, containing the following types to be noted.

(1) Primary key. The primary key is an attribute or group of attributes that identifies the uniqueness of an entity instance. For example, the name of a student entity cannot be used as a primary key because there may be cases of duplication of

Fig. 7.5 Entity categories

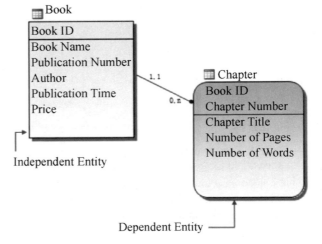

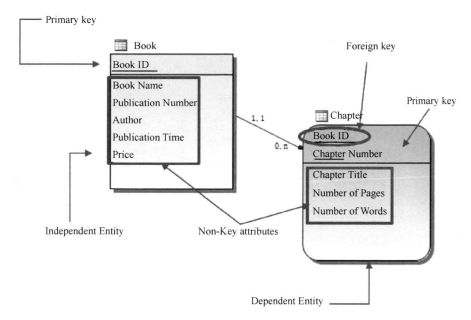

Fig. 7.6 Attributes in entities

name. The school number or ID number can be used as an attribute that uniquely
identifies the student, i.e., it can be used as a primary key.

(2) Optional key. It can identify other attributes or groups of attributes of the entity.

(3) Foreign key. Two entities are linked, and the foreign key of one entity is the
primary key of the other entity. You can also call the primary key entity the
parent entity and the entity with the foreign key the child entity.

(4) Non-key attribute. It is an attributes other than primary key and foreign key
attributes inside an entity.

(5) Derived attribute. It is a field that can be counted or derived from other fields.

The primary key of the book entity shown in Fig. 7.6 is the book ID, while other
attributes are non-key attributes. The primary key of the chapter is the book ID plus
the chapter number, while other attributes are non-key attributes. The book ID in the
chapter entity is a foreign key.

How to distinguish the relation between primary key, foreign key and index? A
primary key uniquely identifies an instance, have no duplicate values, which is a
non-null attribute, and should not be updated. Its role is to determine the uniqueness
of a record and ensure data integrity, so an entity can have only one primary key.

A foreign key is generally the primary key of another entity, which can be
duplicated or null for this entity, and its role is to establish data reference consistency
with the relation between two entities. So an entity can have more than one foreign
key. For example, attribute A is a foreign key in table X, and it is duplicable in table

Table 7.1 Relation between primary key, foreign key and index

	Primary key	Foreign key	Unique index	Non-unique index
Characteristic	Uniquely identifies an instance, no duplicate value, non-null, and should not be updated	Primary key of another entity, can be duplicate and null	An object built on a table, no duplicate value, can have a null value	An object built on a table, can be null and can have duplicate values
Role	Determines the uniqueness of records and ensures data integrity	Establishes data reference consistency and relation between two entities	Improves query efficiency	Improves query efficiency
Quantity	An entity can have only one primary key	An entity can have multiple foreign keys	A table can have multiple unique indexes	A table can have multiple non-unique indexes

X. Because it is a foreign key, it must be a primary key in another table. Suppose *A* is in table *Y* (if any) as a primary key, then attribute *A* is not allowed to be duplicated.

Indexes are physical objects of the database and can be divided into unique indexes and non-unique indexes by uniqueness. A unique index is an object built on a table with no duplicate values and can have a null value. A non-unique index is an object built on a table, which can be null and can have duplicate values. The purpose of indexes is to improve query efficiency and thus speed up queries. The relation between primary key, foreign key and index are shown in Table 7.1.

注意

Primary keys and foreign keys are logical concepts in the logical model, while indexes are physical objects. Many databases can create primary keys when building a table, at which time the attributes of the primary keys are unique non-null indexes.

After determining the entities and important attributes, you also need to understand the relations between the entities. Relations are used to describe how entities are related to each other. For example, if a book "includes" several chapters, "includes" is the relation between these two entities. The relation is directional. The book "includes" the chapter rather than the chapter "includes" the book, so the relation between the chapter and the book is "belonging to".

Cardinality is a service rule that reflects the relation between two or more entities, and the relation cardinality is used to express the concept of "linkage" in the E-R method.

Figure 7.7 shows the illustration of cardinality in IDEF1X. Understanding the meanings of the labels helps to quickly clarify the relation between entities as you see the model structure. From left to right, the first symbol represents a one-to-many relation, where the cardinality for many party is 0, 1, or *n*. The P symbol represents a one-to-many relation, where the cardinality for many party is 1 or *n*. The difference

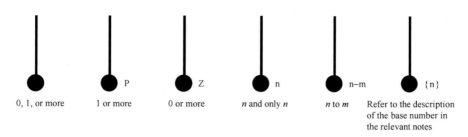

| | P | Z | n | n–m | {n} |
| 0, 1, or more | 1 or more | 0 or more | *n* and only *n* | *n* to *m* | Refer to the description of the base number in the relevant notes |

Fig. 7.7 Cardinality symbols in IDEF1X

between these two relations lies in the presence or absence of 0. If there is 0, it is an optional relation, indicating that the relation may exist, which is expressed as "may" in English, and the opposite is a mandatory relation, indicating that the relation must exist, which is expressed as "must" in English. The Z symbol indicates that the cardinality of the many party is 0 or n. "n" indicates that there are and only n relations, for example, a rectangle has and only has four right angles, then the rectangle and the right angle are in $1 \rightarrow 4$ relations. The n-m symbol represents a range interval relation. For example, the relation between months and days, how many days there are in a month, and the relation between months and days is $1 \rightarrow (28–31)$ as the size of the month and leap years vary. The cardinality relation represented by the $\{n\}$ symbol cannot be illustrated by a simple number, and an annotation is needed to show the value range of this n. Such annotated descriptions are reflected in practical projects as some service rules, for example, the relation between a month and a securities trading day. How many valid securities trading days are contained in a month depends on the dates on which the stock exchange specifies that listing transactions can take place during the month, which varies annually with policy changes and needs to be stated separately.

In summary, the illustration of the cardinality symbols also reflects the important point that the cardinalities reflect different relations, and such relations are likely to reflect important service rules or constraints.

注意

0, n is the expression form of may, which is an optional requirement.
1, n is the expression form of must, which is a mandatory requirement.
In practice, a cardinality of 0 may occur, indicating that a null value (NULL) may occur when two tables are associated.

The significance of cardinality is that it reflects the relation, as shown in Fig. 7.8. First of all, both the left and right sides are "including" relations, and the left side of the relation is 1:1, which means that a chapter must belong to a book, that is, it belongs to and only belongs to. For the example on the left, the values 0 to n are possible expressions for the optional requirement that a book may contain one or more chapters. And the cardinality equal to 0 expression means that a book is not divided into chapters. In practice, when the cardinality is equal to 0, null values may appear when the two tables are associated with each other. The example on the right

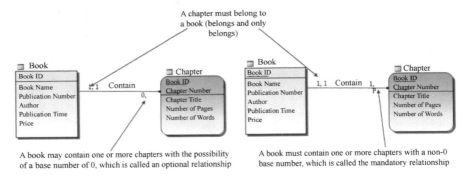

Fig. 7.8   Different cardinalities reflect different relations

takes the values 1 to *n*, which is a certain form of expression for the mandatory requirement that the cardinality is not 0 means that a book must contain one or more chapters.

Identifying relation occurs between independent and dependent entities, where the instance unique identification of a child entity is associated with the parent entity and the primary key attribute of the parent entity becomes one of the primary key attributes of the child entity. The primary key book ID of the parent entity book shown in Fig. 7.6 becomes the primary key attribute component of the chapter.

Non-identifying relation means that the child entity does not need the relation with the parent entity to determine the uniqueness of the instance. At this point the two entities are independent entities with no dependencies. In Fig. 7.6, if the chapter entity does not depend on the book entity and becomes independent, then each chapter number can only have one record, and the same chapters of different books will cover each other, and there is a problem with this design. In this case, the solution is to modify the non-identifying relation into an identifying relation. It can be summarized as follows: according to whether the parent entity and child entity have a foreign key relation, if there is a foreign key, it is a child entity; if there is a primary key, it is the parent entity. The location of the foreign key determines whether the parent entity and the child entity are of identifying or non-identifying relation. If the foreign key appears in the primary key of the child entity, it is an identifying relation; if the foreign key appears in the non-key attribute of the child entity, it is a non-identifying relation.

Recursive relation means that the parent entity and the child entity are the same entity, forming a recursive or nested relation, and the primary key of the entity also becomes its own foreign key. A recursive relation occurs when the entities themselves form a hierarchical relation. In practical applications, such entities of recursive relation are very common. For example, The organization structure includes superior departments and subordinate departments. One department may have one or more subordinate departments, the lowest department has no subordinate department, and the top department has no superior department, as shown in Fig. 7.9.

Fig. 7.9 Recursive relation

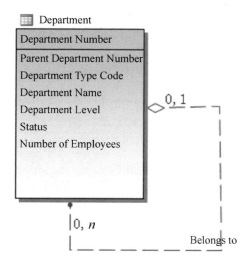

Subtype relation is the relation between a subclass entity and the parent entity to which it belongs. There are two types of subtype relation. One is complete subtype relation, also called complete classification, where each instance of the parent entity to which it belongs can be associated with an instance of the entity in the subtype group, and all instances can be found in the classification case, with no exception. The other is incomplete subtype, also called incomplete classification, where each instance of the parent entity is not necessarily associated with an entity instance in the subclass group, and only some instances can be classified in the subclass, and some instances cannot be classified or do not need to care about the classification. Remember that in practice you must not divide a pocket of other subclasses in order to pursue complete classification, which will bring uncertainty to future service development.

The logic model is summarized as follows.

(1) Entity is the metadata that describes the service.
(2) The primary key is an attribute or group of attributes that identifies the unique-ness of an entity instance.
(3) Relations exist between entities only if there are foreign keys, and no relation can be established without foreign keys.
(4) The cardinalities of the relations reflect the service rules between the relations.

The logic model is as follows.

- A customer can have only one type of savings account.
- A customer can have more than one type of savings account.
- An order can correspond to only one shipping order.
- A product includes multiple parts.

7.4.4   NF Theory

According to the specific service requirements, database design needs to make clear how to construct a database design pattern that meets the requirements, and how many entities need to be generated, which attributes these entities are composed of, and what is the relation between entities. To be precise, these are the questions that need to be addressed in the logical design stage of relational database. The relational model is based on strict mathematical theory, so designing the relational model based on the normalization theory of relational database can construct a reasonable relational model. In the database logic design phase, the process of placing attributes in the correct entity is called normalization. Different NFs satisfy different levels of requirements.

Between 1971 and 1972, Dr. E.F. Codd systematically proposed the concept of 1NF to 3NF, which fully discussed the model normalization issues. Later, others deepened and proposed higher-level NF standards, but for relational databases, it is sufficient to achieve the 3NF in practical applications.

The relational data model designed by following the normalization theory has the following implications.

1. It can avoid the generation of redundant data.
2. The risk of data inconsistency can be reduced.
3. The model has good scalability.
4. It can be flexibly adjusted to reflect changing service rules.

In contrast to normalization in the process of logical model checking, normalization means denormalization when the physical model is built, i.e., violating some normalization rules to improve the performance when the database is applied by enhancing the physical rule attributes.

When determining entity attributes, the question often faced is: which attributes belong to the corresponding entities? This is the question to be addressed by the NF theory. For example, there will be a lot of business dealings between banks and individuals, and the same person may be engaged in business such as saving, spending on credit cards, buying financial products for investment and financial management, and buying cars and houses with loans. For banks, different services are carried out by different departments and service systems. For example, if you spend with credit cards, you have a credit card (credit card number) and a customer number in the credit card system; if you handle financial management, you open a financial account; if you make a deposit, you open a savings account. The individual a bank faces is a person. When building a model, how do you group individuals into a single customer entity? Do you create three entities or use one entity when counting a customer's assets? For customers who do not have a loan relation with the bank, if there is a loan relation in the future, what should the current model consider in advance for this change? These are all questions that need to be addressed in the logical design, and the theoretical basis for this is the NF model.

Fig. 7.10 Relations between NFs

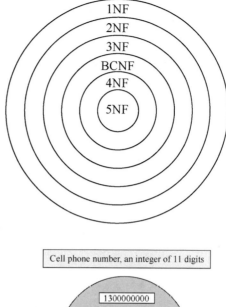

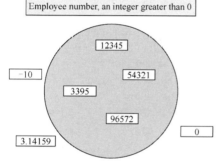

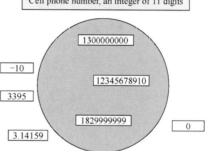

Fig. 7.11 Domain

The one that satisfies the minimum requirements is called the first NF (1NF), the one that further satisfies the requirements based on the 1NF is the second NF (2NF), and so on. A low-level NF relation pattern can be transformed into a collection of several higher-level NF relation patterns by schema decomposition. This process is called normalization, as shown in Fig. 7.10.

Domain is the set of legal values of an attribute, which defines the valid range of values of the attribute. The values inside the domain are legal data. The domain reflects the relevant rules.

For example, the domain of the employee ID shown in Fig. 7.11 is an integer greater than 0, so 0 and -10 are the data outside the domain. For example, if the cell phone numbers are 11-bit length integers, 12345678910 is legal data; however, if we consider the actual situation, it cannot be legal data because different operators have different number segments.

If and only if each attribute contains only atomic values (which cannot be sub-splittable), a relation (table or entity) conforms to the 1NF, and the value of each attribute can only contain one value in the value range (not a subset).

Table 7.2 Customer information table (1)

Customer ID (PK)	Name	Age	Phone number
123	XXX	30	555-666-1234, 333-888-5678
456	YYY	40	555-777-8080 ext. 43, 155-0099-9900
789	ZZZ	50	777-808-9234

Table 7.3 Customer information table (2)

Customer ID (PK)	Name	Age	Phone number 1	Phone number 2
123	XXX	30	555-666-1234	333-888-5678
456	YYY	40	555-777-8080 ext. 43	155-0099-9900
789	ZZZ	50	777-808-9234	

The rules satisfying the 1NF contain the following features.

(1) The attribute value is atomic (non-sub-splittable).
(2) The number of attribute value is single and cannot be a subset inside the value domain.
(3) A primary key is required to ensure that there are no duplicate records in the database.
(4) There is no duplicate group problem for the attributes in the entity, because duplicate groups are prone to producing null values somewhere and unstable structure, that is, the service development that exists in the actual application can bring service instability, and duplicate groups can also lead to ambiguity when used.

For example, in the phone number column shown in Table 7.2, there is a big problem with the phone number attribute: the value format is not uniform, and contains non-numeric characters. The bigger problem is that there are two people with more than one phone number, and the two numbers are subsets of the phone number value field, which violates the feature "the number of attribute value is single and cannot be a subset inside the value domain". This kind of table structure is common in many practical scenarios. Take a list of account followers in social applications as an example. For this dynamic data, commas are often used to separate a series of accounts and they are designed as a field.

If the two phone numbers are split into two fields, they are shown in Table 7.3.

It seems to solve the atomicity problem, but the repeating group problem arises. The repeating group problem technically takes values atomically, but conceptually repeats the same attributes. The reason why we want to avoid the repeating group problem is that the following anomalies are introduced by the repeating group.

(1) Some records produce null values. For example, some customers have only one phone number, without the second phone number, which would result in a null value in the Phone Number 2 field.
(2) The structure may be unstable. For example, some people have three phone numbers or even more, so they require to update the table structure frequently to

Table 7.4 Customer information table (3)

Customer ID (PK)	Name	Age	Phone number
123	XXX	30	555-666-1234
123	XXX	30	333-888-5678
456	YYY	40	555-777-8080 ext. 43
456	YYY	40	155-0099-9900
789	ZZZ	50	777-808-9234

adapt to new situations, which will lead to instability of the model structure, that is, business development brings instability impact to the model.

(3) Ambiguity arise when using data. Which number should be placed first? Which number should be put in the second place? What are the rules? Which telephone number shall prevail when obtaining contact information of customers? All of the above questions can lead to semantic confusion and ambiguity in the use of data for service.

To solve the above problems, the solution is to turn the duplicate group into a high table and put the phone number in the same attribute. This is in line with the 1NF, as shown in Table 7.4.

Atomicity means indivisibility .But to which degree should it be split? Many people are prone to misunderstand the concept of atomicity in practical applications. Generally speaking codes with coding rules are actually composite codes, which are divisible in terms of rules. For example, ID numbers and cell phone numbers can both be further split into data of smaller granularity, such as birth year and gender. However, from the field perspective, the field of ID number is legal as long as it conforms to the coding rules, i.e., it is atomic data and does not need further splitting.

The 2NF means that each table must have a primary key, with other data elements corresponding to the primary key one by one. This relation is often referred to as functional dependence, where all other data elements in the table depend on the primary key, or the data element is uniquely identified by the primary key. The 2NF emphasizes full functional dependence, which simply put, all non-primary key fields are dependent on the primary key as a whole, not some of them.

There are two necessary conditions to satisfy the 2NF: firstly, the 1NF should be satisfied; secondly, every non-primary attribute is fully functionally dependent on any of the candidate keys. It can be simply understood that all non-primary key fields depend on the whole primary key, not a part of it. What is shown in Table 7.5 does not satisfy the 2NF because the order date depends only on the order number and has nothing to do with the part number. So the table will have a lot of redundant data as the order number is repeated.

 A simple tip: If an entity has only one primary key field, then basically the entity is satisfying the 2NF.

注意

Table 7.5 Order and part table 1

Order number (PK,FK)	Part number (FK)	Order date	Number of parts required
1000	1234	2010-08-01	200
1000	5678	2010-08-01	100
2000	1234	2010-11-15	50
3000	7890	2010-09-30	300

Table 7.6 Order and part table (2)

Order number (PK, FK)	Part number (FK)	Number of parts required
1000	1234	200
1000	5678	100
2000	1234	50
3000	7890	300

Table 7.7 Order number table

Order number (PK)	Order date
1000	2010-08-01
2000	2010-11-15
3000	2010-09-30

Table 7.8 Order and customer table

Order number (PK)	Order date	Customer ID	Customer name
1000	2010-08-01	1230008	Mr. Wang
2000	2010-11-15	1290004	Mr. Li
3000	2010-09-30	1280003	Ms. Zhao

Modify Table 7.5 to include the order date and the dependent order number as primary keys to form another entity, then both entities now satisfy the 2NF. This is the normalization, where a first-level NF can be converted into a collection of several higher-level NF relational patterns through schema decomposition, as shown in Tables 7.6 and 7.7.

The 3NF is that all non-primary key fields depend on the whole primary key, not on other attributes of the non-primary key. There are two necessary conditions to satisfy the 3NF: firstly, the 2NF should be satisfied; secondly, every non-primary attribute is not transitively dependent on the primary key. That is to say, the whole non-primary key field of the 3NF depends on the whole primary key instead of the non-primary key attribute. The customer name shown in Table 7.8 depends on the non-primary key attribute customer ID, so the 3NF is not satisfied.

The 3NF is mainly for the field redundancy constraint, which cannot have derived fields in the table. If there are redundant fields in the table, when updating data, the update efficiency will be reduced because of the existence of redundant data, which will easily lead to inconsistent data. The solution is to split the table into two tables and form a primary-foreign key relation, as shown in Tables 7.9 and 7.10.

Table 7.9 Order table

Order number (PK)	Order date	Customer ID (FK)
1000	2010-08-01	1230008
2000	2010-11-15	1290004
3000	2010-09-30	1280003

Table 7.10 Customer table

Customer ID (PK)	Customer name
1230008	Mr. Wang
1290004	Mr. Li
1280003	Ms. Zhao

In 1970, Dr. E.F. Codd, an IBM researcher, published a paper that introduced the concept of relational model and laid the theoretical foundation of relational model. After publishing this paper, he defined the concept of the 1NF, 2NF and 3NF in the early 1970s. In practical applications, it is sufficient for a relational model to satisfy the 3NF.

The KEY—1st Normal Form (1NF)
The WHOLE Key—2nd Normal Form (2NF)
AND NOTHING BUT the Key—3rd Normal Form (3NF)—E.F. Codd

Database design now satisfies at most the 3NF. It is generally believed that although higher NFs have better constraint on data relations, they also make database I/O more busy due to the increase of data relation tables, so in real projects, there are basically no cases that meet the 3NF or higher.

In the data warehouse, the application layer often encounters a star-shaped or snowflake-shaped model. The snowflake-shaped model is a model structure commonly used in business intelligence (BI) systems and reporting systems, named because the dimensions of the fact table are similar to snowflakes after expansion, as shown in Fig. 7.12. This model basically meets the requirements of the 3NF, or at least the 2NF in many scenarios.

7.4.5 Logic Design Considerations

When designing a logic model, some principle issues should be noted. The first is the establishment of naming rules. Similar to other language development, it is advisable to establish naming rules and follow them during logical modeling. The main purpose of establishing naming rules is to unify ideas, facilitate communication and achieve standardized development. For example, in the case of unified naming, the amount is amount, which is abbreviated as amt, and its corresponding physical type is DECIMAL(9,2). This field needs to be accurate to two decimal places when calculating. However, if the naming is inconsistent, for example, some people define the customer ID as cid, and some people define it as customer_id, it is easy to

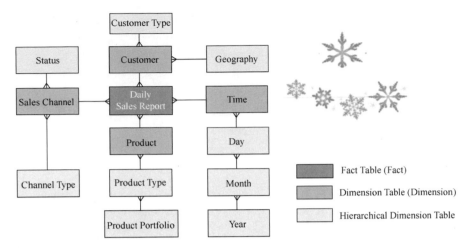

Fig. 7.12 Snowflake-shaped model

question whether the two attributes belong to the same object, which makes different roles have different understandings of the same model.

The naming suggestions for entities and attributes are as follows.

(1) Entity name: capitalize the type domain + entity descriptor (full name, initial capitalization).
(2) Attribute name: use full names with initial capitalization, and some conventional abbreviations are provided after the spaces.
(3) Avoid mixing English and Chinese Pinyin.
(4) If it is abbreviated, it must be the abbreviation of English words, avoid using the acronym abbreviation of pinyin.

Also pay attention to designing the logic model according to the design process, determining the entities and attributes, for example, defining the entity's primary key (PK), defining some non-primary key attributes (Non-Key Attribute), defining non-unique attribute groups and adding the corresponding comment content.

Finally, it is necessary to determine the relation between entities, e.g., use foreign keys to determine whether the relation between entities is identifiable and determine whether the cardinality of the relation is of 1:1, 1:n or n:m. When adding non-key attributes of entities, it is important to consider whether the added attributes conform to the design of the 3NF according to the rules of the 3NF. If the added attributes violate the 3NF, entity splitting is required to determine the relation between the new entity and the original entity. The content of the annotation is generally a literal description of the service meaning, code value, etc.

7.5   Physical Design

7.5.1   Physical Design and Physical Models

Physical design is the adjustment of the physical attributes of the model based on the logical model in order to optimize the database performance and improve the efficiency of service operation and application efficiency. The physical design should be adjusted in conjunction with the physical attributes of the target database product, with the ultimate goal of generating a deployable DDL for the target database.

The main contents include but are not limited to the following.

(1) Non-regularized processing of entities.
(2) Physical naming of tables and fields.
(3) Determining the type of fields, including attributes such as length, precision, and case sensitivity.
(4) Adding physical objects that do not exist in the logical model, such as indexes, constraints, partitions, etc.

Table 7.11 shows the designations of the same concept at different stages. For example, relations in relational theory are called entities in the logical model and tables in the physical model. A tuple in relational theory is an instance in the logical model and a row in the physical model. Attributes in relational theory are called attributes in the logical model and fields of a table in the physical model.

In the comparison between the logical and physical models shown in Table 7.12, what are included in the logical model are entities and attributes, which correspond

Table 7.11 Names of the same concept at different stages

Operational file system	Relational theory	Logic model	Physical model
File	Relation	Entity	Table
Record	Tuple	Instance	Row
Field	Attribute	Attribute	Column

Table 7.12 Comparison of logical and physical models

	Logic model	Physical model
Content	Entities, attributes	Tables, fields
Key value	Primary keys	Indexes, unique constraints
Name definition	Service name	Physical naming (restricted by database product)
Regularization	3NF compliant	Non-regularization based on performance
Redundant data	Without	With
Derived data	Without	With
Users	Service personnel and modelers	Database administrators and developers

to tables and fields in the physical model. As for the key values, the physical model generally does not use primary keys, but more often uses unique constraints and not-null constraints to achieve this. Because the data quality requirement is too high if primary key constraint is used, the constraint requirement is generally reduced in the physical implementation, and the primary key is mainly reflected in the logical concept. In terms of name definition, the logical model is named according to the service rules and the naming convention of real-world objects, while the physical model needs to consider the limitations of database products, such as no illegal characters, no database keywords, and no over-length. In terms of regularization, the logical model design should try to meet the 3NF and be regularized; the physical model pursues high performance and may have to be denormalized, which is non-regularized processing.

7.5.2 Denormalization of the Physical Model

Denormalization, also called non-regularization processing, is the process and technical means that is the opposite of the normalization process, for example, the process of downgrading a model from the 3NF to 2NF or 1NF. The physical model design should take into account the physical limitations of the database in terms of performance and application requirements. Theoretically, if the hardware conditions are unlimited, such as unlimited CPU speed, unlimited memory, unlimited storage space, unlimited bandwidth and so on, there is no need to denormalize. However, it is precisely because of limited resources and limited hardware conditions that the physical model requires denormalization, and denormalization needs to be carried out moderately to avoid possible data redundancy problems and potential risks of data inconsistency.

Frequent table linkage operations can be avoided by adding redundant columns, as shown in Tables 7.13, 7.14, and 7.15. There is a primary-foreign key relation between the order table and the customer table, and if a report can only display the customer number, it is very inconvenient for users. So you need to perform linkage operation to display and output customer names together, which is more convenient for users. However, the linkage operation consumes resources, and in practice, it is common to have more than a dozen code tables associated in one query. Without data redundancy processing, a lot of real-time computing resources will be consumed to perform linkage operations, which will affect query efficiency. Therefore, adding redundant columns and performing pre-linkage operations can improve query efficiency.

Table 7.13 Order table

Order number (PK)	Order date	Customer ID (FK)
1000	2010-08-01	1230008
2000	2010-11-15	1290004
3000	2010-09-30	1280003

Table 7.14 Customer table

Customer ID (PK)	Customer name
1230008	Mr. Wang
1290004	Mr. Li
1280003	Ms. Zhao

Table 7.15 Order and customer table

Order number (PK)	Order date	Customer ID	Customer name
1000	2010-08-01	1230008	Mr. Wang
2000	2010-11-15	1290004	Mr. Li
3000	2010-09-30	1280003	Ms. Zhao

Table 7.16 Sales monthly report of a department

Department number (PK)	Month (PK)	Sales amount/yuan
1000	2019-01	1,000,000
1000	2019-02	1,400,000
1000	2019-03	1,800,000
2000	2019-01	900,000
2000	2019-02	1,300,000
2000	2019-03	2,000,000

Table 7.17 Customer table

Department number (PK)	January sales/yuan	February Sales/yuan	March sales/ yuan	Average monthly sales in Q1/yuan
1000	1,000,000	1,400,000	1,800,000	1,400,000
2000	900,000	1,300,000	2,000,000	1,400,000

Table 7.18 Original customer table

Customer ID (PK)	Customer name	Age
123008	Mr. Wang	65
129004	Mr. Li	50
128003	Ms. Zhao	45
128009	Ms. Zhang	20

The complexity of SQL can be reduced by adding redundant columns and using duplicate groups, as shown in Tables 7.16 and 7.17. This example is a conversion from a high table above to a wide table below, a means often used in the front-end report query process, which is more suitable for fixed class reports with style requirements determined in advance.

Tables 7.18 and 7.19 show the reduction of function calculation by adding derived columns, which is a very common application scenario. For example, extracting customer age information from ID card numbers; classifying users into VIP customers, platinum customers, ordinary customers, etc. based on their spending amounts; and flag suspicious transactions and suspicious accounts after judging

Table 7.19 Derived customer table

Customer ID (PK)	Customer name	Age	Customer group
123008	Mr. Wang	65	Elderly
129004	Mr. Li	50	Middle-aged
128003	Ms. Zhao	45	Middle-aged
128009	Ms. Zhang	20	Youth

them in the AML system. This method is generally used in customer relation management projects. In Table 7.19, users are divided into different groups by age, including elderly, middle-aged and young.

Denormalization is commonly handled by the following means.

(1) Adding duplicate groups.
(2) Performing pre-linkage.
(3) Adding derived fields.
(4) Creating summary tables or temporary tables.
(5) Horizontally or vertically splitting tables.

The negative impact of denormalization is relatively large for OLAP systems, but is more common for OLTP systems, and is generally used to improve the system's high concurrency performance for scenarios that require a large number of transactions. The impact of denormalization needs to be considered more in OLAP systems for the following reasons.

(1) Denormalization does not bring performance improvement to all processing processes, and the negative impact needs to be balanced.
(2) Denormalization may sacrifice the flexibility of data models.
(3) Denormalization poses the risk of data inconsistency.

7.5.3 Maintaining Data Integrity

Denormalization brings the increase of redundant data, which requires certain management measures to maintain data integrity. There are three common processing methods.

(1) Maintain by batch processing. This approach is to modify the replicated or derived columns, and after a certain period of time, a batch of processing jobs or stored procedures are executed to modify the replicated or derived columns. This can only be used in cases where the real-time requirement is not strict.
(2) Add, delete, and modify all designed tables during the same transaction in the application implementation. But be sure to pay attention to the data quality, because it is easy to be neglected when the demand changes frequently, which leads to data quality problems.

(3) Use triggers. The trigger has good real-time processing effect. After the application updates the data of Table *A*, the database will automatically trigger the update of Table *B*, but the cost of using the trigger is that it will cause pressure on the database. The use of triggers in the actual application means a significant negative impact on performance, so there are fewer and fewer scenes using it.

7.5.4 Establishing a Physicalized Naming Convention

Naming convention should be established when physicalizing. Firstly, naming should be based on the physical characteristics of the database, then illegal characters should be avoided in the name, and the reserved keywords of the physical database should be avoided. English words which are meaningful, easy to remember, descriptive, short and unique should be used as far as possible, and Chinese Pinyin is not recommended. The developed naming convention should be unified and strictly observed within the project team. Name abbreviations should be agreed upon. Physical characteristics generally refer to the case sensitivity and the length limit of table names. For example, in GaussDB (DWS), it is specified that the name cannot exceed 63 characters.

Using database reserved keywords may pass at the syntax level, but will bring uncontrollable risks to the subsequent operations and maintenance work, other automated management work and future system upgrades. Generally database object names are case-insensitive when implemented at the physical level, so do not adopt the special use of double quotes to force case differentiation.

Table prefixes can be unified using t, view prefixes unified using v, index prefixes unified using ix. When naming, the corresponding prefix should be added, followed by a meaningful specific name, and the whole name should be in lowercase, as shown in Table 7.20. The examples here are for reference only, which are not mandatory convention.

Table 7.20 Object naming convention

Object	Prefix	Example	Description
Table	t_	t_tablename	t_tablename
Common view	v_	v_viewname	v_viewname
Index	ix_	ix_tablename_columnname	The most commonly used index, denoted by the prefix ix_. If the table name or field name is too long, it is represented by an abbreviation of the table name and field name, using generic abbreviations or de-voweled abbreviations as much as possible
Trigger	trg_	trg_triggername	trg_triggername
Stored procedure	p_	p_procedurename	p_procedurename
Function	f_	f_functionname	f_functionname

7.5.5   *Physicalizing Tables and Fields*

The table-level physicalization operations listed here are only part of the work, not covering all table-level physicalization work.

There are several methods for table physicalization as follows.

(1) Perform the denormalization operation using the methods described earlier.
(2) Decide whether to perform partitioning. Partitioning large tables can reduce the amount of I/O scanning workload and narrow the scope of queries. But the granularity of partitioning is not the finer the better. For example, if you only query monthly summary or conduct monthly query, you only need to partition by month instead of by day.
(3) Decide whether to split the history table and the current table. History table is some cold data with low frequency of use, for which you can use low-speed storage; and current table is the hot data with high frequency of query, for which you can use high-speed storage. History tables can also use compression to reduce the storage space occupied.

For field-level physicalization efforts, first try to use data types with short fields. Data types with shorter lengths not only reduce the size of data files and improve I/O performance, but also reduce memory consumption during related calculations and improve computational performance. For example, for integer data, try not to use INT if you can use SMALLINT, and try not to use BIGINT if you can use INT. The second is to use consistent data types, trying to use the same data type for table linkage operations. Otherwise, the database must dynamically convert them into the same data type for comparison, which will bring some performance overhead. The last is the use of efficient data. Generally speaking, integer data operations (including $=, >, <, \geq, \leq, \neq$ and other conventional comparison operations, as well as GROUP BY) are more efficient than strings and floating-point numbers.

The premise of using efficient data is that the data type must meet the service requirements of the value field. For example, the service context is the amount field with decimals, then you cannot force the use of integers in pursuit of high efficiency.

Integer data is an efficient type compared to string, TINYINT only occupies 1 byte and takes values in the range of 0–255, which is the most efficient. But it belongs to the data type that comes with GaussDB database. At present, the ODBC of GaussDB database is open source odbc driver, with poor compatibility with tinydb. SMALLINT occupies 2 bytes, taking values in the range of −327 68 to +32 767, but the field can only use numbers in the future, and cannot use such characters as a, b, c for expansion. INT occupies 4 bytes, with the range of values from −2 147 483 648 to +2 147 483 647; BIGINT occupies 8 bytes, from −9 223 372 036 854 775 808 to +9 223 372 036 854 775 807; CHAR(1) occupies 1 byte, with efficiency lower than the integer, but supporting characters 0–9, and A–

Z; VARCHAR(1) takes up at least three characters for the leading characters. So there is no absolute standard, just decide according to the actual scenario.

	A certain identification class field takes values of 0,1. If I want to set a data type for this field, which one is appropriate?
Thinking	

Common constraints on the field level are DEFAULT constraints, non-null constraints, unique constraints, primary key constraints and check constraints. If the field value can be completed from the service level, it is not recommended to use DEFAULT constraints to avoid unintended results when data is loaded. It is recommended to add a non-null constraint to a field where a null value clearly does not exist. The primary key constraint is actually equal to the unique constraint plus the non-null constraint, so it should be added if the conditions allow. The check constraint is a requirement for data quality, and data that does not satisfy the constraint will cause SQL execution to fail when inserted into the data table.

Check constraints have little impact on GaussDB (for MySQL) as a whole. In OLTP system, if some data cannot be inserted because the constraint is not satisfied, you can record these failure messages and deal with them by other means instead. However, in GaussDB (DWS) system, it affects the whole job processing system and has relatively more impact. In the OLAP system, the processing of large data volume operations may cause the whole SQL statement or operation to fail because some data records do not meet the check constraints, thus affecting the overall warehouse's data processing process. Therefore, in the OLAP system, the data quality of the local data is constrained by the data application as much as possible, so do not add constraints on the physical tables and fields.

For the creation and use of indexes, here is a list of cases in which indexes are allowed to add, rather than mandatory requirements. Despite the addition of indexes, it is up to the database system to make its own optimization judgments about whether indexes can be used. When using indexes is more efficient and faster, they will be used; if the use is more costly and the efficiency is not significantly improved, the use of indexes will not be forced.

The common index use scenarios are as follows.

(1) Create indexes on columns that are frequently required to be searched and queried, which can speed up the search and query.
(2) Create an index on a column that used as the primary key, which emphasizes the uniqueness of the column and organizes the arrangement structure of the data in the table.
(3) Create indexes on columns that often use joins. These columns are mainly foreign keys, so the speed of association can be accelerated.
(4) Create indexes on columns that often need to be searched based on ranges, because the indexes are already sorted and their specified ranges are contiguous.
(5) Create indexes on columns that often need to be sorted, also because the indexes are already sorted, and these queries can shorten the query time of sorting by index sorting.

(6) Create indexes on the columns that often use the WHERE clause to speed up the judgment of the condition.

The above scenario allows the use of indexes, but it is not necessary. Whether the indexes can be used after being added is determined by the database system itself.

However, creating more indexes will have negative effects, such as the need for more index space; when inserting the base table data, the efficiency of the insertion operation will be reduced because the index data should be inserted at the same time. Therefore, invalid indexes should be deleted in time to avoid wasting space.

Other physicalization means are judged to be used according to the situation, for example, whether to further compress the data, whether to encrypt or desensitize the data, etc.

7.5.6 Using Modeling Software

During the physical design process, we typically use modeling software for both logical and physical modeling. Automation software delivers many benefits, such as forward generation of DDL, reverse analysis of database, and comprehensive satisfaction of various requirements in modeling, so that efficient modeling can be carried out.

Advantages of using modeling software for logical modeling and physical modeling are as follows.

(1) Powerful and rich.
(2) Forward DDL generation and reverse analysis of database.
(3) Free switch of views between logical model and physical model.
(4) Comprehensive satisfaction of various requirements in modeling for efficient modeling.

The following are some of the commonly used modeling software.

(1) ERwin's full name is ERwin Data Modeler, a data modeling tool from CA, which supports all major database systems.
(2) PowerDesigner is SAP's enterprise modeling and design solution that uses a model-driven approach to integrate service and IT, helps deploy effective enterprise architecture, and provides powerful analysis and design techniques for R&D lifecycle management. PowerDesigner uniquely integrates multiple standard data modeling techniques (UML, service process modeling, and market-leading data modeling) with leading development platforms such as. NET, WorkSpace, PowerBuilder, Java, Eclipse, etc., providing business analysis and standardized database design solutions for traditional software development cycle management.
(3) ER/Studio is a set of model-driven data structure management and database design products that help companies discover, reuse and document data assets. It empowers data structures with the ability to fully analyze existing data sources

through regressive database support, and design and implement high-quality database structures based on service requirements. The easy-to-read visual data structure facilitates communication between service analysts and developers at work. ER/Studio Enterprise enables enterprises and task teams to collaborate through a central repository.

(4) dbeaver is a free, open source, universal database tool for developers and database administrators.

(5) pgModeler is a dedicated modeling tool for PostgreSQL databases, developed using Qt and supporting Windows, Linux operating systems and OS X platforms, which uses the classic entity linkage diagram.

7.5.7   Physical Model Products

The products that should be output during the physical model design phase include the following:

(1) A physical data model, usually an engineering file for some automated modeling software;

(2) Physical model naming convention, which is a standard convention that everyone in the project should follow;

(3) Design specification of the physical data model;

(4) DDL table building statements for the target database.

7.6   Database Design Case

7.6.1   Scenario Description

This scenario is a customer placing an order to purchase equipment. A sample order table is shown in Fig. 7.13. After the customer purchases the equipment, he/she needs to fill in the relevant information in the order form.

The current demand is to design the model of the underlying database according to this order style, taking into account the following three requirements.

(1) Record the relevant data information in the database.

(2) Enable to query the information about the order through the database system.

(3) Support some statistical reports of sales volume.

7.6.2   Regularization Processing

The entities and attributes that can be proposed in the order shown in Fig. 7.13 are order number, order date, customer ID, customer name, contact information, ID

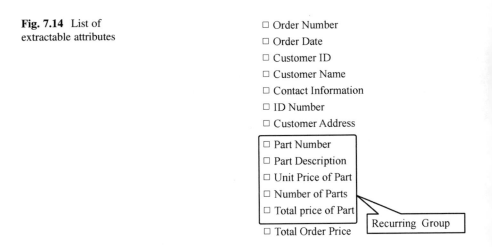

Fig. 7.13 Order form for a customer to purchase equipment

Fig. 7.14 List of
extractable attributes

□ Order Number
□ Order Date
□ Customer ID
□ Customer Name
□ Contact Information
□ ID Number
□ Customer Address

□ Part Number
□ Part Description
□ Unit Price of Part
□ Number of Parts
□ Total price of Part
                              Recurring Group
□ Total Order Price

number, customer address, part number, part description, part unit price, part quantity, part total price, and order total price.

If this information is generated directly into an entity where the design result is a table that needs to cover all the information, then the part number, part description, part unit price, part quantity, and part total price are called duplicate attribute groups that have to appear repeatedly in the entity, as shown in Fig. 7.14. For example, including Part Number 1, Part Description 1, Part Unit Price 1, Part Quantity 1, Part Number 2, Part Description 2, Part Unit Price 2, etc. This situation does not satisfy the 1NF.

For the duplicate group problem of part information, the relevant information of the part is extracted to form a separate entity with several parts for each order, then

Fig. 7.15 Order and order-part entities

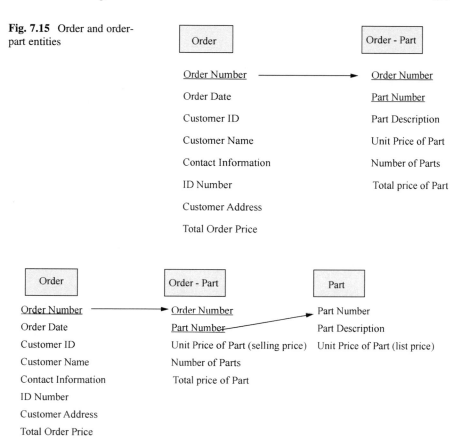

Fig. 7.16 Elimination of partial dependencies

the primary key of the new entity is the order number plus the part number, as shown in Fig. 7.15.

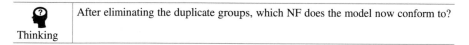

	After eliminating the duplicate groups, which NF does the model now conform to?
Thinking	

There are still partial dependencies on the information of the parts in the current model, so normalization should be continued to resolve the partial dependencies. Extract the partial information that depends only on the part number to form a new entity, the part entity, as shown in Fig. 7.16.

	After eliminating the partial dependencies, which NF does the model now conform to?
Thinking	

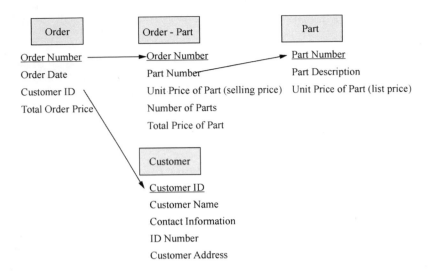

Fig. 7.17   Separate customer information

Table 7.21   Order table

Order number (PK)	Order date	Customer ID (FK)
1000	2010-08-01	123008
2000	2010-11-15	129004
3000	2010-09-30	128003

The problem with the current model is that the customer information depends on the customer ID, and the customer ID depends on the order number. Such dependency has a transferability and is not directly dependent. So a conversion from the 2NF to the 3NF has to be implemented to eliminate this transmissive dependency.

Eliminating the transmissive dependency is to generate the customer information as a separate entity, the customer entity, as shown in Fig. 7.17.

Thinking	After eliminating the transmissive dependency, which NF does the model now conform to?

At this point, the logical model is essentially complete. However, note that the order total price and the part total price are derived fields, which are not strictly considered to meet the requirements of the 3NF, so they should be "erased".

After the regularization process is completed, the entity of the 3NF model is obtained, and the primary key and foreign key are marked in the two-dimensional table. Experience the 3NF model, as shown in Tables 7.21 and 7.22.

Since the part total price attribute has been removed from the order-part table, if you want to get the part total price now, you need to do the operation based on the

Table 7.22 Order-part table

Order number (PK, FK)	Part number (PK, FK)	Sales price	Part quantity
1000	8001	100	3
1000	8002	400	5
2000	8002	200	2
2000	8003	100	1
3000	8004	50	4
3000	8005	80	8

Table 7.23 ORDER table

Field name	Field type	Constraint
Order_Num	INTEGER	NOT NULL, UNIQUE
Order_Date	DATE	NOT NULL
Customer_Id	INTEGER	NOT NULL

order-part table and multiply the part quantity by the sales price. The pseudo SQL code is as follows.

```
select 订单编号, 部件编号, (销售价格*部件数量) as部件合计价格 from 订单部
件表;
```

If you now want to get the order total price, the pseudo SQL code is as follows.

```
SELECT 订单编号, SUM (销售价格*部件数量) AS订单合计金额 FROM 订单部件表;
```

7.6.3 Data Types and Length

After completing the logical model design, the physical model design begins. First, name the table and field according to certain convention, avoid using database keywords, and perform certain case-specific design; then determine the data type at the field level, and if it involves characters, the length of the field definition, then determine its upper limit according to the possible value fields of the actual data; after that determine whether each field needs to add non-null constraints, unique constraints, and other constraints, as shown in Tables 7.23, 7.24, 7.25, and 7.26.

The samples in the above tables are a kind of example, you can adjust them as the actual situation required in practice.

Table 7.24 CUSTOMER table

Field name	Field type	Constraint
Customer_Id	INTEGER	NOT NULL, UNIQUE
Cust_Name	VARCHAR(60)	NOT NULL
Mobile_Num	VARCHAR(30)	
Id_Num	VARCHAR(20)	
Cust_Address	VARCHAR(120)	

Table 7.25 ORDER_ITEM table

Field name	Field type	Constraint
Order_Num	INTEGER	NOT NULL
Item_Id	INTEGER	NOT NULL
Sale_Price	DECIMAL(5,2)	NOT NULL
Item_Quantity	SMALLINT	NOT NULL

Table 7.26 ITEM table

Field name	Field type	Constraint
Item_Id	INTEGER	NOT NULL, UNIQUE
Description	VARCHAR(120)	
Retail_Price	DECIMAL(5,2)	NOT NULL

Table 7.27 Order table

Field name	Field type	Constraint
Order_Num	INTEGER	NOT NULL, UNIQUE
Order_Date	DATE	NOT NULL
Customer_Id	INTEGER	NOT NULL
Total_Price	DECIMAL(9,2)	NOT NULL

? Thinking	If the value type of the set price is DEIMAL(5,2), what is the range of the value field?

7.6.4 Denormalization

The denormalization shown in Tables 7.27 and 7.28 solves some service problems by adding some derived fields. For example, Total_Price states the order total price of a particular order. Item_Total indicate the sales of a part in an order.

Whether to continue to derive fields or perform other pre-association operations depends on the service problems to be solved, the computational complexity, and whether denormalization can speed up these queries.

Table 7.28 order detail table

Field name	Field type	Constraint
Order_Num	INTEGER	NOT NULL
Item_Id	INTEGER	NOT NULL
Sale_Price	DECIMAL(5,2)	NOT NULL
Item_Quantity	SMALLINT	NOT NULL
Item_Total	DECIMAL(9,2)	NOT NULL

Table 7.29 Index selection (1)

Field name	Field type	Constraint	Index selection
Order_Num	INTEGER	NOT NULL, UNIQUE	
Order_Date	DATE	NOT NULL	Partitioning can be considered
Customer_Id	INTEGER	NOT NULL	
Total_Price	DECIMAL(9,2)	NOT NULL	

Table 7.30 Index selection (2)

Field name	Field type	Constraint	Index selection
Order_Num	INTEGER	NOT NULL	
Item_Id	INTEGER	NOT NULL	Add indexes
Sale_Price	DECIMAL(5,2)	NOT NULL	
Item_Quantity	SMALLINT	NOT NULL	
Item_Total	DECIMAL(9,2)	NOT NULL	

Thinking	What is the average monthly sales for Q1? What are the top three parts by sales? You can further refine the derived fields on your own based on some service issues.

7.6.5   *Index Selection*

Taking Tables 7.23 and 7.25 as examples, the operation results of adding indexes are shown in Tables 7.29 and 7.30. Here some partition indexes and query indexes are added. There is no standard answer for adding indexes, and the same needs to be judged according to the actual scenario and data volume. For OLTP, each table needs to add a primary key, and if there is no natural primary key, then a field like sequence can be used as a proxy primary key. For OLAP distributed database, each table needs to further select distribution keys upon careful consideration.

7.7 Summary

This chapter focuses on the New Orleans design methodology to database modeling, and explains the four phases of requirement analysis, conceptual design, logical design, and physical design, with the tasks of each design phase clearly explained. The significance of requirement analysis stage is expounded. The E-R approach is introduced in the conceptual design stage. For the logical design section, the important basic concepts and the 3NF are expounded, and each NF is explained in depth with examples. For the stage of physical design, the denormalization means and the key points in the work are emphasized. The chapter concludes with a small practical case to illustrate the main elements of logical and physical modeling.

7.8 Exercises

1. [Single Choice] The next phase after the logical design phase in the New Orleans design methodology is ( ).

   A. Requirement analysis
   B. Physical design
   C. Conceptual design
   D. Logical design

2. [Multiple Choice] In what ways is the database operating environment efficient? ( )

   A. Data access efficiency
   B. Time cycle of data storage
   C. Storage space utilization
   D. Efficiency of database system operation and management

3. [Multiple Choice] In the process of requirement investigation, which of the following methods can be used? ( )

   A. Questionnaire survey
   B. Interviews with service personnel
   C. Sample data collection, and data analysis
   D. Review or the *User Requirement Specification*

4. [Multiple Choice] Which of the following options are included in the three elements of the E-R diagram in model design? ( )

   A. Entity
   B. Relation
   C. Cardinality
   D. Attribute

5. [Multiple Choice] The linkage between entities are ( ).

   A. One-to-one linkage (1:1)
   B. One-to-null linkage (1:0)
   C. One-to-many linkage (1:n)
   D. Many-to-many linkage (m:n)

6. An entity is a collection of real-world objects that have common attributes and can be distinguished from each other. For example, teachers, students, and courses are all entities, as shown in Fig. 7.2. ( )

   A. True
   B. False

7. [Multiple Choice] The significance of normalized modeling in the logic model design process includes ( ).

   A. Improve the efficiency of database use
   B. Reduce redundant data
   C. Make the model well scalable
   D. Reduce the possibility of data inconsistency

8. [True or False] A model that satisfies the 3NF must satisfy the 2NF. ( )

   A. True
   B. False

9. [Multiple Choice] The physical model has the following characteristics compared to the logical model: ( ).

   A. Strictly observes the 3NF
   B. Can contain redundant data
   C. Mainly for database administrators and developers
   D. Can contain derived data

10. [Multiple Choice] Which of the following are ways to data denormalization? ( )

    A. Add derived fields
    B. Create a summary or temporary table
    C. Perform pre-linkage
    D. Add duplicate groups

11. [Multiple Choice] The effects of using indexes are ( ).

    A. It will take up more physical storage space
    B. With indexes in effect, the efficiency of queries can be greatly improved
    C. The efficiency of inserting base tables will be reduced
    D. Once the index is established, the database optimizer will definitely use the index in queries

12. [True or False] Because partitioning can reduce the I/O scan overhead during data query, the more partitions are created during the physicalization process, the better. ( )

    A. True
    B. False

13. [True or False] The foreign key is the unique identifier that identifies each instance in an entity. ( )

    A. True
    B. False

14. [True or False] Atomicity that satisfies the 1NF is the sub-splitting of each attribute to the smallest granularity that is non-sub-splittable. ( )

    A. True
    B. False

15. [True or False] A relation between entities exists only if a foreign key exists, and a relation between two entities cannot be established without a foreign key. ( )

    A. True
    B. False

16. [Multiple Choice] Which of the following options in the process of building a logical model is within the scope of work for determining the attributes in an entity? ( )

    A. Define the primary key of the entity
    B. Define some of the non-key attributes
    C. Define non-unique attribute groups
    D. Define constraints on attributes

17. [True or False] The data dictionary in the requirement analysis phase of the New Orleans design methodology has the same meaning as the data dictionary in a database product. ( )

    A. True
    B. False

Chapter 8
Introduction to Huawei Cloud Database GaussDB

Database plays an important role in enterprises, and Huawei GaussDB database is one of the "main forces" in Kunpeng ecology.

Databases can be divided into relational databases and non-relational databases. Relational databases include OLTP databases for enterprise production and transactions and OLAP databases for enterprise analysis. For OLTP application scenarios Huawei launched cloud database GaussDB (for MySQL) and GaussDB (openGauss); for OLAP scenarios, it launched data warehouse service GaussDB (DWS). As to non-relational databases (NoSQL), Huawei currently has GaussDB (for Mongo) and GaussDB (for Cassandra).

Database technology innovation is breaking the existing order, and cloud-based, distributed, and multi-mode processing are the main trends in the future. This chapter focuses on the features and application scenarios of Huawei GaussDB (for MySQL) cloud database, and introduces some application cases.

After learning this chapter, readers will master the following contents.

(1) The features of GaussDB database.
(2) Knowledge of Huawei relational database.
(3) Knowledge of Huawei NoSQL.

8.1 GaussDB Database Overview

8.1.1 GaussDB Database Family

Everything from scratch, from weak to strong, means the accumulation of time and the precipitation of experience. The decade whets one sword Huawei officially released GaussDB database series products on May 15, 2019.

In order to pay tribute to German mathematician Gauss, Huawei named its self-developed databases GaussDB. The Kunpeng ecology develops in three technology

© The Author(s) 2023
Huawei Technologies Co., Ltd., *Database Principles and Technologies – Based on Huawei GaussDB*, https://doi.org/10.1007/978-981-19-3032-4_8

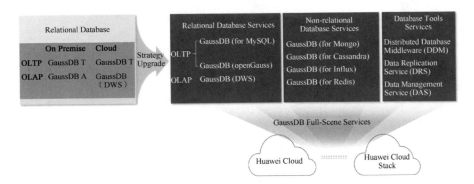

Fig. 8.1 GaussDB full-scene services

directions: chip/media, operating system, and database. Among these, Huawei GaussDB database is one of the "main forces" in Kunpeng ecology.

Databases are generally divided into relational databases and non-relational databases. Non-relational databases include professional document databases, graph databases, etc., which are oriented to refined scenarios and more targeted, but their application areas are narrower, with less market share ($< 20\%$). In the next 5 years, the main market of database is still focused on relational database, whose market share is more than 80%. The current mainstream databases can be mainly divided into two categories of OLTP and OLAP in terms of services orientation. Huawei also targets these two types of services and has launched the transactional database GaussDB (for MySQL) for OLTP scenarios and the analytical database GaussDB (DWS) for OLAP scenarios, respectively. What's more, Huawei GaussDB database holds two important innovations.

(1) It is the industry's first AI-Native distributed database, which integrates AI into the database kernel, making the database more intelligent to achieve self-O&M, self-management, self-tuning, fault self-diagnosis and self-healing. It is the first self-tuning algorithm rooted in deep reinforcement learning under transaction, analysis and mixed load scenarios based on optimization theory.

(2) It supports heterogeneous computing architecture and can take full advantage of multiple algorithms such as X86GPU and NPU to make the database more efficient by releasing diverse computing power. It is also the industry's first ARM-enabled enterprise-class database.

Figure 8.1 shows the GaussDB database upgraded to a full-scene service, relying on Huawei Cloud and Huawei CloudStack. Huawei has seven research institutes around the world engaged in database basic research, with more than 10 years of technical accumulation in the database field, more than 1000 database-specialized talents, and more than 30,000 global database applications. After upgrading to Huawei's self-developed database brand, the business covers both relational and non-relational database services. The business upgrade relies on Huawei Cloud and Huawei Cloud Stack to continuously serve users with cloud services, aiming to improve delivery and O&M efficiency, help users focus on core business innovation, and introduce innovative technologies and new services faster. Rich ecological options, in addition to the commitment to build Huawei ecology, are also compatible with widely used open ecology, such as MySQL, etc., to facilitate users' application migration and development, ensuring continuity of user investment and business.

8.1.2   Typical OLTP and OLAP Databases

OLTP refers to online transaction processing. OLTP, as the main application of traditional relational database, mainly supports the basic daily transaction processing and business activities of enterprises by storing the activity data in query service applications. Typical OLTP systems involve in e-commerce, banking and securities trading systems, etc. The business database of eBay in the US is a very typical OLTP database. OLAP refers to online analytical processing, also known as DSS decision support system, is often referred to as the data warehouse. OLAP, as the main application of the data warehouse system, supports complex analytical operations by storing historical data, focusing on decision support, and provides intuitive and easy-to-understand query results.

GaussDB (for MySQL) database is recommended for systems with high transactional requirements such as business systems, financial systems, sales systems and customer service systems; if a large amount of data generated based on business needs to be stored using data warehouses for subsequent data analysis, data mining, and supporting business decisions, GaussDB (DWS) database is recommended, as shown in Fig. 8.2.

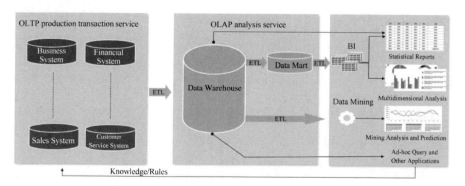

Fig. 8.2 Typical OLTP and OLAP databases

8.2   Relational Database Products and Related Tools

8.2.1   GaussDB (for MySQL)

The cloud database GaussDB (for MySQL) is Huawei's next-generation self-developed distributed database, which is highly scalable, supports massive storage, and is fully compatible with MySQL. Based on Huawei's next-generation DFV storage, it adopts a computing/storage separation architecture and has a massive storage space of 128TB, with no need to separate libraries and tables, and can achieve zero data loss. It combines the high availability of commercial databases with the low cost of open source databases.

GaussDB (for MySQL) employs a multi-node cluster architecture with a write node (master node) and multiple read nodes (read-only nodes) in the cluster, and each node shares the underlying DFV. In general, GaussDB (for MySQL) cluster should be located at the same location as the elastic cloud server instances to achieve the highest access performance.

- Has high user value.
- With 128TB storage space and no sub-library and sub-table, solves the problem of huge amount of data.
- Easy to use, fully compatible with MySQL, with no application modification required.
- With 15 read-only nodes and read/write separation, solves the performance scaling problem.
- With cross-AZ deployment, off-site disaster recovery, realizes high reliability.

An AZ (availability zone) is a collection of one or more physical data centers, and the resources such as computes, networks, and storage are logically subdivided into multiple clusters within the AZ. An AZ is a physical area with independent power and network within a geographic region. AZs communicate with each other within the intranet, but are physically isolated. Each AZ is unaffected by the failure of other AZs and provides low-cost, low-latency network connectivity to other AZs in the same region. The use of GaussDB (for MySQL) within a separate AZ protects users' applications from single-location failures. There is no substantial difference between different AZs in the same region.

There are many needs and pain points in the database market today, as shown in Table 8.1.

The core benefits of GaussDB (for MySQL) are shown in Table 8.2.

In the context of the cloud era, enterprise IT business is deployed across regions and globally, and IT application software is gradually cloud-based and distributed, so the database is also required to be designed based on cloud scenario architecture and have the ability to be deployed across regions in a distributed manner. Huawei Cloud Native distributed database is precisely such a new type of database, following the five design principles below.

Table 8.1 Needs and pain points in the database market

Major needs and pain points	Needs description
Compatible with MySQL	No need to make any modification to the original MySQL application
Massive data storage	Supports large data volume of Internet services
Distributed and highly scalable	Automated database and table splitting or no sub-library and sub-table, with application transparency
Strongly consistent transactions	Supports strong consistency of distributed transactions
Highly available	Supports cross-AZ, high available, cross-region disaster recovery
High concurrency performance	Supports high performance under large concurrency scenarios
Non-middleware architecture	Non-DDM solution (or non-DRDS solution)

Table 8.2 Core benefits

Benefit	Description
Ultra high performance	Million-level qps
High scalability	1 write node and 15 read-only nodes, and 128TB storage space
High reliability	Cross-AZ deployment, and 3 copies of data
High compatibility	MySQL compatibility
Low cost	1/10 of commercial database cost

(1) Decoupling: separation of computation and storage; master-slave decoupling.
(2) Push-down of near data calculation: push-down from I/O intensive load to storage node completion, such as redo processing and page reconstruction.
(3) Full use of cloud storage: independent fault tolerance and self-healing service on the storage layer; shared access (write once and read many).
(4) Full play to the advantages of solid state disk (SSD): avoiding write amplification caused by random writing; less wear and shorter time delay; full use of the random read performance of SSD.
(5) Transfer of performance bottleneck from computing and storage to network: less network traffic; new network technologies and hardware, such as remote direct memory access (RDMA).

When designing the Cloud Native database, Huawei took into account the need for flexibility, including the switch between the host and the standby and the increase of nodes, so as to sink more operations. Huawei Cloud Native benefited from a strong team in hardware and deep cooperation with Huawei's storage department who provided a special platform to sink the operations of the database itself to the storage node. Huawei Cloud Native maximizes the properties of SSDs to improve the performance of the database, in addition to the considerations based on multi-tenancy. It uses new network technologies including AI technology to help users

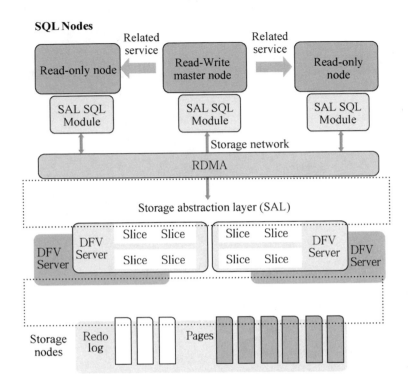

Fig. 8.3 Three parts of database

improve the throughput of data centers, improve the scalability of network applications, and implement auto-tuning.

In fact, Huawei divides the database into three parts: SQL layer, abstraction layer and storage layer. From the physical level, it can be divided into two layers: one is the SQL layer, which adopts a one-master-multi-standby model; the other is the storage abstraction layer, which maintains database services for different tenants, including building pages, log processing, and other related functions, as shown in Fig. 8.3.

For the SQL layer, the plan, query and management transactions can be isolated by managing client connections and parsing SQL requests in the form of one read-write and multiple read-only copies. Meanwhile, Huawei also launched HWSQL and has made many performance improvements based on HWSQL, including query result cache, query plan cache and online DD.

The whole design uniquely features the reduction of frequent page reading operations from memory by SQL replication of multiple nodes. When an update occurs on the master server, the Replicas SQL database also receives the transaction and commits the update list.

There is also a storage abstract layer (SAL). SAL is a logical layer that isolates SQL front ends, transactions, and queries within a storage unit. When manipulating

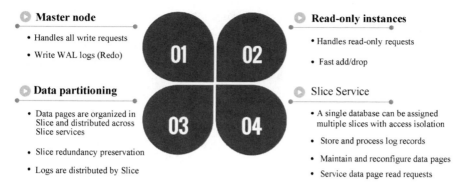

Fig. 8.4 Features of GaussDB (for MySQL)

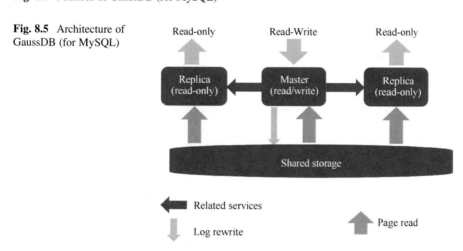

Fig. 8.5 Architecture of GaussDB (for MySQL)

database pages, SAL support accessing multiple versions of the same page. Based on spaceID and pageID, SAL can shard all data, with its storage and memory resources growing proportionally.

In terms of performance, GaussDB (for MySQL) takes full advantage of some features of Huawei. The system container uses Huawei's Hi1882 high-performance chip, so it is better than the general container in terms of performance; the RDMA application greatly reduces computational costs; the Co-Processor achieves data processing with as few resources as possible, reducing the workload of the SQL nodes, as shown in Fig. 8.4.

The architecture of GaussDB (for MySQL) is shown in Fig 8.5.

(1) Ultimate reliability: zero data loss, flash recovery from failure, and support for cross-AZ high availability.
(2) Multi-dimensional expansion: compute nodes expansion in both directions. Horizontal expansion: support for horizontal expansion in 1-write &15-read mode. Vertical expansion: online elastic expansion, and on-demand billing.

(3) Massive storage: single-instance scalable data up to 128TB, no need to split libraries and tables, and fast service go-live on the cloud.
(4) Innovative self-research: Cloud Native distributed database architecture, based on Huawei's new generation of DFV to achieve the separation of computing and storage, to ensure cost effectiveness in scalability; storage on pushed-down database logic, to achieve minimum network load and ultimate performance.
(5) Excellent performance: performance improved up to 7 times of native MySQL, 100% compatibility with MySQL, and industry leading.
(6) Cutting-edge hardware: industry-leading hardware combination based on V5 CPU + Optane DC SSD + RDMA network, and stable and fast data processing.

Kernel optimization of GaussDB (for MySQL) is mainly reflected in the following aspects.

(1) Removal of secondary writes.
(2) Query Cache/Plan Cache optimization.
(3) Innodb Lock Management optimization.
(4) Audit Plugin efficiency optimization.
(5) Community bug fixes.

Hardware enhancements are mainly reflected in the following areas.

(1) Containerization.
(2) Hi1822 offload.
(3) Use of NVMe SSD.
(4) RDMA.

Through the elastic cloud server or devices that can access GaussDB (for MySQL) database, connect to GaussDB (for MySQL) database instance with the corresponding client and import the exported SQL files into GaussDB (for MySQL) database.

The CPU and memory specifications of the cluster can be changed according to the service needs, and if the status of the cluster changes from "changing specifications" to "normal", the change is successful. After GaussDB (for MySQL) 8.0 cluster specifications are changed successfully, the system will adjust the values of the following parameters according to the new memory size: "innodb_buffer_pool_size" "innodb_log_buffer _size" "max_ connections" "innodb_buffer_pool_instances" " query_cache_size".

Users can retrieve the monitoring metrics and alert information generated by the cloud database GaussDB (for MySQL) through the API provided by the cloud monitor.

gaussdb_mysql010_innodb_buf_usage: buffer pool utilization ratio, used to count the ratio of dirty data to data in InnoDB cache, with value ranging from 0 to 1.

gaussdb_mysql011_innodb_buf_hit: buffer pool hit rate, used to count the ratio of read hits to read requests, with value ranging from 0% to 100%.

gaussdb_mysql012_innodb_buf_dirty: dirty block rate of buffer pool, used to count the ratio of used pages to the total data in InnoDB cache, with value ranging from 0 to 1.

gaussdb_mysql013_innodb_reads: InnoDB read throughput, used to count the average number of bytes per second read by InnoDB, with value ≥ 0 bytes/s.

gaussdb_mysql014_innodb_writes: InnoDB write throughput, used to count the average number of bytes per second written by InnoDB, with value ≥ 0 counts/s.

gaussdb_mysql017_innodb_log_write_req_count: InnoDB log write request frequency, used to count the average number of log write requests per second, with value ≥ 0 counts/s.

If the backup policy of the instance is enabled, a full automatic backup will be triggered immediately. The binlog backup does not need to be set by the user; instead, GaussDB (for MySQL) system will automatically do it every 5 min, either full backup or binlog backup is stored on the object storage service.

GaussDB (for MySQL) expands horizontally fast and requires different data to be synchronized compared to traditional addition of read-only copies. GaussDB (for MySQL) only takes about 5 min to add compute nodes due to shared storage, no matter how much data there is.

GaussDB (for MySQL) adopts distributed storage, with storage capacity up to 128TB. The storage is paid on demand, with no need to plan storage capacity in advance, reducing user costs.

GaussDB (for MySQL) delivers faster master-standby reversal, eliminating binlog replication latency, and ensuring guaranteed RTO.

GaussDB (for MySQL) database is fast in crash recovery. and the storage layer is constantly advancing the logs in an asynchronous and distributed manner.

The fast backup recovery and the distributed storage system customized for GaussDB (for MySQL) engine greatly improves the data backup and recovery performance. It also provides powerful data snapshot processing capability through AppendOnly vs. WriteInPlace, storing natural data at multiple time points and multiple copies, and supporting second-level snapshot generation and massive snapshot. Fast rollback at any point in time, based on the multi-point characteristics of the underlying storage system, without incremental log playback, can directly realize rollback by point in time. Parallel high-speed backup and recovery, as well as backup and recovery logic sinking to each storage node, enable local access data to directly interact with the third-party storage system, realizing high concurrency and high performance. Through asynchronous data replication plus on-demand real-time data loading mechanism, the fast instance recovery function enables GaussDB (for MySQL) instance to be fully functional within a few minutes.

GaussDB (for MySQL) is more cost effective with shared DFV storage and only one copy of storage compared to traditional RDS for MySQL. When adding a read-only node, you only need to add one compute node, with no need to purchase additional storage. The more read-only nodes there are, the more storage costs are saved. Compared with the traditional RDS for MySQL, the Active-Active architecture no longer has a backup library, with all read-only in active state, and bear the read traffic, which makes the resource utilization rate higher And compared with the

Table 8.3 Instance specifications for GaussDB (for MySQL)

Specifications	vCPU/pc	Memory/GB
Generic Enhanced	16	64
	32	128
	60	256
Kunpeng Generic Enhanced	16	64
	32	128
	48	192

traditional RDS for MySQL, the log-as-data architecture no longer needs to refresh pages, and all update operations only record logs, removing secondary writes, thus reducing the consumption of precious network bandwidth.

The instance specifications for GaussDB (for MySQL) are shown in Table 8.3.

The financial industry is currently asset-light, and rapid expansion is the driver for its use of cloud databases. However, the whole industry is experiencing the pain point of unpredictable user traffic and generated data, and the user experience is affected at the peak of business, and even the service must be stopped for expansion.

GaussDB (for MySQL) compute nodes support bi-directional expansion, based on cloud virtualization, where the specification can be changed on a single node, which supports 1 write and 15 read nodes, with an expansion ratio of 0.9. It also supports storage pooling, with a maximum of 128TB storage space. The expansion of compute nodes will not bring about an increase in storage costs.

In the enterprise-level market where SaaS applications enter, the business pain points of large Internet companies and traditional large enterprises are huge business, high throughput, and unsolved open source database problems, so it is necessary to adopt complicated solutions such as sub-database and sub-table. Enterprise users generally prefer to commercial databases (eg. SQL Server and Oracle), which cost highly in license.

GaussDB (for MySQL) adopts storage pooling, uses MySQL native optimization, and also has advantages in hardware, such as RDMA, V5CPU, and Optance, and in terms of architecture, database logic is pushed down to release arithmetic power and reduce network overhead.

8.2.2   GaussDB (openGauss)

GaussDB (openGauss) is Huawei's next-generation enterprise-class distributed database, fully self-developed in combination with its own technology accumulation, supporting both centralized and distributed deployment forms; on the basis of supporting traditional business, it provides unlimited possibilities for enterprises to face the challenges of the 5G era.

Table 8.4   Development process and role of openGauss\

2001–2011	Enterprise-class in-memory database
2011–2019	G Line core data warehouse, GaussDB (DWS) Huawei cloud for commercial use; replacement of commercial database with Z Line core business system. Supports more than 40 kinds of key products within the company, with global operators reaching more than 70 and more than 30,000 sets of commercial databases, serving more than 2 billion people worldwide
2019–2020	GaussDB database released globally on May 15, 2019; partner ecology built; compatibility with mainstream industry ecology and interface with finance and other industries
2020 to present	Open source of openGauss centralized version

GaussDB (openGauss) database has advantages as follows.

(1) High performance: high throughput and strong consistency transaction capability. Supports Kunpeng two-way server, bearing 32 nodes with 12 million tpmC to achieve distributed strong consistency.
(2) High availability: active-active and two-site and three-center deployment. High availability within the cluster, no data loss, supporting second-level business interruption; co-location cross-AZ disaster recovery, no data loss, supporting minute-level recovery; support for two-site and three-center deployment.
(3) High scalability: horizontal expansion of capacity and performance on demand. 256-node scalability, and excellent linearity ratio; online capacity expansion.
(4) Easy management: easy migration, easy monitoring, and easy O&M. Compatibility with SQL2003 standard syntax + enterprise expansion package; support for data replication, monitoring O&M, and tool development.

The full open source kernel of openGauss centralized version is the result of Huawei's ten-year effort in database field, which has gone through the process from internal self-use incubation stage to joint-creating productization stage, and then to the open source stage of openGauss centralized version. The development process and role of openGauss are shown in Table 8.4.

As an open source relational database management system, openGauss deeply integrates Huawei's years of experience in the database field. Huawei hopes to attract more contributors in virtue of the charm of open source and jointly builds an enterprise-class open source database community that integrates diverse technical architectures. OpenGauss kernel has experienced long-term evolution and is now giving back to the community. GaussDB database services in Huawei and public cloud are precisely developed based on openGauss, so the kernel will continue to evolve for a long time.

The openGauss kernel is derived from PostgreSQL and focuses on continuously enhancing competitiveness in the direction of architecture, transaction, storage engine, optimizer, etc. It is deeply optimized on ARM architecture chips and compatible with X86 architecture to achieve the following technical features.

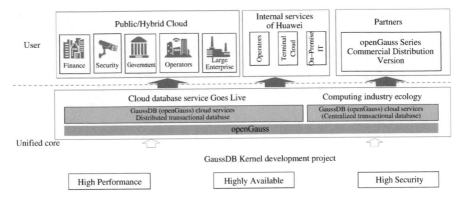

Fig. 8.6 openGauss

(1) Concurrency control technology based on multi-core architecture, NUMA-Aware storage engine, and SQL-Bypass intelligent routing execution technology, releasing multi-core expansion capability of the processor and achieving the performance of 1.5 million tpmC in two-way Kunpeng 128-core scenario.
(2) Support for fast fault reversal with RTO <10s, and full link data protection, to meet security and reliability requirements.
(3) Simplification of O&M through intelligent parameter tuning, slow SQL diagnosis, multi-dimensional performance self-monitoring, online SQL time prediction, etc.

openGauss adopts Mulan PSL v2, which allows all community participants to freely modify, use and reference the codes. The openGauss community has also set up a technical committee to welcome all developers to contribute codes and documents.

Huawei always upholds the overall development strategy of "open hardware, open source software, and enabling partners", and supports partners to build their own brand of commercial databases based on openGauss, so as to support partners to enhance their commercial competitiveness continuously, as shown in Fig. 8.6.

openGauss provides the following support for partners:

(1) Training: Builds training certification system, carries out kernel technology salon, and sets up user groups;
(2) Support: Delivers community support teams;
(3) Developer ecology: Builds a developer ecology jointly; promotes university course development and book publication.

GaussDB database helps Huawei user cloud achieve intelligent business operations. In terms of business requirements and challenges, Huawei user cloud's big data platform centrally stores and manages business-side data with a hybrid architecture of Hadoop + MPP databases. The challenges it faces are as follows:

(1) Rapid business development, with annual data growth of more than 30%;
(2) Real-time analysis capability required for the data analysis platform to achieve intelligent user experience;
(3) Support for independent report development and visual analysis.

To this end, GaussDB database gives the following solutions:

(1) On-demand elastic expansion to support rapid business development;
(2) SQL on HDFS support for real-time analysis of instant exploration scenarios, Kafka stream data entry at high speed, and real-time report generation;
(3) Key technologies such as multi-tenant load management and approximate calculation enabling efficient report development and visual analysis.

These solutions generate the following user benefits:

(1) On-demand capacity expansion without business interruption;
(2) Real-time analysis results thanks to the new data analysis model, with marketing accuracy rate increased by more than 50%;
(3) Response time of typical visual report query and analysis reduced from the past minute level to within 5 s, and report development cycle reduced from the past 2 weeks to 0.5 h.

GaussDB database is suitable for small and medium-sized banks' Internet-based transaction systems, such as mobile apps, websites, etc. It is compatible with the industry's mainstream commercial database ecology, with high performance, security and reliability, etc.

The advantages of GaussDB database are as follows.

(1) Security and reliability. It supports SSL encrypted connection and KMS data encryption to ensure data security; supports database master-standby architecture, and when the host machine fails, where when the master machine fails, the standby machine is automatically upgraded to the master to ensure business continuity.
(2) Ultra-high performance. With high performance and low latency transaction processing capability, the performance of Sysbench data under typical configuration is 30% to 50% higher than that of open source database.

8.2.3 GaussDB (DWS)

Data warehouse service (DWS) is an online data processing database based on public cloud infrastructure and platform, providing out-of-the-box, scalable and fully managed analytical database services. GaussDB (DWS) is a service based on Huawei Cloud's native converged data warehouse, GaussDB database, which is compliant with the ANSI SQL 99 and SQL 2003 standards, providing competitive solutions for petabyte-scale massive big data analysis in various industries.

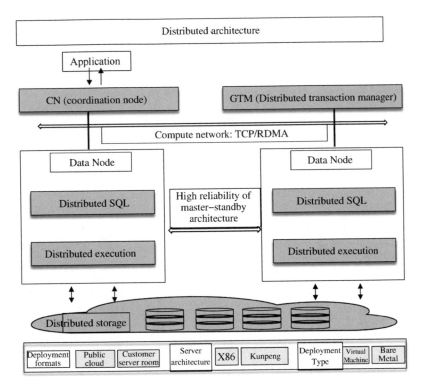

Fig. 8.7 Distributed architecture

GaussDB (DWS) can be widely used in finance, automotive networking, government and enterprises, e-commerce, energy, telecommunications and other fields, and has been selected in the "Magic Quadrant" data management solution list released by Gartner for three consecutive years from 2017 to 2019. It is several times more cost effective than traditional data warehouses, with massive scalability and enterprise-class reliability.

GaussDB (DWS) is distributed and on-demand, with the advantages of distributed architecture, high reliability of master-standby/multi-live design, storage and computing separation, and independent expansion on demand. It is compliant with the standard SQL 2003 and supports transaction ACID feature to provide strong data consistency guarantee; supports X86 and ARM platform servers and is vertically optimized based on Kunpeng chip, which improves performance by 30% compared with the same generation of X86, as shown in Fig. 8.7.

GaussDB (DWS) is based on a non-shared distributed architecture with MPP engine, which consists of many logical nodes with independent and non-shared CPUs, memories, storages and other system resources. In such a system architecture, business data is scattered across multiple nodes, and data analysis tasks are pushed to the data site for execution nearby, so that large-scale data processing can be done in parallel and fast response to data processing can be realized.

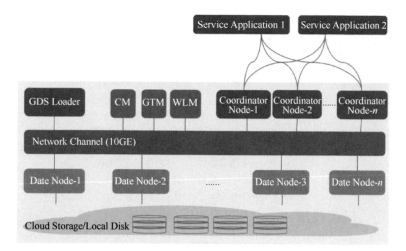

Fig. 8.8 Logical Architecture

The application layer provides data loading tools, ETL (Extract-Transform-Load) tools, BI tools, data mining and analysis tools, all of which can be integrated with GaussDB (DWS) through a standard interface. GaussDB (DWS) is compatible with the PostgreSQL ecosystem and the SQL syntax is processed to be compatible with MySQL, Oracle and Teradata. Applications can migrate smoothly to GaussDB (DWS) with only a few changes.

The interface supports applications to connect to GaussDB (DWS) via standard JDBC 4.0 and ODBC 3.5.

A GaussDB (DWS) cluster (MPP cluster) consists of multiple nodes with the same specifications in the same subnet, which jointly provide services. Each DN in the cluster is responsible for storing data, with disk as the storage medium. The coordinator node (CN) is responsible for receiving access requests from applications and returning execution results to clients. In addition, the CN is responsible for decomposing tasks and scheduling task slices to be executed in parallel on each DN.

Automatic data backup supports automatic backup of cluster snapshots to EB-level OBS, which facilitates periodic backup of the cluster on business idleness to ensure data recovery after cluster abnormalities. Snapshot is a complete backup of GaussDB (DWS) cluster at a certain point in time, recording all configuration data and business data of the specified cluster at that moment.

The tool chain provides the data parallel loading tool GDS (General Data Service), SQL syntax migration tool DSC, and SQL development tool Data Studio, and supports O&M monitoring of the cluster through the console.

GaussDB (DWS)'s logical architecture is shown in Fig. 8.8.

CM: Cluster Manager, which manages and monitors the operation of each functional unit and physical resources in the distributed system to ensure the stable operation of the whole system.

GTM: Global Transaction Manager, which provides the information required for global transaction control and uses multi-version concurrency control mechanism (based on multiple versions and concurrency control protocol).

WLM: Workload Manager, which controls the allocation of system resources and prevents excessive business load from hitting the system, leading to business congestion and system crashes.

Coordinator Node: Acts as the business entry and result return of the whole system; receives access requests from business applications; decomposes tasks and schedules parallel execution of task shards.

Data Node: The logical entity that executes query task sharding.

GDS Loader: Parallel data loading, multiple configurable; supports text file format with automatic error data recognition.

GaussDB (DWS) has the following main features and significant advantages over traditional data warehouses, which can solve the problem of multi-industry ultra-large data processing and common platform management.

(1) Easy use.

One-stop visualization and convenient management: Uses GaussDB (DWS) management console to complete the O&M management work such as application and data warehouse connection, data backup, data recovery, and data warehouse resources and performance monitoring.

Seamless integration with big data: You can use standard SQL to query data on HDFS and OBS without data relocation.

One-click heterogeneous database migration tool: Provides migration tools that support the migration of SQL scripts from MySQL, Oracle and Teradata to GaussDB (DWS).

(2) Easy scalability.

On-demand expansion: Non-shared open architecture, where nodes can be added at any time according to business conditions to improve the data storage capacity and query analysis performance of the system.

Linear performance improvement upon expansion: Capacity and performance improving linearly with the cluster expands, with a linear ratio of 0.8.

Capacity expansion without business interruption: The expansion process supports data addition, deletion, modification and check operations, as well as DDL operations (DROP/ TRUNCATE/ALTER TABLE); table-level online expansion technology, with no business interruption and no perception during expansion.

(3) High performance.

Cloud-based distributed architecture: GaussDB (DWS) adopts fully parallel MPP architecture, where business data is scattered across multiple nodes, and data analysis tasks are pushed to the data site for execution nearby, so that large-scale data processing can be done in parallel and fast response to data processing can be realized.

High performance of query, and trillion data response within seconds: GaussDB (DWS) background realizes parallel execution of instructions in registers through multi-threaded parallel execution of algorithms and vectorized computation engine, and also reduces redundant conditional logic judgments during query through dynamic compilation of underlying virtual machine (framework system of architecture compiler), which helps improve data query performance. GaussDB (DWS) supports row-column hybrid storage, which can provide users with better data compression ratio (column storage), better index performance (column storage), and better point update and point query (row storage) performance at the same time.

Fast data loading: GaussDB (DWS) provides GDS extremely fast parallel large-scale data loading tool.

Data compression under column storage: For inactive early data, it can be compressed to reduce its space occupation and lower down procurement and O&M costs; it can select compression algorithms self-adaptively according to data characteristics, with an average compression ratio of 7:1; compressed data can be accessed directly and transparent to business, thus greatly reducing the preparation time for historical data access.

(4) High reliability.

ACID: It supports distributed transaction ACID feature to provide strong data consistency guarantee.

All-round HA design: All software processes of GaussDB (DWS) have primary and secondary guarantees, and all logical components of the cluster such as CNs and DNs have primary and secondary guarantees; in the case of physical failure of any single point, the system can still ensure reliable and consistent data, while providing services to the outside world; hardware-level high reliability includes disk Raid, switch stacking, NIC bond, and uninterruptible power supply (UPS).

Security: GaussDB (DWS) supports transparent data encryption, and can be docked with database security services, based on network isolation and security group rules to protect system and user privacy and ensure data security; GaussDB (DWS) also supports automatic full and incremental data backup to improve data reliability.

(5) Low cost.

Pay-as-you-go: GaussDB (DWS) is billed according to actual usage and usage length; users just need to pay very low fees and only pay for the actual consumed resources.

Low threshold: Users do not need to invest more fixed costs in the early stage, and can start with a low-specification data warehouse instance, and then flexibly adjust the required resources according to the business situation at any time and spend as needed.

8.2.4   Data Studio

Data Studio's graphical integrated development environment can help database developers to quickly carry out database development.

Data Studio provides various database development and debugging functions, including the following.

(1) Creates and manages database objects (databases, schemas, tables, views, indexes, functions, and stored procedures, etc.).
(2) Database DML, DDL, and DCL operations.
(3) Creates, runs and debugs PL/SQL procedures.

Data warehouse migration is a Data Studio application scenario, as shown in Fig. 8.9.

Smooth migration: GaussDB (DWS) provides supporting migration tools, which can support smooth migration of common data analysis systems such as TeraData, Oracle, MySQL, SQL Server, PostgreSQL, Greenplum, Impala, etc.

Compatibility with traditional data warehouse: GaussDB (DWS) supports SQL 2003 standard, compatible with some syntaxes and data structures of Oracle, supports stored procedures, and can be seamlessly connected with common BI tools, with minimal modification during business migration.

Security and reliability: GaussDB (DWS) supports data encryption and can also be docked with database security services to ensure data security on the cloud.

Big data fusion analysis is also an application scenario for Data Studio, as shown in Fig. 8.10.

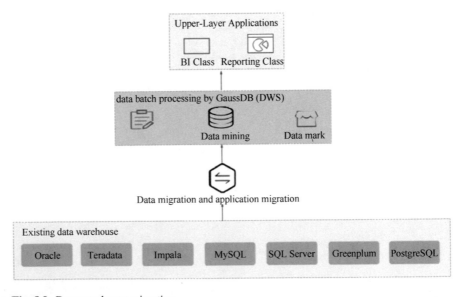

Fig. 8.9 Data warehouse migration

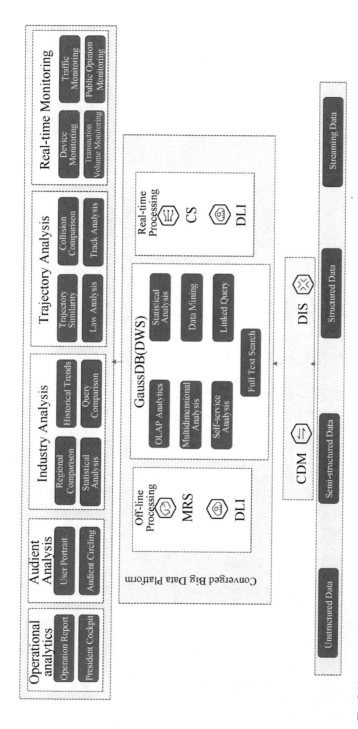

Fig. 8.10 Big data fusion analysis

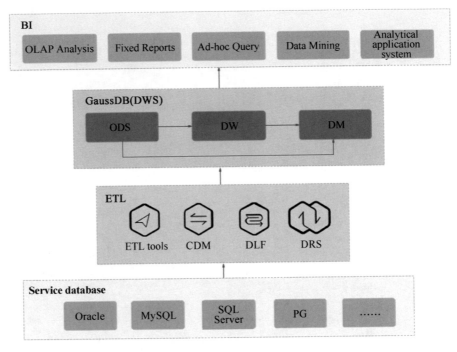

Fig. 8.11 Enhanced ETL and real-time BI analysis

Unified analysis portal: GaussDB (DWS)'s SQL is used as the unified portal for upper-layer applications, and application developers can access all data using familiar SQL.

Real-time interactive analysis: For immediate analysis needs, analysts can get information from the big data platform in real time.

Flexible adjustment: Adding nodes can expand the system's data storage capacity and query and analysis performance, which can support petabyte-scale data storage and calculation.

Data Studio application scenarios also include enhanced ETL and real-time BI analysis, as shown in Fig. 8.11.

Data Migration: It supports multiple data sources, as well as efficient real-time data import in batch.

High performance: It supports petabyte-scale data storage at low cost and trillions of data correlation analysis with second-level response.

Real time: Real-time integration of business data streams helps users optimize and adjust business decisions in a timely manner.

The application scenarios of Data Studio also include real-time data analysis, as shown in Fig. 8.12.

Real-time streaming data entry: IoT, Internet and other data can be written to GaussDB (DWS) in real time after being processed by streaming computing and AI services.

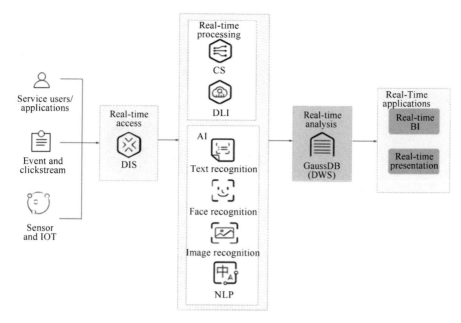

Fig. 8.12   Real-time data analysis

Real-time monitoring and prediction: It analyzes and predicts against data, monitors equipment, and predicts behavior for control and optimization.

AI fusion analysis: The analysis results of AI services on data such as images and text can be correlated and analyzed with other business data in GaussDB (DWS) to achieve fused data analysis.

8.3   NoSQL Databases

8.3.1   GaussDB (for Mongo)

NoSQL, also called "Not Only SQL" and "non-relational", refers to a non-relational database that is different from the traditional relational databases.

There are many significant differences between NoSQL and relational databases. For example, NoSQL does not guarantee the ACID feature of relational databases; NoSQL does not use SQL as the query language; NoSQL data storage can be used without a fixed table schema; NoSQL often avoids the use of SQL JOIN operations. NoSQL features easy scalability, high performance, etc.

Huawei's self-developed distributed multi-mode NoSQL database service with computing-storage separation architecture covers four mainstream NoSQL database services: GaussDB (for Mongo), GaussDB (for Cassandra), GaussDB (for Redis), and GaussDB (for Influx), as shown in Fig. 8.13.

Fig. 8.13 GaussDB
NoSQL

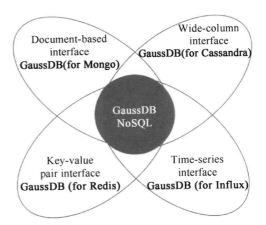

GaussDB NoSQL supports cross-3AZ clusters of high availability, and has the advantages of minute-level computing capacity expansion, second-level storage capacity expansion, strong data consistency, ultra-short latency, and high-speed backup recovery compared with the community version, which is cost-effective and suitable for IoT, meteorology, Internet, games and other fields.

The cloud database GaussDB (for Mongo) is a cloud-native NoSQL database compatible with MongoDB ecology. It features enterprise-class performance, flexibility, high reliability, visual management, etc.

GaussDB (for Mongo), which supports computing-storage separation, extreme availability and massive storage, mainly demonstrates the following benefits.

(1) Separation of storage and computing: The storage layer adopts DFV high-performance distributed storage, and the computing and storage resources are expanded independently on demand.
(2) Extreme availability: It supports distributed deployment with 3–12 nodes, tolerates n-1 node failure, and has three copies of data storage to ensure data security.
(3) Massive storage: It allows up to 96TB storage space.
(4) Autonomy and controllability: It supports Kunpeng architecture.
(5) Compatibility: It is compatible with MongoDB protocol for consistent development experience.

The computing-storage separation architecture of GaussDB (for Mongo) allows computing and storage to expand on-demand separately, effectively reducing costs; based on shared storage, Rebalance does not migrate data; 3AZ disaster recovery is supported.

GaussDB (for Mongo) offloads replica sets to distributed storage, reducing the number of storage copies; all ShardServer can handle business; distributed storage is based on sharded replication, which can better aggregate I/O performance and fault reconstruction performance; RocksDB storage engine guarantees good write performance; local SSD read Cache (cache) is used to optimize read performance;

snapshot-based physical backup avoids logical backups to export data, ensuring better performance; clear backup time points are set; performance is continuously optimized, including infrastructure, thread pool, and storage RDMA; the cluster size is automatically scaled up and down according to the business load, reducing user costs by more than 50%; instantaneous recovery, incremental backup, table-level backup, and arbitrary point-in-time recovery are supported.

User case: JAC's Internet of Vehicles scenario. It meets nearly one million concurrent queries per second, with timely response and stable business operation; the performance of the same concurrency is improved by three times compared with the same cost based on ECS self-built or open source service solution.

8.3.2 GaussDB (for Cassandra)

GaussDB (for Cassandra) is a massively scalable open source NoSQL database suitable for managing large amounts of structured, semi-structured and unstructured data across multiple data centers and clouds. Cassandra is continuously available, linearly scalable, and simple to operate on multiple commercial servers, with no single point of failure. Its powerful dynamic data model allows for flexibility and rapid response. GaussDB (for Cassandra) features the following benefits

(1) Cluster stability: no complete garbage collection problem.
(2) Computing-storage separation: minute-level node capacity expansion; second-level storage capacity expansion.
(3) Active-Active: distributed architecture; n-1 node failure tolerance.
(4) High performance: performance times higher than the community version.
(5) Massive data: single set of instances up to 100TB data.
(6) High reliability: minute-level backup recovery; strong data consistency.

GaussDB (for Cassandra) database supports elastic expansion, super read/write, high availability, fault tolerance, strong consistency, continuous query language (CQL), computing-storage separation, etc., without full GC problem. Its benefits are shown in Table 8.5.

Figure 8.14 shows the GaussDB (for Cassandra) use cases for industrial manufacturing and meteorology industries. The large-scale cluster deployment is suitable for the scenarios of massive data storage in industrial manufacturing and meteorological industries. The full P2P architecture based on consistent hashing ensures high availability of business and easy scalability of nodes, which supports 7×24 real-time writing of multi-sensor terminal data, with minute-level expansion for easily coping with operation or project peak.

8.4 Summary

This chapter introduces the database features, including Huawei relational databases GaussDB (for MySQL), GaussDB (openGauss) and Huawei GaussDB (DWS), and expounds the product features and business value of NoSQL databases, including GaussDB (for Mongo) and GaussDB (for Cassandra).

Table 8.5 Benefits of GaussDB (for Cassandra) database

Compatible Versions	Cassandra 3.11
Backup Recovery	Backup: Supports automatic backup (default retention for 7 days), and manual data backup Recovery: Supports backup restore to new instance
Data Migration	Supports DynamoDB migration to Cassandra (tool)
Elastic Capacity Expansion	Minute-level compute resource expansion, and second-level storage node capacity expansion
Monitoring	Node-level monitoring, including CPU usage, memory usage, network input/output throughput, and active connections
Security	Multiple security policies to protect database and user privacy, such as VPC, subnet, security group, SSL, etc.
Billing	On-demand + packet cycle
Performance	Superb write performance with multi-fold improvement in read-only performance
Highly Availability	Supports 3AZ and single AZ
Node Specifications	4U16G I 18U32G I 16U64G I 32U128G
Number of Nodes	3 - 200

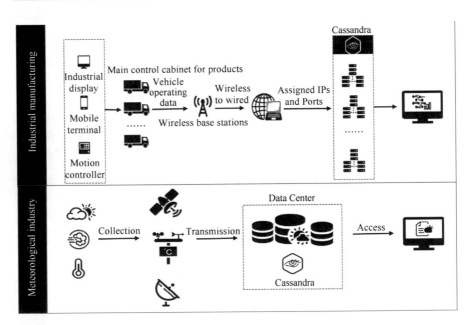

Fig. 8.14 GaussDB (for Cassandra) use cases for industrial manufacturing and meteorology industries

8.5 Exercises

1. [True or False] GaussDB (for MySQL) supports computing-storage separation. ( )

   A. True
   B. False

2. [Multiple Choice] What are the main advantages of GaussDB (for MySQL) database products? ( )

   A. High reliability
   B. High scalability
   C. Ultra high performance
   D. High compatibility

3. [Single Choice] What is the maximum number of read-only nodes that can be added to a GaussDB (for MySQL) cluster? ( )

   A. 12
   B. 13
   C. 14
   D. 15

4. [Short Answer Question] How does GaussDB (for MySQL) automatically perform failover?

5. [True or False] GaussDB (openGauss) is the world's first fully self-developed enterprise-class OLAP database that supports the Kunpeng hardware architecture. ( )

   A. True
   B. False

6. [Multiple Choice] An e-commerce company uses GaussDB (openGauss) database for its business. Which of the following are the advantages of GaussDB (openGauss) database? ( )

   A. Excellent performance
   B. High scalability
   C. Easy management
   D. Security and reliability.

7. [Multiple Choice] GaussDB (openGauss) is based on an innovative database kernel, which supports high-performance transaction processing capabilities in real time. Which of the following are the main features of its high performance? ( )

   A. Distributed strong consistence
   B. Support for Kunpeng two-way server

    C. High throughput and strong consistency transaction capability

    D. Compatibility with SQL2003 standard syntaxes

8. [Single Choice] Which of the following components is responsible for receiving access requests from the application and returning execution results to the client? ( )

    A. GTM

    B. WLM

    C. CN

    D. DN

9. [Multiple Choice] Which of the following product advantages does GaussDB (DWS) have over traditional data warehouses? ( )

    A. High performance

    B. High reliability

    C. Easy use

    D. Easy scalability

10. [True or False] GaussDB (DWS) provides double HA protection mechanism for data nodes to ensure uninterrupted business. ( )

    A. True

    B. False

Index